PROMOTING SAVINGS
IN LATIN AMERICA

Edited by

Ricardo Hausmann and Helmut Reisen

INTER-AMERICAN DEVELOPMENT BANK
DEVELOPMENT CENTRE OF THE ORGANISATION
FOR ECONOMIC CO-OPERATION AND DEVELOPMENT

ORGANISATION FOR ECONOMIC CO-OPERATION AND DEVELOPMENT

Pursuant to Article 1 of the Convention signed in Paris on 14th December 1960, and which came into force on 30th September 1961, the Organisation for Economic Co-operation and Development (OECD) shall promote policies designed:

- to achieve the highest sustainable economic growth and employment and a rising standard of living in Member countries, while maintaining financial stability, and thus to contribute to the development of the world economy;
- to contribute to sound economic expansion in Member as well as non-member countries in the process of economic development; and
- to contribute to the expansion of world trade on a multilateral, non-discriminatory basis in accordance with international obligations.

The original Member countries of the OECD are Austria, Belgium, Canada, Denmark, France, Germany, Greece, Iceland, Ireland, Italy, Luxembourg, the Netherlands, Norway, Portugal, Spain, Sweden, Switzerland, Turkey, the United Kingdom and the United States. The following countries became Members subsequently through accession at the dates indicated hereafter: Japan (28th April 1964), Finland (28th January 1969), Australia (7th June 1971), New Zealand (29th May 1973), Mexico (18th May 1994), the Czech Republic (21st December 1995), Hungary (7th May 1996), Poland (22nd November 1996) and the Republic of Korea (12th December 1996). The Commission of the European Communities takes part in the work of the OECD (Article 13 of the OECD Convention).

The Development Centre of the Organisation for Economic Co-operation and Development was established by decision of the OECD Council on 23rd October 1962 and comprises twenty-four Member countries of the OECD: Austria, Belgium, Canada, the Czech Republic, Denmark, Finland, France, Germany, Greece, Iceland, Ireland, Italy, Japan, Korea, Luxembourg, Mexico, the Netherlands, Norway, Poland, Portugal, the United States, Spain, Sweden and Switzerland, as well as Argentina and Brazil from March 1994. The Commission of the European Communities also takes part in the Centre's Advisory Board.

The purpose of the Centre is to bring together the knowledge and experience available in Member countries of both economic development and the formulation and execution of general economic policies; to adapt such knowledge and experience to the actual needs of countries or regions in the process of development and to put the results at the disposal of the countries by appropriate means.

The Centre has a special and autonomous position within the OECD which enables it to enjoy scientific independence in the execution of its task. Nevertheless, the Centre can draw upon the experience and knowledge available in the OECD in the development field.

Publié en français sous le titre :

PROMOUVOIR L'ÉPARGNE
EN AMÉRIQUE LATINE

*
* *

Foreword

The papers in this volume represent the deliberations of the November 1996 seventh joint OECD Development Centre and Inter-American Development Bank annual conference of the "International Forum on Latin American Perspectives". The conference falls into the context of the Development Centre's research programme entitled "Macroeconomic Interdependence and Capital Flows" and is part of the Centre's external co-operation activities.

Table of Contents

Preface

The International Forum on Latin American Perspectives was created by the Inter-American Development Bank and the OECD Development Centre in 1990 as an initiative for bringing together expertise available in OECD Member countries, particularly in Europe, with the experience of Latin American specialists to discuss topics of current relevance. The Forum provides opportunities for exchanges of views among experts, policy makers and opinion leaders in order to provide new insights and contribute to policy thinking.

This volume presents the results of the seventh annual meeting of the International Forum on Latin American Perspectives, which took place in Paris in November 1996, and focused on whether and how to promote domestic savings in Latin America. The observation that saving rates usually increase only after a sustained period of high growth casts doubt on whether savings should be an intermediate target for economic policy. Though higher savings are clearly important for Latin America's future, the region's efforts in structural reform and towards stabilising inflation have often implied a transitory decline in savings.

The seventh International Forum brought into focus the possible trade-offs involved for economic policy: promoting growth, at the risk of a temporary decline in savings, or targeting higher saving rates, even if this implies a slower pace of economic reform. The meeting also identified appropriate policies for the promotion of savings through domestic financial reform, fiscal policies, tax incentives and the treatment of foreign savings. We hope that the proceedings of the seventh International Forum on Latin American Perspectives will stimulate further debate and influence the formulation of policy priorities throughout the region.

Jean Bonvin
President
OECD Development Centre
Paris

Enrique V. Iglesias
President
Inter-American Development Bank
Washington, D.C.

February, 1997

Opening Remarks

Jean Bonvin

Six years ago, the Inter-American Development Bank and the OECD Development Centre jointly decided to set up the International Forum on Latin American Perspectives. This annual event brings together the expertise available in OECD Member countries with that of Latin American specialists to examine issues of common and topical interest.

The theme of this year's Forum is *"Promoting Savings in Latin America"*.

The choice of this topic suggests that savings are insufficient in the region. Indeed, in the developing world, sub-Saharan Africa is the only region with national saving rates lower than those of Latin America. Moreover, Latin American savings rates have been shrinking even further over the last decade.

By international standards, *government* savings have been fairly high since the early 1980s, but, *private* saving rates have been the lowest in the world.

Our interest in promoting savings results from the observation, in different parts of the world, that savings and income growth are linked.

Though we must admit that the interpretation and policy implications of this relationship between savings and growth remain controversial, the link nevertheless suggests the existence of poverty traps through undersaving or, alternatively, the existence of virtuous circles of saving and prosperity.

The strong link between domestic savings rates and growth can be partly explained by the limited availability of foreign capital over a sustained period of time. This implies that domestic investment must be financed essentially from local sources.

For capital accumulation to result in sustained growth, it must be supported by adequate domestic savings. This has been clearly demonstrated by the extraordinary performance of the East Asian economies. Likewise, in Latin America, high investment rates — mainly financed by domestic savings — are necessary to guarantee the sustained rates of growth required for the eradication of widespread poverty.

Latin America should therefore seek to achieve a domestic savings ratio that is broadly in line with its investment needs. Such a savings ratio is also a key requirement for reducing the region's vulnerability to unexpected — or, rather, predictable — shifts in international capital flows.

The 1995 Mexican crisis showed, among other things, that low domestic savings can raise the probability of sudden capital outflows, and sharpen their negative consequences. In a financially integrated world, high domestic savings contribute to macroeconomic stability which is itself a powerful growth factor.

There is a broad consensus now about the need for higher savings in Latin America, but it is much less easy to agree upon which measures should be adopted to promote them. The lack of consensus on this issue, and the knowledge gap regarding appropriate policies to promote savings, made this 1996 Forum on Latin American Perspectives very timely.

Important channels for the promotion of savings are likely to be found in:

— policy reforms that enhance the sustainability of growth;

— the structure of domestic financial systems;

— fiscal policies and tax incentives; and

— the treatment of foreign savings which all too often tend to crowd out domestic savings.

This, at least, is what is suggested by the papers contained in this volume.

Indeed, the choice between consumption and savings is beset by so many puzzles that we should qualify our claims with doses of caution and moderation.

This is also suggested by recent research at the Development Centre. For instance, it is often claimed that the rise in Chile's savings rates can be attributed to its radical pension reforms. Our recent research suggests, however, that there is no cross-country correlation between the importance of funded pension assets and the level of domestic savings rates. This is not to deny the need for financial policy reform, as is underlined in the results of our research on "Financial Systems, Allocation of Resources and Growth". Such reforms are considered vital to ensure the effectiveness of liberalisation or adjustment measures. The same project also concludes that an efficient financial system is important in mobilising domestic savings to finance economic development.

What is the outlook for Latin America, given these different considerations?

There are grounds for being reasonably optimistic about Latin America's ability to raise its domestic savings rates in the coming decades. Chile has already shown the way. In the 1990s, it succeeded in raising its domestic savings rate well above a quarter of its GDP, thus approaching East Asian levels.

The rest of the region has two strong allies that will assist in increasing domestic savings.

The first is its impressive record of recent policy reform. This has laid solid foundations for strong and sustained growth which, in turn, is likely to stimulate savings, as it did in Chile.

The second ally is demographic: the decline in fertility rates results in lower young age dependency in the future and should stimulate savings.

As the great French economist Jean-Baptiste Say said with respect to our retirement savings:

« Faites des enfants, ou faites de l'épargne »

— "Either have children .... or save!"

Saving Behaviour in Latin America: Overview and Policy Issues

Michael Gavin, Ricardo Hausmann and Ernesto Talvi

Summary and Conclusions

We present here an alternative perspective on the relationship between saving and growth; saving and inflation stabilisation; saving and structural reform; and saving and capital inflows; drawing on the experience of East Asia and Latin America in the last 25 years[1].

Our perspectives on saving are based on the following evidence:

i) higher growth precedes higher saving, rather than the reverse. It is only after a sustained period of high growth that saving rates increase and may do so with a delay that can be quite significant;

ii) the most powerful determinant of saving over the long run is economic growth. According to this view, Latin America's chronically low rate of saving is primarily the consequence, more than the cause, of the region's history of low and volatile economic growth, while the high saving observed in the Asian "miracle" economies is due to their high and less volatile rate of economic growth;

iii) stabilisation and reform policies aimed at raising efficiency and promoting growth may, although temporarily, reduce saving rates for many years, and therefore increase the reliance of the economy on potentially volatile capital flows;

iv) when properly measured, capital inflows are associated with declines in saving which are similar in East Asia and Latin America.

Based on this evidence the policy conclusions of this paper differ from the prevailing views since they de-emphasize saving as an intermediate policy target. They are the following:

i)   the emphasis of policy should be shifted away from saving and concentrate on removing the impediments to growth. This shift of emphasis is non-trivial, since many efficiency raising, growth-promoting policies may result in a temporary, but prolonged, decline in saving rates;

ii) the emphasis of policy should shift away from avoiding the inevitable outcome of inflation stabilisation and many reform policies, i.e., a transitory decline in saving, current account deficit and reliance on foreign saving; and aim at reducing the vulnerability of the economy to external shocks during this transition; and

iii) whatever the merits of polices designed to stimulate a larger participation of FDI, they are unlikely to result in a significant change in the way saving in Latin America responds to capital flows.

We review the policy debate surrounding saving in Latin America. However, we want to make clear from the outset that we do not attempt to produce a balanced presentation of this issue but rather to contribute to a balanced debate on the issue by offering an alternative perspective on saving which is at least as consistent with the evidence as the dominant view.

Saving in Asia and Latin America

Latin America's saving rates are low, especially in comparison with the East Asian "miracle" economies. As Figure 1 illustrates, national saving in Latin America has during the past decade averaged less than 20 per cent of GDP, in comparison with over 30 per cent in six rapidly-growing East Asian economies[2]. Every single economy of Latin America had a saving rate substantially below that recorded in the Asian "miracle" economies, and in several economies of Latin America saving rates were only about one-third the Asian "miracle" average.

Recently, concerns with saving in Latin America have intensified because in many countries of Latin America already low rates of saving have in the past several years declined, in some cases quite significantly.

As Figure 2 illustrates, during the 1990s the rate of national saving fell in 13 countries of the region, in some cases quite dramatically. The decline in private saving has been even more generalised, falling in all countries but three. Thus, if low rates of saving are a cause for concern, the recent past strengthened this concern considerably.

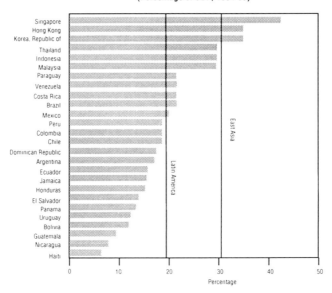

Figure 1. **National Saving in East Asia and Latin America**
(Percentage of GDP, 1984-93)

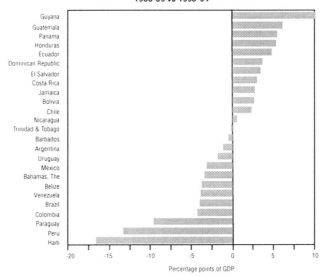

Figure 2. **National Saving in Latin America**
1988-89 vs 1993-94

Why Are Low Saving Rates a Problem?

The dominant view about saving highlights at least two reasons why saving is an important macroeconomic policy issue and can be summarised as follows: Latin America's low rate of saving condemns the region to an uncomfortable choice between low investment and growth, or excessive reliance upon volatile foreign capital which makes the region vulnerable to crises.

From a Long-run Perspective, National Saving Matters for Growth

As Figure 3 illustrates, high rates of saving are highly correlated with high rates of growth. The link between saving and growth is not however a direct one, but operates through the effects of investment on growth.

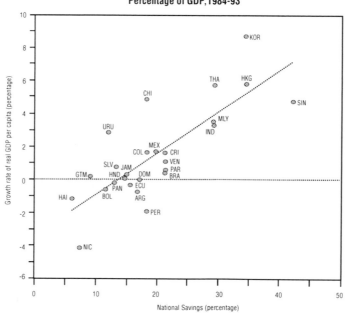

Figure 3. **Saving and Growth, Latin America and E. Asia**
Percentage of GDP, 1984-93

To illustrate this point, Figure 4 shows that there is also a strong link between saving and investment, which suggests that countries that manage to increase their saving rate, and therefore investment, will increase their rate of growth.

16

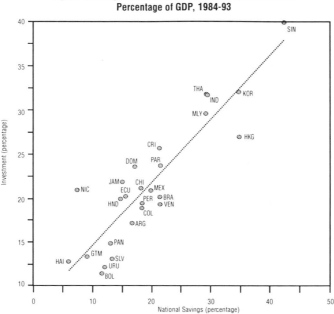

Figure 4. **Saving and Investment, Latin America and E. Asia**
Percentage of GDP, 1984-93

In principle there is no reason to expect a very close link between saving and domestic investment because domestic investment can be financed by foreign saving, through inflows of international capital. One interpretation of this long-run relationship between national saving and domestic investment is that over the long run international capital flows are limited, and thus that a sustained rise in the rate of domestic investment requires a sustained rise in the rate of national saving. The correlation, however, between saving and investment is of course not perfect, therefore there is some scope for boosting domestic investment above domestic saving by encouraging international capital flows, even over a relatively long time horizon. But the correlation between domestic saving and investment is high, suggesting that this scope is limited.

From a Short-run Perspective, Low Rates of Saving Increase Vulnerability

According to the dominant view, low rates of saving are also associated with increased vulnerability to macroeconomic crisis (see for example, Bruno, 1996, and Summers, 1996a, 1996b). A country with a low or declining rate of saving, may occasionally be forced to run large current account deficits to maintain reasonable levels of investment. Excessive reliance on foreign saving unduly exposes the economy to volatile international capital flows. A sudden decline in the inflows of capital might force on the recipient economy a very abrupt and, therefore, disruptive macroeconomic adjustment.

For the tenets of the dominant view, the crisis in Mexico has become associated with that country's low and declining rate of saving and the very large current account deficits during the years leading up to the crisis. In this context, the almost complete insulation of high-saving economies such as Chile and the East Asian "miracle" economies from the financial turbulence that gripped many "emerging-market" economies in the immediate aftermath of the Mexican devaluation, is contrasted with the financial turbulence that affected countries with a less impressive saving performance such as Argentina[3]. International comparisons, and particularly comparisons of Latin America with East Asia, thus provide some support for the idea that saving is an important force for economic stability, as well as growth.

Corresponding to the dominant view on the relationship between saving, growth and stability there is a policy agenda to address the problem of low saving rates in Latin America. This policy agenda focuses on mechanisms to tackle the problem of low saving directly as follows:

i)   Increase national saving by raising public saving;

ii)   Promote private saving by creating a stable and predictable economic environment that rewards savers for thrift and reduces fears that inflation or a collapsing financial system will lead to expropriation of their saving. This implies stabilising inflation, strengthening domestic financial institutions, and increasing the role of market signals in the allocation of saving and investment, i.e., the elimination of "financial repression", and

iii)   Promote contractual saving, in particular through the establishment of fully-funded social security systems.

Much of this agenda is perfectly sensible. In fact, each of these reforms have already been implemented by many countries in the region or, where they have not, they are at the top of the policy agenda. However, although these policies are highly desirable for their potential impact on economic efficiency and growth, they are unlikely to have large, immediate effects on saving in the short to medium term. Furthermore, as we shall see, there is good reason to believe that some of these reforms will have a temporary negative impact on saving in the short term.

Saving and Economic Growth

Econometric studies of the determinants of saving rates (see for example, Edwards, 1994 and CEPAL, 1995) suggest that the long-run behaviour of saving is closely related to an economy's rate of growth and income per capita levels. However, close association does not establish causality and this is a crucial element in the design of policy. As Deaton (1995) points out "the causation is important, not just for understanding the process, but for the design of policy. If saving is merely the passive adjunct to growth or to investment, then policies for growth should presumably be directed at investment (in people, plant or equipment) or at the efficiency of such investment, with saving allowed to look after itself. But if saving is the prime mover, the focus should be on saving incentives, such as tax breaks (...), compulsory saving in (fully-funded) employee provident funds, as in Malaysia, Singapore and Chile, to the design of social security systems, or to the role of financial intermediation in general, improvements in which are variously argued both to increase and decrease saving".

Although the issue is far from settled, the view that growth appears to precede saving rather than the reverse has found support in several papers, including an influential contribution by Carroll and Weil (1994). That paper examined the relationship between saving and economic growth in a sample covering a large number of countries over several decades, and found that past growth predicts future saving rates, while past saving rates do not predict future growth[4].

The fact that increased growth tends to precede increased saving rates suggests that saving may be, to an important extent, caused by, in addition to causing, economic growth[5].

The pattern of strong increases in saving rates *after* an acceleration of growth is illustrated by the experience of the Asian "miracle" economies. Figure 5 shows the (population-weighted) average saving rates for Latin America and the Asian "miracle" economies. Saving rates increased substantially in the Asian "miracle" economies while they remained stagnant in Latin America from the early 1970s. That Asian economies have had a much higher rate of saving than Latin America is a relatively recent phenomenon, resulting from a long and gradual increase in Asian saving from rates that were, in the 1970s, generally below those recorded in Latin America. Only in the late 1970s and early 1980s, *after* the acceleration of growth in Asia, did Asian saving rates rise consistently and substantially above Latin American rates[6].

In Latin America, Chile is another example where strong increases in saving followed the acceleration of growth[7]. Figure 6 shows that Chile's economic recovery began in 1984, when domestic saving was still quite depressed, and the economy was as a result heavily reliant upon capital inflows to finance domestic investment[8]. It was only in the late 1980s, after several years of sustained economic growth, that Chilean saving rates approached the high levels now observed.

The estimated impact of growth on saving is not only statistically significant, but also very large in economic terms. In fact, the differences between East Asian and Latin American growth rates is sufficient to explain the differences in the regions' long-run saving behaviour depicted in Figure 5. Using an econometric model of the determinants of saving rates, which is described in the appendix of this chapter, Figure 7 illustrates the impact of growth on saving by providing an estimate of what Asian saving rates would have been if those countries had had Latin America's rate of economic growth during the past twenty five years.

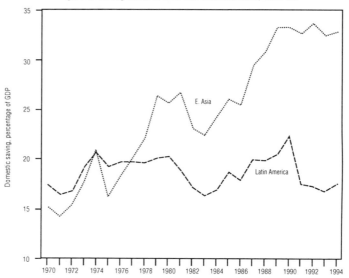

Figure 5. **Saving Rates in Asia and Latin America, 1970-94**

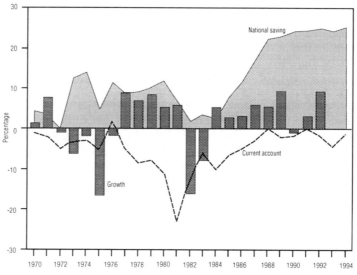

Figure 6. **Growth, Saving and the Current Account in Chile**
(Growth Rate in Percentage, Other Variables Percentage of GDP)

The figure shows that if, during 1970-94, the East Asian "miracles" had experienced the economic growth recorded by Latin America, the Asian saving rate would, other things equal, have been even *lower* than that recorded in Latin America. This implies that essentially all of the difference between saving rates in Latin America and the Asian "miracle" economies is explained by differences in their growth performance.

This does not mean that other determinants of saving are unimportant but that they are unlikely to account for much of the long-run difference in Latin American and East Asian rates of saving, or for the recent, sustained increase in Chilean saving rates. For example, the econometric model of this paper and other work by other authors find that although improvements in the terms of trade typically increase saving, the effect appears to be purely transitory, as economic theory would predict, and therefore unlikely to explain the differences in long-run behaviour[9]. Other determinants of saving, such as the distribution of income, the age distribution of the population and demography may also be statistically relevant[10], but none of these factors can account quantitatively for the dramatic shift from relatively low to very high saving rates that occurred in the Asian "miracle" economies since the early 1970s, and in Chile since the mid-1980s.

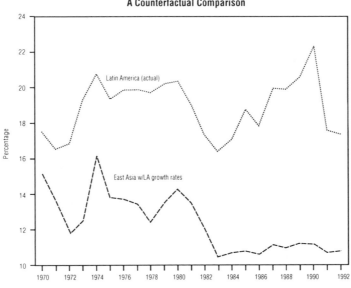

Figure 7. **Can Growth Explain Asia's Higher Saving Rate?**
A Counterfactual Comparison

Policy Issues

The main policy implication of the view that growth is the prime mover and not saving, is that policy efforts should concentrate on removing the impediments to growth rather than trying to establish programmes aimed directly at promoting saving that are likely to be of dubious effectiveness and may involve economic inefficiencies.

Of course, policy impediments to saving should be removed, but policy should be mainly concerned with establishing an environment conducive to high and sustained rates of growth, trusting saving to follow in response to the incentives that such an environment provides.

Although policies aimed at increasing saving may exhibit a substantial overlap with those aimed at removing impediments to growth, the shift of emphasis in the policy objective from saving to growth is non-trivial. As we will argue in the following section, many efficiency-raising, growth promoting policies are likely to have an adverse effect on saving, that although temporary, may last for many years.

Saving, Stabilisation and Structural Reform

In line with the policy agenda suggested by the prevailing views on saving, Latin America's economic reforms of the past decade have included: fiscal consolidation; inflation stabilisation; financial liberalisation and reform, and in some countries, the creation of mechanisms for contractual saving via the replacement of pay-as-you-go with fully-funded social security systems[11]. Trade liberalisation has also been pervasive, and although not usually mentioned in the context of policy towards saving it may nonetheless have a substantial impact on the saving rate.

Fiscal Consolidation

A cornerstone of the region's economic reform efforts has been fiscal consolidation, which has brought budget deficits from nearly 10 per cent of GDP in the early 1980s to about 3 per cent in recent years. While public saving increased significantly in most of Latin America, private saving declined in several countries, leading to a reduction in total saving, as is illustrated in Figure 8.

Both theory and evidence suggest that increased public saving is likely to generate a reduction in private saving[12]. This means that, in order to raise domestic saving by one dollar, governments may need to increase public saving by 2 or more dollars. Doing so is not costless: raising taxes imposes important costs on the economy and may reduce economic growth, and reducing spending may make it impossible to carry out worthwhile public programmes.

This does not mean that governments in the region should not strengthen their fiscal position. It does mean that, if done efficiently, it is unlikely to yield large increases in aggregate saving. Moreover, it is easier and more efficient to improve public saving in a growing economy with stable and moderate tax rates.

As we will discuss below, further deepening of the region's recent fiscal consolidation, grounded in meaningful reforms of the region's budgetary institutions, remains one of the Latin America's priorities, but this is likely to be an expensive means of raising total saving.

Figure 8. **Public and Private Saving in Latin America**
(Percentage of GDP)

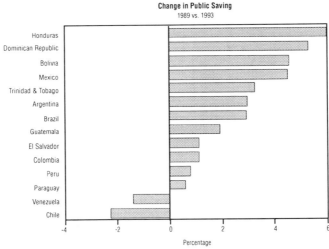

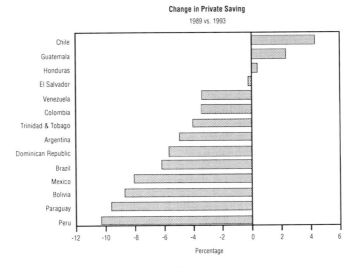

Inflation Stabilisation

The second element of the policy prescription emphasises the importance not only of raising domestic saving, but also of ensuring that it will remain in the domestic economy to finance domestic investment. After all, high saving will provide little support for economic development if the saving leaves the economy in the form of capital flight. An important reason for such capital flight is fear that wealth will be confiscated in a bout of unexpectedly high inflation. Thus a second item on the policy agenda for saving is inflation stabilisation.

On this front, too, substantial progress has been made in Latin America (see Figure 9). With the recent Brazilian stabilisation, extreme inflation has essentially vanished from the continent. While, in 1990, 10 of the region's 26 countries experienced inflation rates greater than 40 per cent, only 4 countries did so in 1994 and 1995.

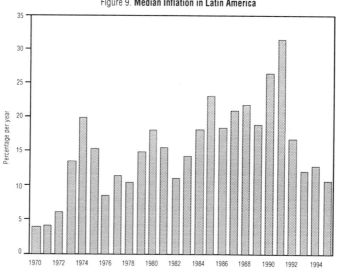

Figure 9. **Median Inflation in Latin America**

Inflation stabilisation is a particularly relevant example to illustrate how efficiency raising, growth promoting policies may reduce saving in the short to medium run, since it is a well established empirical regularity that exchange rate-based stabilisations are expansionary and generate a consumption boom and a corresponding decline in saving in the initial stages (see for example, Kiguel and Liviatan, 1992 and Végh, 1992). It is only later that consumption contracts and the economy falls into recession. An important reason for the decline in Latin American rates of saving during the 1990s is the major inflation stabilisation programmes that have been pursued in many countries (see IDB, 1996b).

24

To illustrate the potential economic significance of the relationship between inflation stabilisation and saving we used the model described in the appendix to simulate the impact of a major inflation stabilisation, that reduces the rate of inflation from 1 000 per cent per year to zero, and increases in the long-run rate of economic growth by 2 per cent per year. The results are illustrated in Figure 10.

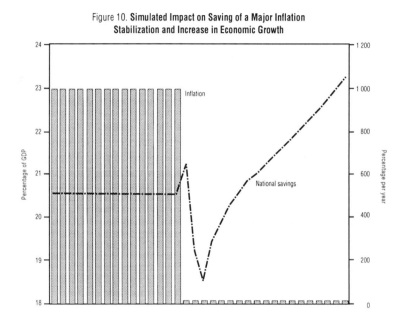

Figure 10. **Simulated Impact on Saving of a Major Inflation Stabilization and Increase in Economic Growth**

The econometric model predicts a 2 percentage point decline in the rate of saving in the immediate aftermath of the stabilisation. The effect is transitory, and eventually the higher economic growth leads to a higher rate of saving. While transitory, however, the model predicts that it will take five years for saving to recover its pre-stabilisation levels.

Even in the long run, the impact of inflation stabilisation on saving is ambiguous. The statistical work prepared for this chapter (as described in the appendix) as well as other studies, including Held and Uthoff (1995) and Morandé (1996), indicate that lower inflation, when controlling for other determinants of saving rates, is associated with lower rates of saving[13]. The available evidence thus suggests that inflation stabilisation, whatever its other good effects, has almost certainly the short-run effect of reducing, rather than increasing saving, and an ambiguous impact in the long run.

Financial-System Reform

The policy agenda emphasises the need not only to provide a stable currency, but also to build a financial system in which domestic savers can be rewarded for thrift and have confidence in its soundness.

Here, too, many countries in the region have made substantial progress; domestic financial institutions have been privatised, and markets have been largely freed from quantitative credit restrictions and interest-rate ceilings. While there remains much to be done, one key objective, at least, was largely fulfilled: confidence in the domestic financial system has increased and this increase in confidence was reflected in a large increase in the size of domestic financial systems in many countries, as domestic and foreign savers both became more willing to place their savings there. As had been the objective, this provided domestic banks with funds to invest domestically.

However, while a deeper financial system may have positive effects on saving in the long run, the resulting increase in the size of the domestic financial system has had little effect on saving in Latin America in the short run. As Figure 11 illustrates, short-run changes in financial depth, as measured by the size of the domestic banking system bears little relationship to changes in national saving in the region. Mexico, Brazil and Bolivia, for example, recently experienced large increases in financial depth but saving rates were largely unaffected in Bolivia and declined in Mexico and Brazil.

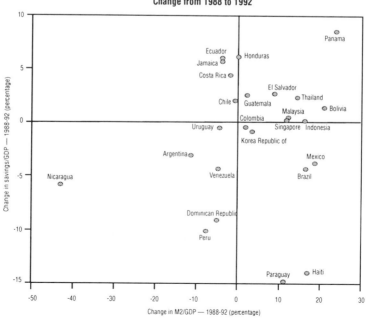

Figure 11. **Financial Depth and National Saving Latin America
Change from 1988 to 1992**

Mexico presents an extreme, but nonetheless revealing example of the short-run consequences of rapid growth in domestic financial intermediation[14]. That country saw a large increase in the demand for domestic bank deposits during 1990-94, driven in large part by the country's success in stabilising inflation. At the same time the government was using privatisation revenue to repay its loans from the banking system. The result was a large increase in resources available for commercial banks to lend.

As Figure 12 illustrates, Mexican bank lending to the private sector rose from less than 10 per cent of GDP in 1989 to nearly 40 per cent in 1994. This lending financed some investment, which recovered substantially during 1990-94, but much of the lending also went to consumers. The greater availability of credit relaxed constraints on consumption spending, and was almost certainly a major factor underlying the substantial decline in Mexican saving during the years leading up to the 1995 crisis. Thus, a policy of financial liberalisation that was justified, in part, by a desire to raise saving appears to have had, at least in the short run, exactly the opposite result.

Figure 12. **Mexican Bank Lending to the Private Sector**
(Percentage of GDP)

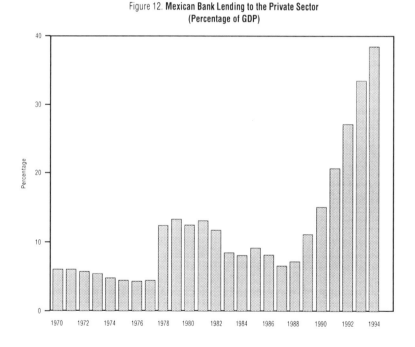

Contractual Saving

Another element of the policy response to the problem of low saving in Latin America is the implementation of contractual saving schemes, particularly fully-funded social security systems.

Fully funded social security systems have several advantages. First, they reduce the governance problem inherent in pay-as-you-go systems due to the fact that future taxpayers are not represented in political decision making about levels of social-security benefits that they will be required to provide. Second, there is also evidence from the Chilean experience that fully-funded social security systems can provide an important impetus to development of domestic capital markets.

However, the effects on saving are not likely to be large unless the reform is accompanied by fiscal tightening. The largest and most direct impact of social security reform on saving is that generated by cleaning up the fiscal disarray typically created by pay-as-you-go social security systems. The reform requires that today's workers save for their own retirement. The question is who pays for today's pensioners? Saving increases to the extent that current taxpayers do, but if the government accommodates this obligation through an increase in the deficit, there is no direct effect on national saving.

In Chile the reform implied a major fiscal adjustment to pay for the current pensioners and the direct effect on public saving was therefore significant, roughly 3 per cent of GDP, though small in comparison with the increase in total saving registered over the past decade, roughly 15 per cent of GDP[15]. Reforms in other Latin American countries have not involved a similar fiscal adjustment, and the impact of reform on saving is therefore likely to be much smaller (Ayala, 1995).

One of the most important effects of pension reform is its contribution to financial-market development. This appears to have also been the case in Chile. Such development is likely to promote a more efficient allocation of both domestic and foreign saving flows to the economy, since there is evidence that deep financial markets act as "shock absorbers".

Trade Liberalisation

Trade liberalisation is not usually associated with the issue of saving. However, trade liberalisation can lead to a transitory decline in saving and an increase in investment. Such liberalisation generally reduces the cost of imported consumer durable goods and capital goods, leading to a temporary burst of spending on such goods, as consumers and firms adjust upward their stock. During this transitory period of stock adjustment, conventional measures of saving decline[16].

As Calvo has suggested, trade liberalisation can also lead to a reduction in saving if it is perceived as transitory. If liberalisation is perceived to be temporary, consumers may have an even stronger incentive to purchase imported consumption goods during the time when they are temporarily inexpensive, thus leading to a transitory consumption boom and decline in the rate of saving.

Figure 13 illustrates the behaviour of saving and investment before and after trade liberalisation for fifteen Latin American countries and lends support to the idea that, on impact, trade liberalisation reduces saving and deteriorates the current account balance.

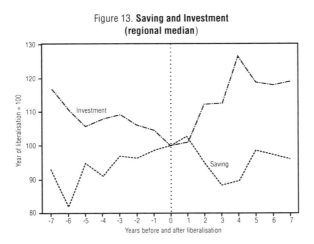

Figure 13. **Saving and Investment**
(regional median)

Policy Issues

Stabilisation and reform policies which are intended to raise efficiency and promote growth trigger complex dynamics. In many cases, these reforms will generate a transitory decline in saving, particularly if there is a substantial lag between the implementation of the reforms and the arrival of the higher output. Higher output (and income) should eventually, according to our model, lead to higher saving.

The fact that highly desirable economic reforms may have a transitory adverse impact on saving has important implications. First, it highlights the importance of properly diagnosing a decline in saving, which may result not from inadequate policies but from the reverse. Second, it is important to ensure that growth-friendly policies will not be foregone or delayed because of the possibility of a transitory, adverse impact on saving.

Since there may be a reasonably long delay between the recovery of growth and the saving response, the economy is likely to be reliant upon capital inflows, until it reaches a high-growth, high-savings equilibrium. In this transition, the economy may be vulnerable to external shocks or a sudden loss of confidence.

Since shocks to the economy in this phase may derail the reform process and thwart growth, complementary policies that make the economy more resilient need to be implemented, so that the inevitable shocks can be absorbed without aborting the positive effects of reforms on growth and saving. Policies aimed directly at raising saving are unlikely to be the most effective means of reducing vulnerability. Instead the stress points in the economy, where shocks can trigger collapse, must be strengthened.

We focus here on two particularly important areas that have been weak links in many Latin American economies, and where appropriate policies can substantially improve a country's "shock resistance" and ability to bridge the transition to high savings: domestic financial systems and fiscal policy[17].

The domestic financial system: The domestic financial system is crucial because it will be called upon to intermediate some, though not all, of the potentially volatile capital flows during the transition. For example, foreign direct investment and equity portfolio investment are not intermediated by banks, but foreign deposits in the domestic banking system clearly are. This intermediation is, of course, an essential function of banks, but it carries with it the potential for instability and crisis because the intermediation involves a transformation of term structure and a transfer of risk, and because implicit or explicit public insurance of the banking system generates strong problems of moral hazard.

The transformation of term structure carried out by banks means that savers obtain liquid bank deposits, which banks use to fund longer-term lending commitments. This is not inherently bad, but it can exaggerate swings in capital flows and their macroeconomic consequences[18], and creates the potential for financial crisis if depositors attempt to withdraw their deposits from the system more rapidly than banks' lending commitments can be wound down. Unless the financial system possesses sufficient liquid reserves to manage such liquidity shocks, even a brief and unwarranted panic by depositors can bring the financial system to its knees, potentially crippling the real economy and creating the very macroeconomic crisis that depositors feared. Banks generally benefit from implicit or explicit insurance, they therefore have inadequate incentives to remain sufficiently liquid, and there might be a role for policy to ensure that they do.

Financial intermediation also means that the risk of lending is shifted from savers, the value of whose deposits is largely unaffected by the return on the bank's loan portfolio, to shareholders of the bank and, because of implicit public insurance schemes, to taxpayers. This poses a strong moral hazard problem, and in particular creates the danger that a surge of capital inflows will generate a lending boom, in which excessively risky and potentially wasteful projects are funded because the costs of particularly bad outcomes largely fall upon taxpayers not the bank managers responsible for making the loans. This creates the need to institute a conservative bank supervisory system that enforces appropriate capital-adequacy standards and, as necessary, to adjust domestic monetary policy to forestall such credit booms[19]. This may reduce somewhat the efficiency of bank intermediation, but failing to do so leaves the economy open to periodic macroeconomic and financial crises of the sort that have too often interrupted Latin American growth and development.

Fiscal policy: The transition to a high-growth high-saving equilibrium will generally involve periods of transitory spending booms. These will have favourable fiscal implications because taxes are mainly levied on domestic spending. The danger is that the transitory fiscal benefits will generate permanent public spending commitments or permanent reductions in tax rates. These changes weaken fiscal sustainability but do not necessarily show up in a deterioration of the observed fiscal deficit. However, the structural fiscal situation will be vulnerable and fiscal deficits will appear when the boom subsides[20].

The problem of an inadequate reaction of fiscal policy is a deep one, and may arise because of problems in securing the collective action required to generate an appropriate response. Anticipating this, financial markets may lose confidence in the sustainability of fiscal policy, even if the country currently exhibits relatively low deficits, as did Mexico in 1994.

Solving this problem probably requires deep reforms in the budgetary institutions that shape fiscal policy determination in the region[21]. Here we point out that, while future fiscal policy reforms are essential to secure the economic stability required for sustained growth, our perspective departs from the conventional wisdom in two key respects. First, the focus on ensuring macroeconomic stability makes it clear that the issue is not merely raising rates of public saving with the aim of increasing total national saving. The real need is to create institutional structures that provide real assurance that fiscal policy will be well managed in good times. If the institutional reforms are effective, they will permit larger deficits in bad times, thus promoting a more counter-cyclical fiscal policy, but not necessarily one with higher public saving on average. Second, our perspective highlights the need to tackle problems in the formulation of fiscal policy by addressing the underlying institutional and political causes of suboptimal fiscal policy making, rather than simply exhorting governments to behave themselves.

Saving and Capital Inflows[22]

Another context in which saving has recently arisen as a policy issue is in the macroeconomic response to large capital inflows. The dominant view is that East Asia has invested these inflows, while Latin America has mainly consumed them. The associated decline in Latin American saving is blamed for the region's greater vulnerability to interruptions in the flow of international capital.

Lawrence ("Larry") Summers, Under-secretary of the U.S. Treasury and Michael Bruno, Chief Economist at the World Bank have espoused this view:

"Policy makers must look at how capital flows are being used. For nations as well as for people, borrowing to finance investment is seen as healthy, but borrowing to finance consumption is much more problematic. When the lion's share of inflows is being used for investment, there is the presumption that the economy is generating the capital to repay these obligations....Similarly, the national saving rate can offer some evidence as to whether capital inflows are being used to finance unsustainable consumption or investment..." (Summers, 1996a)

"In both Latin America and East Asia, private capital inflows in recent years have amounted to some 3 to 4 per cent of GDP. But as Larry Summers noted, whether this is a good thing or not depends on whether those inflows went to finance investment or consumption. On this score, the two regions differ: capital flows to East Asia (except the Philippines) primarily financed private investment, whereas in Latin America as a whole (but not in Chile), they financed an increase in consumption..." (Bruno 1996).

Figure 14 illustrates the behaviour of capital flows to East Asia and Latin America. There is a very similar pattern in both regions: during the 1978-82 period capital flows were very large, they declined substantially during 1983-89, and increased once again during the 1990-94 period[23].

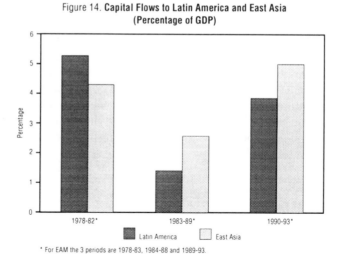

Figure 14. **Capital Flows to Latin America and East Asia (Percentage of GDP)**

* For EAM the 3 periods are 1978-83, 1984-88 and 1989-93.

32

As Figure 15 shows, in both Latin America and Asia, the inflows were eventually reflected in larger current-account deficits, with the Asian current account moving somewhat further into deficit than that of Latin America. In some individual countries of Asia, notably Thailand, current account deficits in the early 1990s exceeded the 8 per cent of GDP recorded by Mexico before the crisis, and have remained in the neighbourhood of 6 per cent of GDP in recent years.

Figure 15. **The Current Account in Latin America and Asia**
(Percentage of GDP)

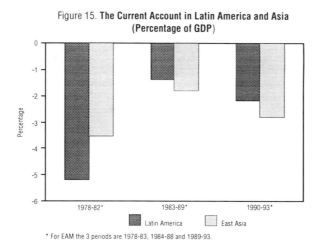

* For EAM the 3 periods are 1978-83, 1984-88 and 1989-93.

However, as was pointed out by Summers and Bruno, and illustrated in Figure 16, the two regions differ in the way current account deficits were allocated between higher investment and lower saving. While current account deficits mainly financed investment in East Asia they financed consumption, i.e., declines in saving, in Latin America.

This perception is somewhat misleading, in that it fails to make a clear enough distinction between trend and short-run movements in saving. While it is true that the Asian saving rate did not fall during the capital inflows episode of 1990-94, it had been growing rapidly since the mid-1970s, and Asian saving rates *did* fall in relation to this increasing trend. Indeed, once the trend is subtracted from the actual saving rate to estimate the cyclical or short-run component, a remarkable similarity emerges between the East Asian and the Latin American experience. This is illustrated in Figure 17.

This figure graphs the cyclical component of saving rates in East Asia and Latin America, defined as the difference between the actual saving rate and a simple trend line. The correlation between the short-run fluctuations in Latin American and East Asian saving rates is very high, and it is very hard to explain except as the response to a common, international shock.

Figure 16. **Saving, Investment and the Current Account**

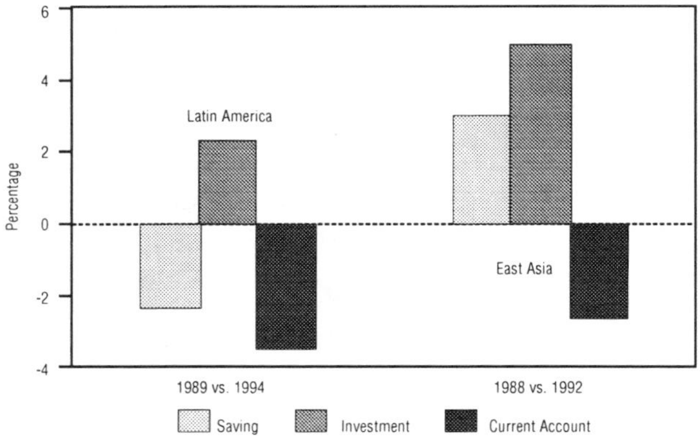

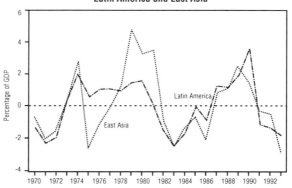

Figure 17. **Cyclical Component of National Saving
Latin America and East Asia**

Even more striking is the strong similarity in the Asian and Latin American relationship between changes in the current-account balance and cyclical fluctuations in saving rates.

Figure 18 shows that saving is inversely correlated with current account deficits in Latin America. This is of course not surprising. Much recent commentary has focused on this fact and how it has increased Latin America's economic vulnerability.

Perhaps more surprising is the very similar relationship between current accounts and the cyclical component of saving in East Asia, as illustrated in Figure 19. In contrast with the widely held view, which asserts that current account deficits in Asia have been associated with increased investment rather than reduced saving, fluctuations in the East Asian current account are, as in Latin America, associated with reductions in saving, when measured relative to a long-run trend.

34

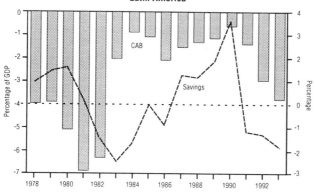

Figure 18. **The Current Account and Cyclical Component of Saving**
Latin America

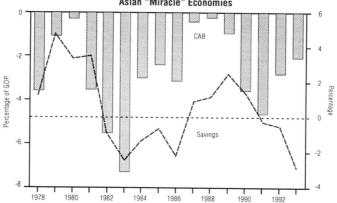

Figure 19. **The Current Account and Cyclical Component of Saving**
Asian "Miracle" Economies

The similarity of the *short-run* response of saving and investment to capital-flow shocks in Latin America and East Asia suggests two things: first, that attention should be directed away from short-run and towards long-run saving (and investment) behaviour, where the differences between the regions are much larger and arguably more significant. Second, one is led to search elsewhere for explanations of Latin America's greater financial vulnerability.

Policy Issues

Several explanations have been offered to account for the different response of saving to capital inflows in Latin America and East Asia. One of them emphasises the different composition of capital flows, i.e., East Asia receives a larger share of total flows in the form of FDI than Latin America, as mainly responsible for the different response of saving in both regions (see for example, Calvo, Leiderman and Reinhart, 1994).

The policy prescription of this view says that Latin America should find ways to change the composition of capital inflows to stimulate a larger participation of FDI in total flows. This policy would ensure that a larger share of the resources made available by capital inflows are invested and not consumed.

Given the evidence we have presented, whatever the merits of policies designed to increase the participation of FDI in total capital flows, they are unlikely to result in a significant change in the way saving in Latin America responds to those flows.

Notes

1. We use the term East Asia to refer to the six rapidly growing economies of Hong Kong, Indonesia, Korea, Malaysia, Singapore and Thailand.

2. In recent years Chile's saving rate has increased dramatically, and, around 25 per cent, now approaches East Asian levels.

3. It should be noted that many countries with an equally poor saving performance, such as Colombia, were also largely immune to the "tequila effect".

4. Technically, the paper asked whether saving "Granger causes" growth and vice versa. One variable "Granger causes" another if observations of the first variable help predict subsequent movements in the second, after taking into account the predictive value of the second variable's own history. The paper found that growth "Granger causes" saving, while saving appears not to "Granger cause" growth.

5. A plausible mechanism through which growth may "cause" saving operates through the need to provide self-finance for at least a portion of the many profitable investments available in a high-growth economy, in an environment of imperfect capital markets. Birdsall, Pinckney and Sabot (1995) argue for the importance of this mechanism in the context of low-income economies, and Liu and Woo (1994) provide evidence on its empirical importance for Chinese Taipei.

6. Granger causality test performed for the Asian "miracle" economies are consistent with the results obtained by Carroll and Weil (1994). In all cases growth was high early and saving high later.

7. For a comprehensive and formal treatment of saving behaviour in Chile, see Agosín, Crespi and Letelier (1996) and Morandé (1996).

8. This reliance can be seen in the large current-account deficits in the early stages of the economic recovery.

9. Held and Uthoff (1995) actually find a negative effect of the terms of trade on saving.

10. For example, Edwards (1994) finds some evidence that the age dependency ratio (the fraction of the population either younger than 15 or older than 65 years of age) is negatively related to domestic saving rates. In some specifications of his model a more equal distribution of income is associated with a higher saving rate, but this result was not robust.

11. Social security reform has been undertaken in Argentina, Chile, Colombia, Peru and Uruguay and are underway in Brazil and Mexico.

12. See Edwards (1994) for evidence that private saving in Latin America tends to decline by about 50 cents for every dollar by which public saving increases. Economic theory provides an explanation for this, though not everyone considers the theory entirely plausible: a budget surplus in the current period implies lower debt service, and therefore lower taxes, in future periods. Looking forward, consumers realise that, because of the lower future taxes, they can afford to consume more, thus saving less, in the current period. The increase in public saving is therefore offset by a decrease in private saving. Some theories suggest that the offset should be complete, but most empirical estimates of the offset suggest that it is about 50 per cent.

13. Edwards (1994) finds no significant impact of inflation on national saving. The results in Held and Uthoff (1995) break down if the sample of countries is restricted.

14. See Gavin and Hausmann (1995) for discussion of other countries in the region.

15. See, for example, Agosín, Crespi and Letelier (1996).

16. Although most countries' accounts consider it so, it is debatable whether an increase in spending in consumer durables really represents a decline in saving at all, because the purchases of consumer durables are really a form of investment in an asset that will yield benefits, potentially for a considerable period of time.

17. Such policies were the focus of the special chapter of the 1995 Report on Economic and Social Progress.

18. Goldfajn and Valdés (1995).

19. See the proceedings of the IDB/Group of 30 conference on Banking Crises in Latin America, and in particular Gavin and Hausmann (1995) and Rojas-Suárez and Weisbrod (1995b).

20. See Talvi (1996) for a theoretical statement of this problem, and Talvi (1995) for an empirical discussion in the Uruguayan context.

21. This problem is being explored in an ongoing research project in the Office of the Chief Economist of the Inter-American Development Bank. See Alesina, Hausmann, Hommes and Stein (1995), Hausmann and Stein (1996), and Eichengreen and Hausmann (1996), and Gavin, Hausmann, Perotti and Talvi (1996).

22. For a formal treatment of the issues presented in this section see Reinhart and Talvi (1996).

23. This is not surprising due to the significant role of external factors in determining the size and direction of capital flows to developing countries (see Calvo, Leiderman and Reinhart, 1993).

Bibliography

AGOSÍN, M., G. CRESPI and L. LETELIER (1996), "Explaining Chile's Increase in Saving", Working Paper, Regional Research Network, Inter-American Development Bank, Washington, D.C.

ALESINA, A., R. HAUSMANN, R. HOMMES and E. STEIN (1995), "Budgetary Institutions and Fiscal Performance in Latin America", working paper, Office of the Chief Economist, Inter-American Development Bank, Washington, D.C.

AYALA, U. (1995), "Social Security Reform in Latin America", manuscript, Office of the Chief Economist, Inter-American Development Bank, Washington, D.C.

BIRDSALL, N., T. PINCKNEY and R. SABOT (1995), "Inequality, Savings and Growth", manuscript, Inter-American Development Bank, Washington, D.C.

BRUNO, M. (1996) ,"Comment", in HAUSMANN, R. and L. ROJAS-SUÁREZ (eds.), *Volatile Capital Flows: Taming their Impact on Latin America,* Johns Hopkins University Press for the Inter-American Development Bank, Washington, D.C.

CALVO, G., L. LEIDERMAN and C. REINHART (1993), " Capital Inflows and Real Exchange Rate Appreciation in Latin America: The Role of External Factors", IMF Staff Papers, vol. 40, No.1, IMF, Washington, D.C.

CALVO, G., L. LEIDERMAN and C. REINHART (1994), "Inflows of Capital to Developing Countries in the 1990s: Causes and Effects", working paper No. 302, Office of the Chief Economist, Inter-American Development Bank, Washington, D.C.

CARROLL, C. and D. WEIL (1993), "Saving and Growth: A Reinterpretation", *Carnegie-Rochester Conference Series on Public Policy,* vol. 40, June.

DEATON, A. (1995) "Growth and Saving: What Do We Know, What Do We Need to Know, and What Might We Learn?", manuscript, Princeton University, Princeton, NJ.

EDWARDS, S. (1994), "Why Are Saving Rates so Different Across Countries? An International Comparative Perspective", working paper No. 5097, NBER.

EICHENGREEN, B. and R. HAUSMANN (1996), "Reforming Fiscal Institutions in Latin America: The Case for a National Fiscal Council", working paper, Office of the Chief Economist, Inter-American Development Bank, Washington, D.C.

GAVIN, M. and R. HAUSMANN (1996), "The Roots of Banking Crisis: The Macroeconomic Context", Inter-American Development Bank, Washington, D.C.

GAVIN, M., R. HAUSMANN and L. LEIDERMAN (1995), "The Macroeconomics of Capital Flows to Latin America: Experience and Policy Issues", in HAUSMANN, R. and L. ROJAS-SUÁREZ (eds.), *Volatile Capital Flows: Taming their Impact on Latin America,* Johns Hopkins University Press for the Inter-American Development Bank, Washington, D.C.

GAVIN, M., R. HAUSMANN, R. PEROTTI and E. TALVI (1996), "Managing Fiscal Policy in Latin America", working paper No. 326, Office of the Chief Economist, Inter-American Development Bank, Washington, D.C.

GOLDFAJN I. and R. VALDÉS (1995), "Balance of Payments Crises and Capital Flows: The Role of Liquidity", manuscript, MIT.

HAUSMANN, R. and E. STEIN (1996), "What are Appropriate Budgetary Institutions for Latin America", in HAUSMANN, R. and H. REISEN (eds.), "Securing Stability and Growth in Latin America: Policy Issues and Prospects for Shock-Prone Economies", OECD Development Centre and Inter-American Development Bank, Paris.

HELD, G. and A. UTHOFF (1995), "Indicators and Determinants of Savings for Latin America and the Caribbean", working paper No. 25, CEPAL.

INTER-AMERICAN DEVELOPMENT BANK (1995a), "Overcoming Volatility", in *Economic and Social Progress in Latin America: 1995 Report,* Johns Hopkins University Press for the Inter-American Development Bank, Washington, D.C.

INTER-AMERICAN DEVELOPMENT BANK (1995b), "A Macroeconomic Assessment of Latin America", manuscript, Office of the Chief Economist, Washington, D.C.

INTER-AMERICAN DEVELOPMENT BANK AND GROUP OF 30 (1996a), *Banking Crises in Latin America,* Inter-American Development Bank,Washington, D.C.

INTER-AMERICAN DEVELOPMENT BANK (1996b) "Macroeconomic Developments in Latin America and the Caribbean", in *Economic and Social Progress in Latin America: 1996 Report,* Washington, D.C.

KIGUEL, M. and N. LIVIATAN (1992), "The Business Cycle Associated with Exchange Rate-Based Stabilisation", *The World Bank Economic Review*, Vol 6.

LIU, L. and W. WOO (1994) "Saving Behavior Under Imperfect Financial Markets and the Current Account Consequences", *The Economic Journal,* 104, May.

MILESI-FERRETTI, G. M. and A. RAZIN (1996) "Current Account Deficits and Capital Flows in East Asia and Latin America: Are the Nineties Different From the Early Eighties", manuscript, IMF, Washington, D.C.

MORANDÉ, F. (1996) " Saving in Chile: What Went Right?", working paper No. 322, Office of the Chief Economist, Inter-American Development Bank, Washington, D.C.

REINHART, C. and E. TALVI (1996), "Capital Inflows and Saving Behavior in Asia and Latin America: A Reinterpretation", working paper, Office of the Chief Economist, Inter-American Development Bank, Washington, D.C.

ROJAS-SUÁREZ, L. and S. WEISBROD (1995a) "Achieving Stability in Latin American Financial Markets in the Presence of Volatile Capital Flows", working paper No. 304, Office of the Chief Economist, Inter-American Development Bank, Washington, D.C.

Rojas-Suárez, L. and S. Weisbrod (1995b) "Banking Crises in Latin America: Experience and Issues", Office of the Chief Economist, Inter-American Development Bank, Washington, D.C.

Summers, L. (1996a) "Comment", in Hausmann, R. and L. Rojas-Suárez (eds.), *Volatile Capital Flows: Taming their Impact on Latin America,* Johns Hopkins University Press for the Inter-American Development Bank, Washington, D.C.

Summers, L. (1996b) "Ten Lessons to Learn", *The Economist,* Dec. 23-Jan. 5.

Talvi, E. (1995) "Fiscal Policy and the Business Cycle Associated with Exchange-Rate Based Stabilisation: Evidence from Uruguay ", working paper No. 313, Office of the Chief Economist, Inter-American Development Bank, Washington, D.C.

Talvi, E. (1996) "Exchange-Rate Based Stabilisation with Endogenous Fiscal Response", working paper No. 322, Office of the Chief Economist, Inter-American Development Bank, Washington, D.C.

Végh, C. (1992), "Stopping High Inflation: an Analytical Overview", *IMF Staff Papers*, IMF, September , Washington, D.C.

Appendix

This appendix presents the results obtained from the estimation, on a 26 country data set —six East Asian "miracle" economies and 20 Latin American countries— of the determinants of saving. The estimation was performed on a panel of annual data for the period 1970-93, utilising a new data set on saving assembled by the International Monetary Fund.

The specification of the saving model is in line with both economic theory and with the previous empirical literature on saving (see for example Edwards, 1994 and Held and Uthoff 1995). This specification also allows for a simple dynamic structure, which in turn allows us to capture the dynamic adjustment of the economic system to its long-run equilibrium, in response to temporary and permanent shocks.

The variables included in the saving model are the following: growth of GDP per capita (ggcap) and GDP per capita (gcap) which were obtained from Summers and Heston; inflation (infl), capital flows (kflows) and changes in the terms of trade (gtot) which were obtained from the IMF's International Financial Statistics.

The results of the regression are presented in the Table A1:

The results of the regression indicate that saving is *i)* positively affected by the rate of growth, i.e., faster growing economies should, other things being equal, enjoy higher saving rates; *ii)* positively affected by the level of income per capita; and *iii)* negatively related to the availability of foreign saving (capital flows). A permanent improvement (deterioration) in the terms of trade, temporarily increases (decreases) the saving rate but has no permanent effects. A permanent reduction (increase) in the rate of inflation, reduces temporarily the saving rate, which later increases (decreases) to a level which is close to, but still lower (higher) than, the one prevailing before the reduction (increase) in the inflation rate.

Table A1. **Dependent variable – National Saving**
Included observations: 416

Variable	Coefficient	Std. Error	T-Statistic	Prob.
GCAP (-1)	2.75E-05	5.87E-06	4.685077	0.0000
GGCAP	0.102982	0.035269	2.919924	0.0037
KFLOWS	-0.206742	0.050839	-4.066629	0.0001
GTOT	0.053568	0.008768	6.109410	0.0000
GTOT(-1)	0.028714	0.009629	2.982002	0.0030
GTOT(-2)	0.014147	0.008428	1.678498	0.0940
INFL	-0.000687	0.000242	-2.841819	0.0047
INFL(-1)	0.002024	0.000273	7.420894	0.0000
INFL(-2)	0.000758	0.000293	2.586022	0.0101
INFL(-3)	-0.000472	0.000272	-1.735052	0.0835
C	0.110729	0.028247	3.920071	0.0001
AR(1)		0.023399	38.04861	0.0000

R-squared	0.840481	Mean dependent var	0.198719
Adjusted R-squared	0.836137	S.D. dependent var	0.090120
S.E. of regression	0.036481	Akaike info criterion	-6.593527
Sum squared resid	0.537657	Schwartz criterion	-6.477257
Log likelihood	793.1751	F-statistic	193.5099
Durbin-Watson stat	2.103030	Prob(F-statistic)	0.000000

Inverted AR Roots   .89

A Comment by Daniel Cohen

The paper by Gavin, Hausmann and Talvi is "dangerous". Although presented at a conference on "Promoting Saving in Latin America", it deduces that policy makers should not promote saving. The basis for their conclusion is simply that increased growth seems to precede a rise in saving — Granger causality — while the opposite is not true.

Before turning to whether that has actually been demonstrated, such inverse causality would have radical implications, as the authors stress. To mention just two examples, stabilising inflation usually decreases saving and fiscal consolidation reduces private saving, but we should not be concerned.

The appendix convincingly shows that growth Granger causes savings. Consumption theory offers many possibilities of finding this type of correlation and this is supported by causal evidence offered by the authors. On the other hand, while reverse causality was not presented, it would be harder to accept. To give one example, let us recall Alwyn Young's insightful portrayal of Asian growth in "The Tale of Two Cities" for the NBER annual or his Quarterly Journal of Economics paper "The Tyranny of Numbers". What Young proves is that Asian growth owes very little to total factor productivity and much to capital and labour inputs. The most striking example is Singapore, where total factor productivity is almost nil but two-thirds of its recorded growth (6 per cent explained for a 9 per cent average) is due to capital accumulation, i.e. its high saving rate. Young makes it fairly clear that reforms such as a funded pension plan and the government's fiscal surplus were the outcome of a growth-oriented policy, not the *endogenous* response to higher growth. However, that is not the main point. According to the authors, if growth leads saving, then it should be highly correlated with capital accumulation. Indeed, if growth began on its own, it must be reflected by a strong surge in total factor productivity (TFP) which would create its own capital accumulation response. Hence, a high positive correlation between the two should be observed.

Incidentally, such positive correlation was predicted by endogenous growth theories of the first kind (emphasising capital accumulation spill-over) and Young's papers were in part intended to deflate that view by showing the other correlation.

Other studies have come to same conclusion. A paper of mine in the Journal of Economic Growth shows that physical and human capital accumulation confirms the "convergence hypothesis" while TFP does not. If TFP were driving capital accumulation the converse should be observed.

Having said this, if a large part of the Asian miracle is an endogenous response to growth rate but that growth itself is in part generated by saving, then the conclusion would be that there is a large multiplier associated with thrift and there should be policies which aim at "promoting saving in Latin America".

Bibliography

COHEN, D. (1996),"Tests of the 'Convergence Hypothesis': Some Further Results", *Journal of Economic Growth,* Vol. 1, No. 3, September.

YOUNG, A. (1992),"A Tale of Two Cities: Factor Accumulation and Technical Change in Hong Kong and Singapore", in O.J. BLANCHARD and S. FISCHER, eds., NBER macroeconomics annual, MIT Press, Cambridge and London.

YOUNG, A. (1995), "The Tyranny of Numbers: Confronting the Statistical Realities of the East Asian Growth Experience", *The Quarterly Journal of Economics*, 110, 3, August.

A Comment by Marco Pagano

This paper offers an interesting and provocative argument with strong policy conclusions. The premise of the argument is that, in the long run, growth determines saving, rather than the reverse. It follows that low saving rates cannot be blamed for the low and volatile growth performance typical of most Latin American countries, as recently argued by Bruno (1996) and Summers (1996), among others. An important corollary of this argument is that in Latin America policies should not be aimed at increasing saving, but at stimulating growth.

The argument naturally raises three questions. First and foremost, is the premise correct? Second, even assuming that it is not — i.e. conceding that the saving rate affects the level of the growth rate — can low saving rates be also held responsible for the high volatility of growth rates in Latin America? Third, can growth-promoting policies reduce saving, at least in the short run, i.e. is there a potential policy conflict?

Is the Premise Correct?

The existence of a *contemporaneous* positive correlation between saving and growth is a robust empirical finding, documented by Modigliani (1970) and (1990), Maddison (1992), Bosworth (1993), and Carroll and Weil (1994) among others. There also is evidence that *growth leads saving*, and not vice versa. For instance, Carroll and Weil (1994), who estimate panel regressions using the Summers-Heston data, report unidirectional Granger causality from growth to saving. A similar result is found by Deaton and Paxson (1993) on time-series data for Chinese Taipei and by Jappelli and Pagano (1996) on Italian time-series data for the 1862-1990 interval. The article by Gavin, Hausmann and Talvi reports a comparable result for a panel of East-Asian and Latin American countries based on IMF data.

However, Granger causality tests do not solve the causality issue. Even if changes in growth tend to precede changes in saving, we cannot ignore that the growth rate is an endogenous variable, in the sense that there may be important (contemporaneous) feedbacks from saving to growth. Some of the leading models in macroeconomics predict precisely this: an increase in the steady-state saving rate causes a transitory increase in growth according to the standard neoclassical growth model with exogenous productivity growth, and a permanent increase in growth according to endogenous growth models[1].

The causal relationship from growth to saving is itself not easily or unambiguously explained. The model routinely used to rationalise it, i.e. the life-cycle hypothesis, is increasingly questioned for its inconsistencies with microeconomic evidence. According to the life-cycle model, increases in growth induce increases in saving only via the process of aggregation: an increase in income growth raises the resources of the young (who are net savers) relative to those of the old (who dissave). In the basic version of the model, Modigliani (1986) further assumes generation-specific productivity growth and flat individual earning profiles. Under these assumptions, an increase in aggregate productivity does not affect individual saving rates, but causes an increase in aggregate saving, due to the increased income share and number of young households relative to the retired. The trouble is that microeconomic data for several countries show that the fall in the aggregate saving rate associated with the productivity slowdown of the 1980s and 1990s did not result from aggregation across households, but rather from an across-the-board decline in individual saving rates — a result that is hard to reconcile with the life-cycle model (see Bosworth, Burtless and Sabelhaus, 1991, for a study based on US, Canadian and Japanese data; Paxson, 1996, for an analysis of repeated cross-sectional data for the United States, Britain, Chinese Taipei and Thailand; and Jappelli and Pagano, 1996, for a study of Italian repeated cross-sectional data).

In short, both the direction of causality between saving and growth and the interpretation of their causal relationships are still open issues. Actually, they are among the most unsettled issues in current macroeconomics, as shown by the recent surveys by Deaton (1996) and Schmidt-Hebbel, Servén and Solimano (1996). Even for the countries where the correlation between growth and saving has lately been strongest, i.e. the fast-growing East Asian economies, the debate rages between those who attribute their growth performance chiefly to their fast capital accumulation (Young, 1994, 1995) and those who credit it to their extraordinary manufacturing export performance, and regard capital accumulation as its effect (Pack and Page, 1994a, 1994b).

Given this state of affairs, the premise of the paper appears far too bold: we cannot rule out that the low South American saving rates are an important contributor to the disappointing growth performance of these countries.

Can Low Saving Rates be Held Responsible for *Volatile* Growth?

Even if one were to concede that low saving rates have contributed to Latin America's slow growth, it is much harder to argue that they may have contributed to its volatility. Summers (1996) has claimed, especially with reference to the recent Mexican crisis, that a low domestic saving rate generates high dependence on foreign saving, which in turn exposes the performance of the domestic economy to the vagaries of international capital flows. Here, the authors' objection is valid: with free capital mobility, domestic saving is at least as loose-footed as foreign capital in response to the danger of expropriation by policy-makers, via hyperinflation, capital levies, etc. In the presence of large potential policy shocks, a high domestic saving rate does not buy insurance against capital flight.

The likely culprit for volatile growth in Latin America is the instability of national monetary and fiscal policies, rather than the low domestic saving rates. Incidentally, this very policy instability is likely to be one of the key determinants of the low level of the domestic saving rate in most Latin American countries. This is confirmed by the Chilean exception, whose stable monetary and fiscal policies have been associated with high saving rates. With sound and foreseeable monetary and fiscal policy, Latin American countries would likely achieve both more stable growth and higher domestic saving. Here there is no policy tradeoff, at least in the long run.

However, it is worthwhile asking if such a tradeoff might still exist in the short run. In other words, if a country introduces policies intended to promote stability of the long-run growth performance — such as a sounder monetary and fiscal policy — can it actually experience a short run decline in saving? This leads us to the third question.

Can Growth-promoting Policies Reduce Saving?

Gavin, Hausmann and Talvi give a positive answer to this question, and they are correct to do so. A sudden and drastic fiscal and monetary stabilisation can lead to a consumption boom, especially if coupled with an exchange-rate-based disinflation. This is documented by abundant evidence for developing countries which start from high inflation (see Rebelo and Végh, 1993, and Easterly, 1996, among others), but there is also related evidence concerning sharp fiscal stabilisation in developed countries with relatively mild inflation (Giavazzi and Pagano, 1990, 1996; Alesina and Perotti, 1995, 1996). Many competing explanations have been offered for this non-Keynesian outcome:

— the monetary stabilisation induces a sudden drop in the nominal interest rate, but inflation fails to adjust as quickly, so that in the short run there is a real interest rate drop, which stimulates consumption via a wealth effect;

— the fiscal stabilisation induces the private sector to expect less public spending, and therefore less taxes and inflation in the future, so that households perceive their permanent disposable income to be higher and are induced to consume more;

— the fiscal stabilisation creates the feeling that the government has managed to avoid "disaster" (e.g., future default on public debt) or simply greater tax distortions tomorrow, so that the private sector perceives its permanent disposable income to be higher, and goes on a consumption binge.

49

These effects may be compounded if the fiscal and monetary stabilisation is preceded or accompanied by domestic capital-market liberalisation, if the latter increases the availability of lending to households. On one hand, the liberalisation of the household credit market has an independent negative impact on the saving rate (Jappelli and Pagano, 1994); on the other, it amplifies the effects of policy shocks which raise consumers' future after-tax incomes, since it allows people to borrow more abundantly in response to their increased permanent income. This is illustrated by the Mexican expansion of the early 1990s, where microeconomic evidence suggests that the household credit market liberalisation added considerable fuel to the consumption boom (Calderón Madrid, 1996).

This indicates that there can be a short-run tradeoff between the stabilisation policies needed for stable growth and the level of the saving rate. In itself, this tradeoff should not be a source of undue policy concern, as the authors point out: for instance, its existence should not scare the policy-makers away from implementing stabilisation policies, provided these policies are internally consistent. A high domestic saving rate may be important as a long run contributor to growth, but it makes no sense as a short-run policy objective.

Note

1. Besides posing an interpretation problem, the VAR results reported by Carroll and Weil (1994) and by Gavin, Hausmann and Talvi also suffer from a potentially serious econometric problem: panel data regression estimates are inconsistent in the presence of fixed effects and lagged dependent variables.

Bibliography

ALESINA, A. and R. PEROTTI (1995), "Fiscal Expansions and Fiscal Adjustments in OECD Countries", *Economic Policy*, 21.

ALESINA, A. and R. PEROTTI (1996), "Reducing Budget Deficits", *Swedish Economic Policy Review*, Vol. 3, 1, Spring.

BOSWORTH, B.P. (1993), *Saving and Investment in a Global Economy*, The Brookings Institution, Washington, D.C.

BOSWORTH, B.P., G. BURTLESS and J. SABELHAUS (1991), "The Decline in Saving: Evidence from Household Surveys", *Brookings Papers on Economic Activity*, 1, Washington, D.C.

BRUNO, M. (1996), "Comment", in R. HAUSMANN and L. ROJAS-SUÁREZ, eds., *Volatile Capital Flows: Taming their Impact on Latin America*, Johns Hopkins University for the Inter-American Development Bank, Washington, D.C.

CALDERÓN MADRID, A. (1996), "Determinantes del ahorro interno en México: ¿A que se debió la caída en el ahorro privado durante los años previos a la crisis de 1994?", paper prepared for the IDB Conference on "Determinants of Domestic Savings in Latin America", Bogota, June, unpublished.

CARROLL, C.D. and D.N. WEIL (1994), "Saving and Growth: a Reinterpretation", *Carnegie-Rochester Conference Series on Public Policy*, 40.

DEATON, A. (1996), "Growth and Saving: What Do We Know, What do We Need to Know, and What Might We Learn?", Princeton University, Princeton, NJ, November, unpublished.

DEATON, A. and C. PAXSON (1993), "Saving, Growth, and Ageing in Taiwan", in D.A. WISE, eds., *Studies in the Economics of Aging*, Chicago University Press for NBER, Chicago, IL.

EASTERLY, W. (1996), "When is Stabilization Expansionary? Evidence from High Inflation", *Economic Policy*, 22.

GIAVAZZI, F. and M. PAGANO (1990), "Can Severe Fiscal Contractions be Expansionary? Tales of Two Small European Countries", *NBER Macroeconomics Annual*, 5.

GIAVAZZI, F. and M. PAGANO (1996), "Non-Keynesian Effects of Fiscal Policy Changes: International Evidence and the Swedish Experience", *Swedish Economic Policy Review*, Vol. 3, 1, Spring.

JAPPELLI, T. and M. PAGANO (1994), "Saving, Growth and Liquidity Constraints", *The Quarterly Journal of Economics*, 109, 1, February.

JAPPELLI, T. and M. PAGANO (1996), "The Determinants of Saving: Lessons from Italy", paper prepared for the IDB Conference on "Determinants of Domestic Savings in Latin America", Bogota, August, unpublished.

MADDISON, A. (1992), "A Long-run Perspective on Saving", *Scandinavian Journal of Economics*, 94, 2.

MODIGLIANI, F. (1970), "The Life-cycle Hypothesis of Saving and Intercountry Differences in the Saving Ratio", in W.A. ELTIS, M. FG. SCOTT and J.N. WOLFE, eds., *Induction, Trade, and Growth: Essays in Honour of Sir Roy Harrod*, Clarendon Press, Oxford.

MODIGLIANI, F. (1986), "Life Cycle, Individual Thrift, and the Wealth of Nations", *American Economic Review*, 76.

MODIGLIANI, F. (1990), "Recent Developments in Saving Rates: a Life-cycle Perspective", Frisch Lecture, Sixth World Congress of the Econometric Society, Barcelona, August.

PACK, H. and J.M. PAGE, Jr. (1994*a*), "Accumulation, Exports, and Growth in the High Performing Asian Economies", *Carnegie-Rochester Conference Series on Public Policy*, 40.

PACK, H. and J.M. PAGE, Jr. (1994*b*), "Reply to Alwyn Young", *Carnegie-Rochester Conference Series on Public Policy*, 40.

PAXSON, C. (1996), "Saving and Growth: Evidence from Micro Data", *European Economic Review*, 40.

REBELO, S. and C.A. VÉGH (1993), "Real Effects of Exchange-rate-based Stabilization: An Analysis of Competing Theories", *NBER Macroeconomics Annual*, 10.

SCHMIDT-HEBBEL, K., L. SERVÉN, and A. SOLIMANO (1996), "Saving and Investment: Paradigms, Puzzles, Policies", *The World Bank Research Observer*, 11, 1, February.

SUMMERS, L.H. (1996), "Ten Lessons to Learn", *The Economist*, December 23-January 5.

YOUNG, A. (1994), "Accumulation, Exports, and Growth in the High Performing Asian Economies", *Carnegie-Rochester Conference Series on Public Policy*, 40.

YOUNG, A. (1995), "The Tyranny of Numbers: Confronting the Statistical Realities of the East Asian Growth Experience", *The Quarterly Journal of Economics*, 110, 3, August.

Financial Development, Savings and Growth Convergence: A Panel Data Approach

Jean-Claude Berthélemy and Aristomène Varoudakis

Recent empirical studies of growth have emphasised the financial system's importance as a factor which can promote long-run economic growth (for example, see King and Levine, 1993*a* and 1993*b*). A better mobilisation of savings, efficient risk diversification and the evaluation of investment projects, are some of the financial system's functions which explain this positive influence on growth. Until now, these empirical studies have been based on internationally comparative cross-country data. They customarily cover the 1960-85 period for which the Summers and Heston (1991) data set is available for a large number of developed and developing countries.

In this study, we use panel data econometrics to examine the contribution to growth of the financial system's development. Our estimates distinguish between two possible mechanisms for this contribution. One involves increased capital efficiency, thanks to a better allocation of resources which is achieved by the financial system's development. To study this mechanism we estimate a conditional convergence equation in which we control for the mobilisation of saving by holding constant the investment ratio. The second involves a better mobilisation of savings, which increases the investment ratio and, in this way, enhances growth. This mechanism is studied by estimating an investment equation.

The analysis of the paper is therefore closely related to the issue of savings promotion to ensure sustained growth in the long run. We are particularly interested in the analysis of savings promotion in connection with the development of the financial sector of the economy. Moreover, our analysis bears some resemblance to the one developed in the paper by Gavin, Hausmann and Talvi (1996), in so far as it acknowledges the reciprocal relationship that may exist between savings and growth. Our working hypothesis is that the development of the financial sector increases savings, which strengthens long-run growth. At the same time, faster growth promotes saving and the development of financial markets, enhancing the efficiency of financial intermediaries and leading to further development of the financial sector. Such a cumulative process may be at the origin of multiple equilibria of financial development and growth (see Berthélemy and Varoudakis, 1996), the analysis of which is at the heart of our empirical approach.

Some of our results concerning conditional convergence and the explanatory factors of growth are close to those found in cross-section studies. Nevertheless our estimates do not corroborate the presumed positive influence of the financial system's development on growth. Our explanation of this apparent paradox involves the possibility that there are multiple equilibria and threshold effects linked to the financial system's development. The possibility of multiple equilibria implies that the effects of the financial system's development are probably not appropriately taken into account by linear regressions. The reason is that these phenomena lead to discontinuities in growth, linked to threshold effects.

In testing this hypothesis we suggest a search method of threshold effects linked to the financial system's development which is applicable to both mechanisms — namely, increased productive efficiency, and promotion of savings. This methodology was used in the research on convergence clubs with cross-section data by Berthélemy and Varoudakis (1995 and 1996). It is adapted here to panel data econometrics by using estimates of the fixed effects of the regressions of conditional convergence and of the investment ratio. It should be stressed that by increasing the number of observations, panel data estimations can take into account individual differences of growth which are ascribed to factors other than those incorporated in the regression — probably institutional factors. The potential importance of these individual effects, which are at the origin of major differences in the growth of economies, has been recently demonstrated by Islam (1995).

In the second section, we present the base estimates of the conditional convergence equation in panel data. The third section studies financial development's threshold effects on productive efficiency by analysing the fixed effects of the conditional convergence regression. The fourth section uses panel data to examine financial development's effects on the investment ratio. In the fifth section we extend the study of threshold effects to the analysis of the fixed effects of the regression of the investment ratio.

Financial Development and Growth: From Cross-section to Panel Data Estimations

Our panel data estimates are based on a specification of a growth equation close to that proposed by Mankiw, Romer and Weil (1992). This equation makes a log-linear approximation of growth in the neighbourhood of the economy's long-run equilibrium. This equilibrium is defined by a Solow model augmented by introducing human capital as an additional factor of production. With panel data this equation has the following form:

$$ln(y_{i,t}) - ln(y_{i,t-1}) = \alpha_i - \beta ln(y_{i,t-1}) + \gamma_K \big(ln(s_{\kappa,t}) - ln(\delta + g^* + n_{i,t})\big) + \gamma_H ln\, h_{i,t} + Z_{i,t} + \eta_t + \varepsilon_{i,t} \quad (1),$$

y_t is the real per capita GDP of period t, s_k is the investment ratio, h is the stock of human capital, g^* is the exogenous rate of technical progress and n is the rate of population growth. The vector Z_t contains other control variables which can influence growth by their effect on the efficiency of the allocation of resources and production techniques. The economy's openness, the level of financial development, the existence of inflationary pressures are examples of such control variables.

The η_t terms express fixed temporal effects which are represented by dummy variables corresponding to each period. They convey the fixed effects of temporal shocks on growth which are not taken into account by the other explanatory variables (oil shocks, international debt crisis, etc.). The α_i terms represent time-invariant fixed effects by country. It should be recalled that in this approach all sample countries are supposed to have the same aggregate production function. The fixed effects allow for the characteristics of each country's own production function, for example, linked to the possession of natural resources, to the development of institutions and to other factors not directly taken into account by the production function. As Islam (1995) shows, these fixed effects essentially reflect the efficiency of labour at the beginning of the estimation period.

Our initial sample consisted of 82 countries observed during six five-year periods from 1960-65 to 1985-90. According to equation 1, the control variables were, first, those suggested by Mankiw, Romer and Weil (1992): a) The logarithm of the real per capita GDP at the beginning of each period (LGDP) to represent a conditional convergence effect on observed growth. b) The logarithm of the investment ratio (LINV) adjusted by subtracting $g^* + \delta + n_i$ (with $g^* + \delta = 0.05$). c) The logarithm of the stock of human capital, approximated by the average number of years of schooling of the population over 25 years of age (LH). Unlike in international cross-section estimations, recent studies have shown that the various indicators of human capital no longer have significant effects on growth as soon as the estimations take the temporal dimension into account (Knight, Loayza and Villanueva, 1993; Islam, 1995). This apparent paradox can be resolved by assuming that the effects of human capital accumulation on growth depend on policies in other areas of the economy, in particular the extent of trade openness (Berthélemy, Dessus and Varoudakis, 1997). This hypothesis is taken into account in our regressions by introducing an interactive variable (LHOP) in the regression, defined as the product of the logarithms of the stock of human capital and of the coefficient of openness.

The additional control variables in the vector Z_i are: a) The logarithm of the coefficient of openness (LOPEN), measured by the sum of imports and exports as a percentage of GDP. Since trade openness is supposed to promote efficiency in the allocation of resources, the coefficient's expected sign is positive. b) The logarithm of the average inflation rate during each period (LINF). A higher inflation is supposed to introduce distortions in investment by discouraging long-term investments. Moreover, inflation's variability probably increases with its level, which is an additional cause of distortions that can slow growth. *c)* The logarithm of the M2/GDP ratio, considered an indicator of the economy's financial system's development (LM2). The financial system is a source of economic growth insofar as it reduces transactions costs, permits risk diversification and improves selection of investment projects.

Our conditional convergence equation has been estimated by the fixed effects method, correcting for the heteroscedastic bias of standard errors by White's estimator. Because of the lack of data on the inflation rate of some countries, our estimations finally covered an unbalanced sample of 82 countries, consisting of 475 observations, with a minimum of four observations per country. The results of the estimation are as follows[1]:

$$LGDP_t - LGDP_{t-1} = \underset{(7.29)}{-0.061} \ LGDP_{t-1} + \underset{(3.86)}{0.025} \ LINV_t - \underset{(0.01)}{0.0002} \ LH_t + \underset{(2.08)}{0.013} \ LHOP_t$$

$$+ \underset{(1.80)}{0.018} \ LOPEN_t - \underset{(4.97)}{0.049} \ LINF_t - \underset{(2.50)}{0.013} \ LM2_t$$

$$- \underset{(3.22)}{0.024} \ \eta_1 - \underset{(1.71)}{0.012} \ \eta_2 - \underset{(1.86)}{0.010} \ \eta_3 - \underset{(0.89)}{0.004} \ \eta_4 - \underset{(5.70)}{0.018} \ \eta_5 \quad , \tag{2}$$

$$\overline{R}^2 = 0.525 \qquad \text{S.E.R.} = 0.021 \qquad \text{n. obs. } 475$$

Some of our results are close to those obtained by cross-section estimations. The coefficient of the lagged GDP is negative and significant, indicating conditional convergence. The investment ratio and trade openness have the expected positive coefficients. The coefficient for inflation indicates a significant negative influence on growth. On the other hand, the coefficient for the stock of human capital does not indicate that education has any direct influence on growth. Nevertheless, the coefficient of the interactive variable LHOP is positive and significant, confirming the assumption that the effect of human capital on growth depends on the economy's openness to trade[2]. The most surprising result of this estimation is the coefficient of LM2, which is negative and significant, indicating that the financial system's development hinders growth. This is exactly the opposite of the results obtained by previous cross-section econometric studies[3].

Multiple Equilibria, Financial Development and Growth: A Fixed Effects Analysis

The working hypothesis which we will consider to explain this paradox involves the possible existence of multiple growth equilibria linked to the financial system's level of development[4]. Various mechanisms that could be at their origin have been studied by Saint-Paul (1992), Zilibotti (1994), and Berthélemy and Varoudakis (1994). In the latter study, the proposed mechanism is based on reciprocal externalities between the financial sector and the real sector: the financial system's development increases the efficiency of investment and enhances growth, but at the same time the real sector's growth promotes saving and the development of financial markets, which have a positive effect on the efficiency of financial intermediation.

Such interactions generate two stable equilibria: a "high equilibrium" with high growth and normal development of the financial sector and a "low equilibrium" with weak growth, where the economy does not succeed in developing its financial sector. Between the two there is an unstable equilibrium which defines a threshold effect of the financial system's development on growth. Beyond this threshold the economy converges towards an equilibrium with high growth, while below the threshold it remains confined in a poverty trap.

In a hypothetical distribution of economies around this critical threshold (LM2*), the relationship between the observed growth rate and the measure of the financial system's development (after controlling for the influence of other growth factors) would look like a function in the form of steps, as shown in Figure 1.

Figure 1.

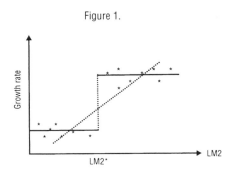

This suggests that the effect of the financial system's development on growth is mainly a step effect which reflects a discontinuity in the growth process. This discontinuity is linked to changes in the characteristics of the long-term equilibrium towards which the economy is converging. In the presence of threshold effects, it is inappropriate to express financial development's contribution to growth by linear functions which will inevitably ignore these discontinuities. If there is such a threshold effect, no relationship between LM2 and the growth rate can appear in an estimation by panel data with fixed effects insofar as the underlying "stairs" will most probably be captured by the fixed effects themselves.

The channel linked to productivity growth can be studied by analysing the determinants of the fixed effects of growth associated with different economies, which can be identified thanks to panel data estimates. It should be recalled that these "country fixed effects" theoretically represent the initial level of labour productivity (see Islam, 1995) which, in turn, is linked to efficiency of investment and thus to the financial system's efficiency.

Our research strategy involves three stages. First, the fixed effects associated with the 82 countries of our sample have to be obtained from the estimations of equation 2 above. Indeed, these fixed effects reveal a major variability in productive efficiency between countries. Second, we identify the factors explaining these international differences in productive efficiency. Lastly, we try to detect threshold effects linked to the financial system's development by analysing the structural stability of the econometric relationship for the fixed effects.

We tried a number of variables which might explain international differences in productive efficiency like trade openness, the availability of human capital, the level of the financial system's development, public expenditure as a percentage of GDP and socio-political instability. The only variables having a significant influence on the fixed effects (FIX) are human capital (LH) and the financial system's size, as measured by LM2[5]. That is illustrated by equation 1.1 of Table 1. It shows that the stock of human capital and the financial system's size both have a significant positive influence on productive efficiency.

Table 1. **Regressions for the Fixed Effects of the Conditional Convergence Equation**
(dependent variable: FIX)

Independent variables	eq. 1.1	eq. 1.2 *	eq. 1.3 **	eq. 1.4
Intercept	0.467	0.373	0.473	0.465
	(32.1)	(10.62)	(27.14)	(45.22)
LH	0.058	0.060	0.053	0.056
	(9.62)	(7.17)	(7.00)	(9.91)
LM2	0.021	-0.036	0.007	
	(2.59)	(1.70)	(0.43)	
DUM				-0.033
				(4.05)
$\bar{R}^2$	0.674	0.535	0.583	0.707
SER	0.034	0.036	0.028	0.032
Nb obs	82	44	38	82

* M2/PIB < 36.5% (44 countries)   ** M2/PIB ≥ 36.5% (38 countries)
DUM = 1 for the first group of countries, 0 for the others.
Estimation method OLS; Student's t in parentheses.
Source: Authors' calculations.

The positive influence of LM2 on the fixed effects tends to confirm the beneficial impact of the financial system's development on growth, meeting the conclusions of empirical cross-section studies of conditional convergence. However, insofar as the relationship between the fixed effects and the financial system's size gives rise to threshold effects, as in the case of multiple equilibria, the estimated relationship can simply be a spurious regression. It could falsely depict the impact of LM2 on growth linearly, as a result of the step effect implicit in multiple equilibria, as shown by the upward-sloping, discontinuous line of Figure 1.

To test this hypothesis, we used a search method of "convergence clubs", originated by Durlauf and Johnson (1992). This method has also been used by Berthélemy and Varoudakis (1995) and (1996) to test for the existence of multiple equilibria linked to the development of the financial system in the framework of a cross-section study of conditional convergence. In the present context, this method first involves sorting the sample of 82 countries according to a criterion of financial development (LM2). Then it implies testing the structural stability of the estimated relationship (equation 1.1) by successive Fisher tests, each time advancing the sample's break point by one observation.

Figure 2 presents the estimated values of Fisher's tests (curve F), as well as the probability of rejecting by error the null hypothesis of equal coefficients on the samples defined by different break points (curve P). The tests suggest that there was a break point — at a 1 per cent significance level — for M2/GDP = 0.365, corresponding to the 45th observation in the sample. This break point defines a group of 44 countries with a low level of financial development and a second group of 38 countries with a developed financial system, which seem to follow different growth trajectories. Unlike the results from the whole sample shown by equation 1.1, an analysis of the fixed-effects equation's parameters, estimated for these two groups of countries (Table 1, equations 1.2 and 1.3), no longer reveals a positive effect for the financial development variable on productive efficiency. On the other hand, the coefficient associated with human capital remains almost identical for the two groups of countries.

Figure 2. **Stability Test for Fixed Effects of Growth: Sample Sorted According to M2/GDP**

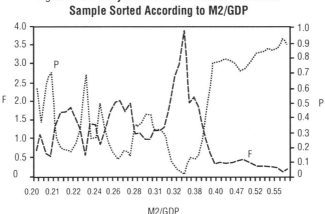

The main difference between the two groups resides in the effect of the financial development variable LM2. It seems to be negative in the countries with a financial system of a size lower than a critical threshold and is not significant for the financially developed countries. The negative coefficient of LM2 for the first group seems to be consistent with the result illustrated by equation 2, in which an expansion of the financial system in countries where there is financial repression can be detrimental to growth. The fact that the coefficients of LM2 are not significant for both the first and second groups seems to corroborate the hypothesis that the influence of the financial system's development on productive efficiency is transmitted by a threshold effect rather than in a linear manner.

That is confirmed by equation 1.4 of Table 1 which is estimated from the whole sample, but when replacing LM2 by a dummy variable (DUM) which allows for this threshold effect of financial development. As can be seen, the coefficient associated with this variable is negative and highly significant. Moreover, this equation has better statistical properties than its counterpart, equation 1.1, which includes the anomalous effect of LM2. This result suggests that the financial system's development eventually has a positive effect on productive efficiency, and thus on growth, which however has the form of a step effect, as illustrated in Figure 1.

Financial Development and Investment: A Panel Data Analysis

The second mechanism by which the financial system's development can affect growth is by a better mobilisation of savings, which leads to a greater investment ratio. The close link existing between these two variables has been well documented by Feldstein and Horioka (1980). To assess the importance of this mechanism, we estimated a regression for the investment ratio of the same sample of 82 countries in panel data as for the conditional convergence equations.

The dependent variable is the logarithm of the investment ratio (LINV). We used four control variables for the international differences in the investment ratio and their changes over time: *a)* The logarithm of the M2/GDP ratio (LM2), which in the present context reflects the impact of the financial system's development through better mobilisation of savings. *b)* The logarithm of the coefficient of the economy's openness used previously (LOPEN). By promoting the diffusion of new technologies and improving competitiveness, trade openness can raise capital productivity and increase the incentive to invest. *c)* The logarithm of the stock of human capital. *d)* Dummy variables (η_t) for fixed temporal effects which are supposed to represent the impact of various shocks on the investment ratio.

Equation 2.1 of Table 2 is estimated by the fixed effects method on a sample of 82 countries for five periods of five years from 1960 to 1985 (406 observations). The results reveal a positive, significant influence for both financial development and trade openness. The stock of human capital has a positive effect but is not significant. The temporal fixed effects show a decreasing trend in the investment ratio over time.

Despite their plausibility, the robustness of these results could be called into question because of the reciprocal relationship between the size of the financial sector and the volume of savings, and thus the investment ratio. If financial development contributes to the investment ratio's growth by mobilising savings more efficiently, the greater volume of savings increases demand for intermediation services and, in turn, contributes to the financial system's development. This hypothesis is confirmed by equation 2.2 which explains on the same sample in panel data the international differences in M2/GDP.

The independent variables are[6]: *a)* The value of LM2 lagged by one period, on the assumption that there is a conditional convergence trend towards the long-term equilibrium value of M2/GDP. *b)* The logarithm of the coefficient of trade openness (LOPEN) on the assumption that the demand for financial intermediation services increases with an economy's integration in world trade. *c)* The logarithm of public expenditure as a percentage of GDP (LGOV). A large ratio can lead to growth of the monetary base and a greater volume of financial intermediation, if public spending is not inflationary and the state does not repress the financial sector to finance public expenditure. *d)* The logarithm of the inflation rate (LINF), inasmuch as a high inflation increases the opportunity cost of holding money, thus being detrimental to the financial system's development. *e)* The logarithm of the stock of human capital (LH), on the assumption that a high level of educational attainment increases both the efficiency of financial intermediaries and consumer demand for their services, thus promoting the financial system's growth. *f)* The logarithm of the investment ratio (LINV).

The estimated coefficients have the expected sign and are significant. The results confirm that the investment ratio has a large positive influence on the M2/GDP ratio. This reciprocity between the two variables could be at the origin of a simultaneity bias in the estimation of the coefficient of LM2 in the investment ratio equation. To test this hypothesis, we estimated equation 2.1 with LM2 replaced by an instrumental variable. The latter was constructed by using the predicted values of LM2 from equation 2.2 (LM2), from which the investment ratio has been excluded.

The results are illustrated by equation 2.3 of Table 2. As can be observed, the influence of trade openness and human capital on the investment ratio remain practically unchanged (the effect of human capital even becoming significant). On the other hand, LM2 no longer has a significant effect on the investment ratio. This result is similar to that found in the conditional convergence regressions 2 and 3. It *a priori* calls into question the relevance of the hypothesis that the financial system's development can contribute to mobilising savings better and, by that means, promotes investment and growth.

Financial Development and Investment: Analysis in Terms of Fixed Effects

To study this paradox further, we follow the same procedure as before on the effects of LM2 on growth. The existence of multiple growth equilibria implies that the influence of the financial system's development on the investment volume is not expressed linearly but rather takes the form of a "step effect", like the one previously identified. Moreover, this effect is probably not expressed through the multiplicative coefficient of LM2 in the investment equation but rather through the fixed effects, which can capture the discontinuity in the mobilisation of savings resulting from crossing a critical threshold in financial development.

Table 2. **Financial Development and Investment: Panel Data Estimations**

Independent variables	eq. 2.1	eq. 2.2	eq. 2.3	eq. 2.4
		dependent variable		
	LINV	LM2	LINV	LINV
LM2	0.239			
	(3.06)			
LOPEN	0.293	0.087	0.332	0.330
	(4.15)	(1.90)	(4.14)	(5.00)
LH	0.129	0.180	0.187	0.252
	(1.58)	(3.53)	(2.09)	(3.96)
LM2F			0.029	
			(0.26)	
LM2(-1)		0.582		
		(8.81)		
LINV		0.177		
		(4.21)		
LGOV		0.177		
		(3.10)		
LINF		-0.164		
		(2.29)		
η_1	0.302		0.258	0.216
	(5.18)		(4.44)	(3.74)
η_2	0.309		0.282	0.270
	(6.35)		(5.85)	(5.30)
η_3	0.261		0.243	0.301
	(6.64)		(6.22)	(6.85)
η_4	0.134		0.129	0.255
	(3.71)		(3.55)	(6.41)
η_5				0.135
				(3.33)
$\bar{R}^2$	0.898	0.929	0.892	0.884
SER	0.212	0.159	0.218	0.229
No obs	406	406	406	492
Fisher Test [1]	20.76**	2.69**	19.83**	26.72**
Hausman Test [1]	124.1**	39.1**	87.9**	10.79*

Estimation by the fixed effects method. The heteroscedastic bias of the standard errors was corrected by White's method. Student's t is in parentheses.

In the first three regressions, the number of observations was reduced by the introduction of a lagged value of LM2 and by the absence of some data on the inflation rate. Equation 2.4 which does not use these variables was estimated for the whole sample.

1 * (**) indicate that the test was significant at the 5 per cent or 1 per cent level respectively.

Source: Authors' calculations.

To test this hypothesis, we first obtained the fixed effects from the equation for the investment ratio — eliminating the LM2 variable which is not significant. The results of this estimation by the fixed effects method are shown under equation 2.4 in Table 2. It should be observed that in all the investment-ratio equations Fisher's test strongly rejected the hypothesis of common intercepts.

As with the fixed effects of the growth equation, the fixed effects of the investment-ratio equation (FIXINV) are explained by two variables: a) The logarithm of the stock of human capital and b) the logarithm of the M2/GDP ratio. Equation 3.1 of Table 3 shows the results obtained by estimation of this equation on a cross section of the whole sample of 82 countries. The coefficient for human capital is positive but not significant enough. On the other hand, the positive influence of LM2 is highly significant. To verify if this influence does not conceal a threshold effect similar to that identified before, we made a structural stability test of this regression by sorting the whole sample by increasing order of LM2. As before, this was done by successive Fisher tests, each time advancing the sample's break point by one observation. The results of this procedure are shown in Figure 3.

Table 3. **Regressions for the Fixed Effects of the Investment Equation**
(dependent variable: FIXINV)

Independent variables	eq. 3.1	eq. 3.2 *	eq. 3.3 **	eq. 3.4
Intercept	-1.784	-2.637	-1.729	-1.913
	(9.09)	(1.83)	(11.31)	(33.19)
LH	0.115	0.577	0.032	
	(1.43)	(1.91)	(0.53)	
LH×DUM2				0.590
				(3.11)
LM2	0.373	0.132	0.266	
	(3.36)	(0.17)	(2.48)	
DUM2				-0.961
				(5.35)
$\bar{R}^2$	0.225	0.09	0.111	0.268
SER	0.459	0.691	0.317	0.447
No obs	82	22	60	82

* M2/PIB < 21.5% (22 countries)   ** M2/PIB ≥ 21.5% (60 countries)
DUM2 = 1 for countries of the first group, 0 for the others.
Method of estimation OLS; Student's t is in parentheses.
Source: Authors' calculations.

The data indicate that there was a break point for M2/GDP = 0.215 at a significance level below 5 per cent. Twenty-two countries are located under this threshold and 60 countries above. The difference between these two groups of countries concerns both the influence of human capital and financial development. As regression 3.2 for the 22 countries with limited financial development shows, human capital is a factor having a relatively significant positive influence on the propensity to invest. On the other hand, LM2 does not have a significant effect. In the group of 60 countries whose financial system is above the threshold, human capital does not have a notable influence on investment but LM2 has a significant positive effect.

Figure 3. **Stability Test for Fixed Effects of Investment: Sample Sorted According to M2/GDP**

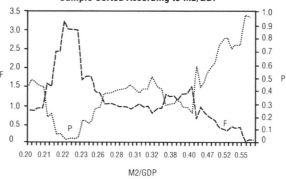

M2/GDP

Our presumption is that these results reveal a step effect of financial development on the "natural" propensity to invest, analogous to that previously found. This is confirmed by regression 3.4 in which LM2 is replaced by a dummy variable (DUM2) which allows for the break point at M2/GDP = 0.215. Using the same dummy variable, this equation also allows for the fact that human capital only seems to have a significant influence on the fixed effects of investment for the countries under this threshold of financial development. As can be observed, this regression has better statistical properties than regression 3.1, which incorporated LM2. Moreover, the coefficient of human capital is now significant. The dummy variable is negative and highly significant. That indicates that countries under the threshold of financial development that we identified have significantly poorer investment performances. Crossing this threshold makes possible better mobilisation of savings and improves these performances.

However, it should be noted that this second threshold of financial development is considerably lower than that for the direct effects of M2/GDP on productive efficiency and growth (0.215 against 0.365). This divergence is probably explained by the difference in the two functions that the financial system fulfils in the growth and economic development process. It can be reasonably assumed that a better mobilisation of savings, which leads to an increase in the volume of investment, of course requires a sufficiently dense, but not necessarily sophisticated, network of financial intermediation. Efficient collection of savings essentially depends on a good network of financial intermediaries in the territory and the disposal of financial instruments that are sufficiently attractive and allow an efficient diversification of risks. On the other hand, improved allocation of savings to different investment projects which contributes to enhanced capital productivity requires a larger and more diversified financial system that is capable of efficiently evaluating and monitoring various productive activities. Besides the presence of financial intermediaries, this also requires some minimum development of financial markets, which cannot be based on a banking system (and thus on a M2/GDP ratio) that is too small. Thus it is natural enough that the threshold of financial development which is relevant for mobilisation of savings is lower than the threshold for the quality of allocation of savings to investment — which affects productive efficiency.

Moreover, it is fairly instructive to study the growth and investment performance of different groups of countries in relation to the development of their financial system and the two thresholds that have just been identified. Table 4 presents the average annual per capita GDP growth rate, the investment ratio and the M2/GDP ratio during the 1960-90 period for six groups of countries (calculated as the average of individual country data). These groups have relatively homogenous economic characteristics, either because of geographical proximity of their member countries, or because of the similarity of market mechanisms, institutions and economic policies they share (the OECD countries).

Table 4. **Comparative Growth and Investment Performances (1960-90)**

	Per capita GDP growth rate	Inv/GDP	M2/GDP
OECD countries (except Mexico)	3.20	0.264	0.644
Southeast Asia	4.89	0.233	0.518
North Africa and Middle East	2.93	0.171	0.466
Latin and Central America	1.29	0.178	0.262
South Asia	1.88	0.121	0.259
Sub-Saharan Africa	0.63	0.136	0.202

Source: Authors' calculations.

Of these groups, it can be seen, only the OECD countries, Southeast Asia and North Africa/Middle East have a level of financial development higher than the first threshold relating to the allocation of resources and productive efficiency. The size of the financial systems of Latin American and South Asian countries is lower than this threshold — but greater than 0.215 relating to the mobilisation of savings and investment. Finally, the sub-Saharan African countries are under both financial development thresholds.

In light of the result previously obtained, it is not surprising that the growth rate of the three last groups of countries under the first threshold (0.365) was significantly less than that of the first three groups. Having a financial system whose size is less than the second threshold (0.215), the sub-Saharan African countries also have a very low investment ratio. That is also the case for the South Asian countries, despite their position above this threshold. The low per capita income — which is comparable to sub-Saharan Africa — is a factor that could explain the low saving rate in these countries. The Latin American countries are of special interest inasmuch as they are between the two thresholds. The fact that their financial system's size is greater than the threshold of 0.215 seems to permit a reasonable mobilisation of savings, as shown by an investment ratio comparable to countries of North Africa and the Middle East. Being however under the 0.365 threshold of financial development, they seem to suffer from a low quality of allocation of savings to investment, which is harmful to the productivity of capital. This is reflected to an extremely weak rate of growth, despite the relatively good investment performances of these economies.

Conclusion

We have shown that the validity of empirical cross-section results of the financial system's contribution to growth seems to be called into question by panel data estimations. Our explanation of this paradox is based on the existence of multiple equilibria related to the financial sector's development. Threshold effects associated with multiple equilibria introduce discontinuities which are not captured by linear estimations. Such discontinuities are captured by the fixed effects of panel data estimations. Following a disaggregated approach, we tried to identify two channels which transmit the threshold effects to growth. The first is based on the quality of the allocation of resources to investment and affects growth through capital productivity. The second is based on the mobilisation of savings by the financial system, which determines the volume of investment and, in this way, exerts an influence on growth.

Our analysis of the stability of the econometric relationships for the fixed effects of growth and investment revealed the existence of two thresholds of financial development, each associated with one of these two mechanisms. The first threshold, relatively low, concerns the efficiency of the mobilisation of savings, while the second, relatively higher, concerns the quality of resource allocation to investment. This analysis permits a better understanding of the financial system's contribution to growth during different phases of its development, and assists in identifying the appropriate policies and structural reforms during each phase.

With respect to Latin America, our results produce instructive information. According to our criteria, the average level of financial development in the region is currently relatively low, though there are, of course, exceptions, if only because of imperfections in the indicator we have chosen. This is the case of Chile, which was able to develop a dynamic financial market owing to the establishment of pension funds. Nonetheless, with an average level of financial development comparable to

South Asia's and distinctly inferior to that of Southeast Asia, Latin America will certainly need a more developed financial system to be able to accelerate its growth. According to our results, the problem is not so much generating savings, but of their efficient allocation. From this point of view, we concur with the analysis by Gavin, Hausmann and Talvi (1996) who consider that the collection of savings should not be seen as a priority for economic policy.

The current state of Latin American financial systems is clearly part of the heritage of the financial repression of the past. Such policies greatly reduced the dynamism of the financial sector. Our analyses suggest that, insofar as there exist persistence effects due to the presence of multiple equilibria, the relatively recent liberalisation policies have not been able to restore the necessary dynamism to the financial system. An efficient financial system for allocating savings requires the creation of well functioning financial institutions and instruments, which takes time after a long period of financial repression. Any voluntarist policy which allows progress in this area, for example, the creation of a solid financial market, could contribute significantly to enhancing the prospects for growth in Latin America.

Notes

1. Fisher's test [F81.381) = 3.28] confirms the individual effects specification in relation to a common constant specification for all countries. Moreover, Hausman's test [$\chi^2(7)$ = 69.2] confirms the fixed effects specification in comparison to a random effects estimation for the constant term.

2. Some theoretical arguments for this influence are presented by Berthélemy, Dessus and Varoudakis (1997), where the effect of trade openness is also established more explicitly by the estimation of a varying coefficient model using panel data.

3. For example, see King and Levine (1993a), (1993b) and Levine and Zervos (1993).

4. Before turning to this analysis we tested the hypothesis that the positive effects of the financial system's development (as expressed by an increased M2/GDP ratio) on growth can only be fully seen after financial reform has been undertaken. When the financial system is repressed an increase in the M2/GDP ratio can be harmful to growth. It can reflect inflationary monetary growth inasmuch as financial repression is often used by governments with public deficits to increase the inflationary tax. Moreover, it can reflect a poor allocation of savings to investment, which will have negative effects on growth because of the allocative distortions resulting from the financial system's repression. To test this hypothesis we attempted to synthesise the effect of financial reforms on the allocation of resources by a single dummy variable which equals 1 for the periods before the reform and 0 for the post-reform periods, including the period in which it is implemented (and countries which never implemented financial repression policies). This variable was defined in accordance with the classification of countries and dates of reform suggested by Johnston and Pazarbasioglu (1995). This variable turns out to exert a significantly negative influence on growth. However, the financial system's development effect on growth in the economies that reformed their financial system is not significant and its sign remains contrary to the one expected. It should be noted that the weakness of this effect can also reflect financial crises which resulted from experiences with financial liberalisation that failed, especially in Latin American countries. The financial system's negative contribution to growth during these phases has been established for the countries of this region with a panel data approach by De Gregorio and Guidotti (1995).

5. Human capital's influence on the fixed effects of a conditional convergence regression has also been established by Islam (1995). In cross-section regressions for fixed effects, we use the logarithm of the average value of the stock of human capital and the M2/GDP ratio during the 1960-90 period for each country.

6. See also Berthélemy and Varoudakis (1996) for the estimation of a financial development equation with cross-section data.

Bibliography

BERTHÉLEMY, J.-C. and A. VAROUDAKIS (1994), « Intermédiation financière et croissance endogène », *Revue Économique*, 45.

BERTHÉLEMY, J.-C. and A. VAROUDAKIS (1995), "Thresholds in Financial Development and Economic Growth", *The Manchester School*, 63, Supplement.

BERTHÉLEMY, J.-C. and A. VAROUDAKIS (1996), "Economic Growth, Convergence Clubs, and the Role of Financial Development", *Oxford Economic Papers*, 48.

BERTHÉLEMY, J.-C., S. DESSUS and A. VAROUDAKIS (1997), "Human Capital and Growth: The Role of the Trade Regime", Technical Paper, OECD Development Centre, Paris.

DE GREGORIO, J. and P.E. GUIDOTTI (1995), "Financial Development and Economic Growth", *World Development*, 22.

DURLAUF, S.N. and P.A. JOHNSON (1992), "Local versus Global Convergence Across National Economies", *Discussion Paper No. 131*, LSE Financial Markets Group, January.

FELDSTEIN, M. and C. HORIOKA (1980), "Domestic Saving and International Capital Flows", *Economic Journal*, 90.

ISLAM, N. (1995), "Growth Empirics: A Panel Data Approach", *Quarterly Journal of Economics*, 110.

JOHNSTON, R.B. and C. PAZARBASIOGLU (1995), "Linkages Between Financial Variables, Financial Sector Reform and Economic Growth and Efficiency", *IMF Working Paper No 95/103*, October.

KING, R.G. and R. LEVINE (1993a), "Finance, Entrepreneurship and Growth: Theory and Evidence", *Journal of Monetary Economics*, 32.

KING, R.G. and R. LEVINE (1993b), "Finance and Growth: Schumpeter Might Be Right", *Quarterly Journal of Economics*, 108.

KNIGHT, M., N. LOAYZA and D. VILLANUEVA (1993), "Testing the Neoclassical Theory of Economic Growth: A Panel Data Approach", *IMF Staff Papers*, 40.

LEVINE, R. and S. ZERVOS (1993), "Looking at the Facts: What we Know about Policy and Growth from Cross-Country Analysis", *American Economic Review*, 83.

MANKIW, G.N., D. ROMER and D.N. WEIL (1992), "A Contribution to the Empirics of Economic Growth", *Quarterly Journal of Economics*, 107.

SAINT-PAUL, G. (1992), "Technological Choice, Financial Markets and Economic Development", *European Economic Review*, 36.

SUMMERS, R. and A. HESTON (1991), "The Penn World Table (Mark 5): An Expanded Set of International Comparisons 1950-1988", *Quarterly Journal of Economics*, 106.

ZILIBOTTI, F. (1994), "Endogenous Growth and Intermediation in an 'Archipelago' Economy", *Economic Journal*, 103.

A Comment by Jorge Braga de Macedo

This paper builds on the two-way interaction between growth and financial development by introducing the promotion of savings. It uses panel data estimation techniques to suggest the existence of two thresholds of financial development. Under the higher threshold, the quality of resource allocation to investment is inadequate. Under the lower threshold, there is inadequate mobilisation of savings as well. Table 4 reports averages for the 1960-90 period of growth of per capita income, investment and broad money (M2) output ratios for large groups of countries. The conclusion is that if M2 is on average below 22 per cent of Y (typical of sub-Saharan Africa where it is 20 per cent), there is inadequate mobilisation of savings, and if M2 is below 37 per cent of Y (typical of Latin and Central America and South Asia where it is 26 per cent), there is inadequate investment. North Africa and Middle East, Southeast Asia and the OECD countries (except Mexico) are above both thresholds, with 47 per cent, 52 per cent and 64 per cent respectively.

The pattern is far from clear with period averages and it would become even less defined if the entire data set were presented. While one is sympathetic to the topic and approach the authors chose, the results in their present form are of limited usefulness for policy making. Thus it seems preferable to go back to the early literature showing how growth in national income increases the demand for money which induces financial development and sustains growth.

Both its empirical and theoretical strands start with Raymond Goldsmith's major book *Financial Structure and Development* whose conclusions are still worth citing: "Both (economic theory and economic history) assure us that the existence and development of a superstructure of financial instruments and financial institutions, is a necessary, though not a sufficient, condition for economic growth... Both however fail to answer the question in which we are primarily interested: Does finance make a difference...? The question certainly cannot be settled before the theory of finance is developed much further in the direction of analysing the process of financial development and its relation to economic growth in operational testable terms and before we possess a substantial number of intensive case studies, for different representative countries and periods, that use the framework of such a financial theory. We are still, it seems, many years from that crucial point" (1969).

The quest for a quantitative answer to Goldsmith's question continued with Ronald McKinnon's influential book *Money and Capital in Economic Development*, published in 1973. The interaction is quite complex though and McKinnon (1986) recognised the dangers of all-out capital account liberalisation for growth prospects : "The existence of moral hazard in banks... implies that the government should probably impose a ceiling on the standard loan (and deposit) rate of interest" (1986).

My own comments on this used medical metaphors: financial repression is bad but cures that are worse than the disease should be avoided. This is the message that we probably associate with Carlos Diaz Alejandro's well-known account of how the credibility of Chile's liberalisation policy was undermined by the rescue of Banco Osorno in 1977. "Goodbye Financial Liberalization, Hello Financial Crash", it anticipates similar developments in the US, Europe (first Scandinavia and now central Europe) and Japan, showing once again how Latin America is a laboratory of economic experimentation. The authors' approach should be judged against this background.

The authors address similar topics in several other theoretical papers and conclude a simulation exercise with the proposal of subsidising the banking sector, whose practical implementation is of course fraught with moral hazard problems, as is evident from the examples just mentioned. The problem of adverse selection in monitoring projects with uncertain returns has been shown, by Mc Kinnon (1986) in particular, to become worse under macroeconomic instability of the kind often experienced in Latin America. We may now add the Portuguese experience, Scandinavia in the early 1990s, and central Europe more recently.

Indeed, this is one of the arguments contained in the European Commission's report *One Market One Money* (1990) in favour of a change in regime towards financial stability in countries at the periphery of an integrated area, especially if there are multilateral surveillance procedures which deal with fiscal policy and encourage the adoption of multi-year fiscal adjustment strategies and pre-pegging exchange rate regimes. In a paper with Bill Branson (1995), we asserted that this is the case for the central and eastern European periphery. In this respect, the independence of the central bank, the nature of budgetary procedures and perhaps even the existence of an independent national debt board come readily to mind.

However, as Goldsmith emphasised, the lessons of economic history are also relevant. The Portuguese experience with currency convertibility shows that floating is associated with political and financial instability, which is why *real* convergence was fastest under democracy when the *real* was convertible into gold at a fixed price between 1854 and 1891 (Macedo *et al.* 1996). The period since 1989, when there was bipartisan support for a constitutional amendment to privatise banks, and especially since convertibility was restored in 1992, shows how international financial markets preceded voters in taking Portugal as a financially mature borrower.

The major objective of economic policy in the government elected in October 1991 underscored the convergence programme Q2 approved by the Ecofin council in Brussels on 16 December 1991. The main credibility-enhancing measures in Q2 were:

— no monetary financing beginning with the 1992 budget;

— an incomes policy designed to bring inflation down to single digits in 1992;

— nominal ceilings on non-interest expenditure (required for central government and recommended for general government) which in the revised programme (PCR) of November 1993 were updated until 1997 (and have not yet been revised);

— a stable and convertible exchange rate relative to the ecu.

A few weeks after the 1992 wage and price agreement and the budget were approved, the escudo entered the ERM and all controls on the capital account were gradually eliminated from 13 August to 16 December 1992. After the Treasury returned to international financial markets in 1993, borrowing in yen, DM and dollars, Portugal received an upgrade to AA- by Moody's Investors Services in the spring 1993 and launched the first ever global issue in ecu in early 1994. Yet trade unions, employers, and even political circles had grown accustomed to inflation and, coupled with the European recession and the threat of early elections, stability at home was undermined after 1993. Thus the reputation acquired in 1992-93 was reinforced by the change in government in 1995 ("the political landslide was a financial nonevent", as noted in Macedo, 1996).

Ireland's success in overcoming the "geographic fundamentals" in January 1993 provides similar evidence of the benefits of the change in regime in 1987. The same could be said for the northern European periphery and that the recent Finnish decision to join the ERM reveals the same pattern as Portugal's. These countries need a stable convertible currency as a sign of their commitment to stable policies in the future, together with social understanding and acceptance of such policies, as evidenced in bipartisan electoral support. As in the Portuguese context, "selling stability at home, earning credibility abroad" may well apply to many small open economies at the periphery of financially integrated areas — a category that increasingly applies to Latin American countries.

Returning to Berthélemy and Varoudakis after this long detour through the literature, they use longitudinal data growth empirics, as described in Islam's excellent survey which they cite, to verify the insights of Goldsmith and McKinnon. But they enjoy less than full success.

The measure of financial development used (broad money over gross domestic product) has the wrong sign in the equation. Instead of changing the measure, from the many suggestions offered in Goldsmith, the authors change the specification. The paper then lists several attempts at obtaining the right sign, first by allowing for monetary reforms, but without really trying to define whether a monetary reform might involve a change of regime in the sense of *One Market One Money* "through intensive case studies", as suggested above. They then identify fixed effects and thresholds for the 1960-90 period, summarised in their Table 4, already mentioned. Perhaps a refinement of the methodology of Jeffrey Sachs and Andrew Warner (1995) for the definition of growth convergence could make such arguments persuasive. But further research is necessary before we reach Goldsmith's crucial point when the relation of the process of financial development to economic growth can be analysed in operationally testable terms.

Bibliography

BERTHÉLEMY, J.-C. and A. VAROUDAKIS (1996), in this volume.

BRANSON, W.H. and J.B. DE MACEDO (1995), "Macroeconomic Policy in Central Europe", CEPR Discussion Paper 1445, August.

COMMISSION OF THE EUROPEAN COMMUNITIES (1990), "One Market One Money", *European Economy*.

DIAZ- ALEJANDRO, C. (1985) "Goodbye Financial Liberalization, Hello Financial Crash", *Journal of Development Economics*.

GOLDSMITH, R. (1969), *Financial Structure and Development*, Yale University Press, New Haven.

MACEDO, J.B. DE (1996), "Portugal and European Monetary Union: Selling Stability at Home, Earning Credibility Abroad", *Monetary Reform in Europe*, F. TORRES (ed.), Catholic University Press, Lisbon.

MACEDO, J.B. DE, B. EICHENGREEN and J. REIS (1996), *Currency Convertibility: The Gold Standard and Beyond*, Routledge, London.

MCKINNON, R. (1973), *Money and Capital in Economic Development*, Brookings Institution, Washington, D.C.

MCKINNON, R. (1986), "Financial Liberalization in Retrospect: Interest Rate Policies in LDCs", in *The State of Development Economics Progress and Perspectives*, G. RANIS and T. P. SCHULTZ (eds.), Basil Blackwell, New York.

SACHS, J. and A. WARNER (1995), Economic Convergence and Economic Policies, *Brookings Papers on Economic Activity*, Washington, D.C.

A Comment by José De Gregorio

This is another interesting contribution from Berthélemy and Varoudakis to our understanding of the mechanisms through which financial markets affect economic growth.

Methodology

The framework of the author's analysis is based on the extended version of the Solow model popularised by Mankiw, Romer and Weil (1992). A constant returns-to-scale production function with physical capital *(K)*, human capital *(H)*, and labour *(L)* as factors of production is assumed. The production function (using small letters to denote variables measured per unit of labour) can be written as:

$$y_t = \alpha_t k_t^{\alpha} h_t^{\beta},$$
(1)

where α is a technological parameter. Output can be consumed or saved. Savings, in turn, may take the form of increased physical or human capital. The model assumes constant savings rates for physical and human capital, denoted by s_k and s_h, respectively[1].

The economy converges gradually to the steady state per-capita income level, y^*, at a rate υ which depends on the parameters of the model:

$$ln(y_t) - ln(y_{t-1}) = \upsilon[ln(y^*) - ln(y_{t-1})].$$
(2)

After some transformations, the following regression (equation (1) in BV) can be derived:

$$ln(y_{i,t}) - ln(y_{i,t-1}) = \alpha_i + Z_{i,t} - \beta ln(y_{t-1}) + y_k[ln(s_{ki,t}) - ln(\delta + g^* + n_{i,t})] + y_h ln(h_{i,t}) + \eta_t + \epsilon_{i,t}.$$
(3)

The notation is explained by Berthélemy and Varoudakis. First, this is not an equation for long-run growth, but for transitional growth, that is, growth on the path to the steady state. Economies with low levels of income, other things equal, grow faster since capital is more productive. The transition may be slow, and current estimates indicate that half of the adjustment occurs in a period of 30 years (Barro and Sala-i-Martin, 1995)[2], but in the absence of exogenous productivity growth (growth of α) the economy converges to a constant level of output per capita.

Second, not all the economies converge to the same steady state. Economies with higher levels of steady state per capita income *(y*)* grow faster. The steady state level of income depends on savings rates, depreciation, and other characteristics of the economy. The authors examine whether the level of development of the financial market increases the steady state level of per-capita income, and through this channel induces countries to grow more rapidly in the transition path. Differences in y^* across countries are captured by the coefficients α, which are assumed to be country specific, but *time invariant*, and Z, which is variable across countries and over time. The vector Z includes variables that have been shown to affect economic growth, such as inflation (De Gregorio, 1993; Fischer, 1993) and openness (Edwards, 1993; Lee, 1993). In addition, the authors include M2 as a fraction of GDP, called LM2 in the paper, to proxy for the degree of financial deepness. Regressions like this have been estimated by King and Levine (1993) and De Gregorio and Guidotti (1995), showing that in a cross-section of countries, financial deepness exerts a positive effect on economic growth. In addition, De Gregorio and Guidotti (1995) show that the effects come mainly through the effects that financial deepening has on the efficiency with which capital is allocated, rather than on the volume of resources allocated to investment. Berthélemy and Varoudakis attempt to go beyond these results by analysing whether the effect is a monotonic one or there is some possibility for multiple equilibria. If there were multiple equilibria we could find two type of countries: those experiencing high growth and high degree of financial development, and those experiencing low growth and low degree of financial development. However, the multiple equilibria should be interpreted with caution, all economies grow at g^* in the steady state, and therefore, it would be necessary to argue that there are two equilibria for y^*, and hence, two possible transitional dynamics.

Finally, long-run growth is assumed to be exogenous [rate of growth of α in equation (1)] and equal to g^* for all countries. This simplification is made to avoid complicated nonlinearities since g^* would appear not only as shown directly in equation (3), but also in some of the parameters of the regressions. This is a shortcoming of the authors' framework because, in general, we would expect that countries would have different rates of productivity growth depending on the same variables that affect the steady state level of income.

Main Results

Berthélemy and Varoudakis start by showing that including LM2 in regression (3) yields a negative coefficient, which is at odds with theoretical presumption and other existing evidence for the relationship between financial development and economic growth. The authors argue that this may be the result of two possible factors: the lack of control for financial reform and/or the existence of multiple equilibria.

The Role of Financial Reforms

Regarding financial reform the authors argue that LM2 may only be a relevant variable in countries that have experienced financial reforms. In countries that have an underdeveloped financial market, the monetary aggregate M2 may not be a good measure of financial development. Moreover, in those cases M2 may be very large because money may be the only instrument available for savings. This is, for example, the case of Eastern European countries in the aftermath of market-oriented reforms, where the so called monetary overhang was the result of the non-existence of instruments other than money for savings.

Nevertheless, we could raise the questions of whether M2 is a good indicator of financial development at all. As discussed in De Gregorio and Guidotti (1995), the problem with using monetary aggregates to proxy for financial development stems from a confusion on the role of financial markets. They have mainly two functions (Fama, 1990). The first is credit allocation, by which they channel funds from savers to investors, and this is the standard link between financial markets and economic growth. The second role is to provide transaction services or mediums of exchange. M2 is more related to this latter role, than to credit allocation. Cases could be conceived of where financial markets are very sophisticated, but have a low degree of monetization. This is the typical case of high-inflation countries, where efficient financial markets may provide alternatives to money as medium of exchange.

Perhaps one would like to see the results of this paper extended to other indicators of financial development, such as the ratio of domestic bank credit to the private sector to GDP or liquid liabilities of the financial system.

The authors rule out this explanation as the reason for the lack of significance of LM2 in the growth regression, since, although the dummy for financial reform is significant, LM2 remains not significant after the dummy is included.

Multiple Equilibria and Thresholds

An alternative explanation is that there is a non-linear relationship between financial development and economic growth. More precisely, there could be a threshold for LM2, denoted by LM2*. For economies with LM2>LM2* growth would be high, and for LM2<LM2* growth would be low. The authors estimate a cross-section regression for the estimated values of α_i in equation (3), as a function of several variables, one of which is LM2. They then test whether there is a threshold value for LM2. They estimate the threshold at a level of LM2 equal to 36.5 per cent. This leads to a number of comments:

—   Why is α assumed to be time invariant? There is no reason to assume that countries cannot cross the threshold, and during the whole period, 1960-90, they belong only to one of the two groups of countries: those in the low-growth financial-underdevelopment equilibrium and those in the high-growth financially-developed equilibrium;

—   Multiple equilibria are assumed, rather than compared to other similar possibilities. There is no reason to rule out the possibility that the relationship between LM2 and growth is highly non- linear, but without involving multiple equilibria;

—   The method used to estimate the threshold is rather indirect and perhaps inefficient. Since the set of variables belonging to Z are assumed to vary across countries and over time, one may wonder why LM2 is not included as one of those variables directly in the growth regression without the need of estimating α. Moreover, given that Z already includes openness and inflation, it is not clear why they should be also regressors in the equation for α.

Finally, and to analyse fully the channels through which financial development affects growth, the authors analyse the effect of LM2 on savings-investments. They conclude, consistent with evidence discussed in Jappelli and Pagano (1994), that financial development does not increase savings. This is a finding common to other literature and is due to the fact that financial development increases the returns to savings, encouraging them, but, financial development also relaxes borrowing constraints, thereby reducing the need for savings.

Financial Development and the Virtuous Cycle of Savings and Growth

A large body of literature has shown that high growth induces high savings. Beyond the traditional aggregate effect emphasized in the life-cycle theory, by which young generations — those who are supposed to save — are larger in number and/or have higher productivity, at the individual level it is also observed that as individuals' income grow savings increase (Carroll and Weil, 1994; Gavin, Hausmann and Talvi, 1996). On the other hand, most of the literature, both empirical and theoretical, on economic growth emphasizes the role of investment, and hence savings, on fostering growth. For example, for East Asian countries Young (1994) has convincingly argued that their high savings rate have been a key factor in explaining output growth; similarly, Jappelli and Pagano (1994) show directly that higher savings result in higher growth.

The two relationships described above can be written as:

$g = g(s, X)$

$s = s(g, Y),$

where g is the growth rate, s is the savings rate, X is a set of other variables affecting growth , and Y is a set of other variables affecting savings. Since $\partial g/\partial s$ and $\partial s/\partial g$ are both positive, it is possible for the above system to display multiple equilibria. The usual problem is that if there are two equilibria, as the threshold proposed by Berthélemy and Varoudakis would suggest, one would be stable and the other unstable[3].

An alternative is to consider that X changes over time, because, for example, it includes financial development, which increases with the degree of development of the economy. Figure 1 shows how the rates of growth and savings would evolve in such an economy.[4] As the economy grows, financial markets develop, with the increase in X from X_1 to X_2, resulting in an upward shift in the $g(s,X)$ schedule. This change results in an equilibrium with higher growth and savings in a more financially developed economy. Of course, financial development could also affect the savings rate directly and negatively. In this case, financial development would also enter Y, and this effect would tend to offset the effects of growth on savings, shifting the $s(g,Y)$ schedule to the left. In this case, growth and financial development would occur simultaneously while the effects on savings would be unclear.

This simple framework can help to understand the positive correlation between savings and growth, where growth and savings feedback to each other. Financial development, by channeling investment funds toward the most productive activities could allow an economy to trace a path of higher growth and savings.

Figure 1. **Interactions Between Savings, Growth and Financial Development**

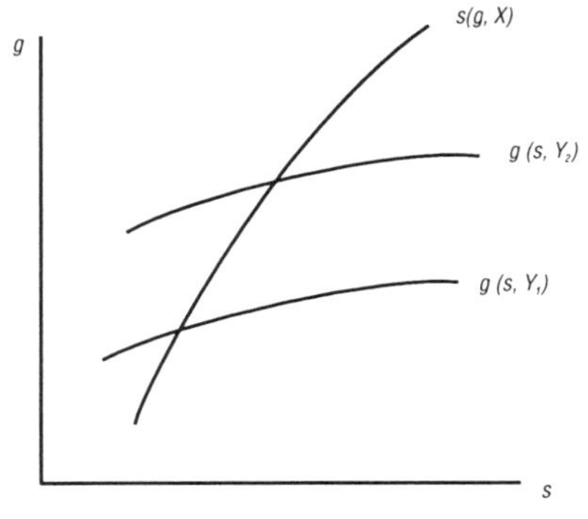

Notes

1. Note that final goods, human capital, and physical capital are produced with exactly the same technology, which is of course a simplification.

2. Recent estimates, using dynamic panel estimations, find greater values for the speed of convergence. See Islam (1995) and Caselli, Esquivel and Lefort (1996).

3 Berthélemy and Varoudakis (1996) present a formal model with multiple equilibria, and two stable equilibria, and financial development that helps to underpin the theoretical background for the threshold effects discussed in this chapter.

4. In Figure 1, two equilibria would arise if the schedule $g(s, Y)$ would cut $s(g, X)$ twice, but one of those equilibria would be unstable.

Bibliography

BARRO, R. and X. SALA-I-MARTIN (1995), *Economic Growth*, McGraw Hill.

BERTHÉLEMY, J.-C. and A. VAROUDAKIS (1996), "Economic Growth, Convergence Clubs, and the Role of Financial Development", *Oxford Economic Papers*, 48.

CARROLL, C. and D. WEIL (1994), "Savings and Growth: A Reinterpretation", *Carnegie Rochester Conference Series on Public Policy*, 40.

CASELLI, F., G. ESQUIVEL and F. LEFORT (1996), "Reopening the Convergence Debate: A New Look at the Cross-Country Growth Experience", *Journal of Economic Growth*.

DE GREGORIO, J. (1993), "Inflation, Taxation, and Long-Run Growth", *Journal of Monetary Economics*, 31.

DE GREGORIO, J. and P. GUIDOTTI (1995), "Financial Development and Economic Growth", *World Development*, 23.

EDWARDS, S. (1993), "Openness, Trade Liberalization, and Growth in Developing Countries", *Journal of Economic Literature*, 31.

FAMA, E. (1990), "Banking in the Theory of Finance", *Journal of Monetary Economics*, 6.

FISCHER, S. (1993), "The Role of Macroeconomics Factors in Growth", *Journal of Monetary Economics*, 32.

GAVIN, M., R. HAUSMANN and E. TALVI (1996), "Saving Behavior in Latin America: Overview and Policy Issues", mimeo, Inter-American Development Bank, Washington, D.C.

ISLAM, N. (1995), "Growth Empirics: A Panel Data Approach", *Quarterly Journal of Economics*, 110.

JAPPELLI, T. and M. PAGANO (1994), "Savings, Growth and Liquidity Constraints", *Quarterly Journal of Economics*, 109.

KING, R. and R. LEVINE (1993), "Finance, Entrepreneurship, and Growth: Theory and Evidence", *Journal of Monetary Economics*, 32.

LEE, J.W. (1993), "International Trade, Distortions, and Long-Run Economic Growth", *IMF Staff Papers*, 40.

MANKIW, G., D. ROMER, and D. WEIL (1992), "A Contribution to the Empirics of Economic Growth", *Quarterly Journal of Economics*, 107.

YOUNG, A. (1994), " Lessons from the East Asian NICs: A Contrarian View", *European Economic Review*, 38.

Financial Markets and the Behaviour of Private Savings in Latin America

Liliana Rojas-Suárez and Steven R. Weisbrod

Recent concerns about the availability of funding sources for domestic investment in Latin America have resulted in a number of studies of savings behaviour in the region. While there are several competing hypotheses about the determinants of savings, a review of the recent literature indicates that the stylised facts of savings in Latin America can be summarised by four features: First, Latin American national savings rates are lower, relative to GDP, than in many other developing countries; second, for the region as a whole, national savings rates have shown a declining trend in the 1990s; third, higher foreign savings are inversely correlated with national savings rates; and fourth, the improvement in the public savings rate during the 1990s has been largely offset by a deterioration in private savings[1].

In addition to the four features described above, there is a fifth stylised fact that has been largely ignored in the literature on savings in Latin America; namely, in contrast to industrial countries and other developing countries, corporations in the region save much more than households. A related fact accompanies this observation: generally speaking, Latin American corporations distribute few profits; for all practical purposes, most of corporate profits are saved in the form of retained earnings.

There are many arguments for explaining the most prominent features of savings in Latin America. For example, the low savings ratios in the region are attributed to factors such as low per capita economic growth on a sustained basis, demographical features resulting in a higher dependency ratio than in other parts of the world, and the persistence of high current account deficits. There are also competing arguments to explain the reduction in national savings rates during the 1990s. Some analysts claim that, by increasing expected permanent income, the introduction of market reforms in the early 1990s has resulted in an increase in private sector consumption — and, therefore, a reduction in private savings. In contrast, others hold a more pessimistic view, by arguing that, because the reforms were not expected to be permanent (especially financial and trade liberalisation), households increased consumption expenditures (decreased savings) on the expectation that the value of real savings would decline after the reversal of the reform efforts.

This chapter complements previous studies by arguing that the low private savings ratio in Latin America can be associated with the limited confidence of households and businesses in domestic financial institutions. Previous studies have established a relationship between private savings and financial markets either by using a measure of "financial depth" [see for example, Edwards (1995)] or a measure of "borrowing constraints" [see, for example, Schmidt-Hebbel, Webb and Corsetti (1992) and Jappelli and Pagano (1994)]. In the former case, deepening of financial markets — usually defined as the ratio of a monetary aggregate to GDP — is associated with increased private savings rate. In the latter case, the lack of access to credit is associated with a higher savings rate: even if the private sector wants to consume more by dissaving, borrowing constraints would prevent them from doing so. Under this hypothesis relaxing borrowing constraints, through, say, financial liberalisation, would reduce the private savings rate.

This paper offers an alternative view by claiming that the private savings rate relates positively to the confidence of the private sector in the strength of the financial system and that the latter concept can be approximated by the ratio of corporate demand for bank liquid assets to household demand for bank liquid assets.

The argument is derived from the analysis of corporate and household behaviour in the uncertain financial environment that characterises Latin America. As is well documented[2], remaining fragilities in Latin American financial markets have resulted in making households reluctant to hold domestic assets in the formal financial markets. Indeed, households as well as small enterprises can cover a significant proportion of their demand for liquidity by holding cash (or by borrowing from informal markets)[3]. In contrast, large and medium-size firms need to hold liquid assets in the formal financial markets because of two fundamental reasons. First, for this kind of firm, maintaining liquidity is essential to maintaining the production process. For example, they must pay taxes and cover workers' contributions to social insurance, even when the financial system does not perform well. They must also use deposits to pay other firms operating in the formal sector for inventory, supplies, etc[4]. Second, in the risky financial environment of Latin America, corporate borrowers must find some means of protecting themselves from the uncertainty of fund availability. With the exception of a few large corporations, the Latin American corporate sector has limited access to relatively cheap sources of foreign funds and even those firms with access find that they are shut out of international markets on short notice at the first sign of financial problems in their home country. The desire of the corporate sector to assure access to bank loans under conditions of uncertainty encourages corporations to accumulate liquid bank balances.

Thus, it is expected that a financial market where confidence is low would be associated with a higher ratio of corporate to household holdings of liquid bank assets than that prevailing in strong financial markets. *Ceteris paribus*, this high ratio would, in turn, be associated with a low private savings ratio.

To assess the validity of the arguments stated above, we analyse cross-country flows of funds and financial data for industrial, newly industrialised, and Latin American countries. An important limitation of the analysis is the scarcity of data available for Latin American countries. Indeed, data on holdings of liquidity by corporations and households is only available for a few countries and for a short period of time. This limitation precludes the use of econometric methods of analysis to test fully specified models of savings. Therefore, the conclusions derived should be taken as preliminary.

Notwithstanding these caveats, the evidence supports our hypothesis. Latin American countries, where private savings rates are lower than in other developing countries and most industrial countries, display the highest corporate to household bank deposit ratios among the three groups of countries considered here. The evidence also indicates that the ratio of corporate to household deposit holdings is strongly correlated with another indicator of the fragility of the banking system, such as the cost of bank liquidity. The ratio of corporate to household deposit holdings is also inversely correlated with a more traditional measure of financial market depth, such as the ratio of liquid financial assets to GDP.

The Stylised Facts

As is well documented in the literature, the national savings rate differs significantly across regions of the world[5]. Marked differences in savings rates are also evident among industrial countries and among groups of developing countries. The extent of these differences is shown in Table 1 which presents the recent behaviour of gross domestic savings ratios, which include capital consumption allowances, as a percentage of GDP for industrial, Latin American and South East Asian countries. Clearly, in each of the three periods considered in the table, Latin America has displayed the lowest average and median savings rates among the three groups of countries. An important feature is that, in contrast to South East Asia where the average savings rate shows an increasing trend, the average national savings rate in Latin America during the 1990s is similar to that of the 1970s; this despite the comprehensive stabilisation programmes and the structural reform efforts undertaken by this group of countries in the early 1990s.

Data for private savings rates show even more dramatic features for Latin America (see Table 2). First, average private savings rates in the region, which by the 1970s were higher than those experienced in South East Asia, declined during the 1990s and were only slightly above half of the level reached by South East Asia. Second, in Latin America, the median savings rate, i.e., the "typical" savings rate in the region, was much smaller than the average savings rate.

Table 1. **Gross National Savings Rates by Region**
(percentage of GDP)

	1970-81		1982-89		1990-94	
	average	median	average	median	average	median
Industrial Countries	23.8	23.4	20.6	20.2	20.0	19.0
Latin America	17.9	17.3	15.5	15.2	17.1	16.7
South East Asia	22.9	21.3	30.2	30.7	33.2	34.2

Source: IMF database

Table 2. **Private Savings Rates by Region**
(percentage of GDP)

	1970-81		1982-89		1990-94	
	average	median	average	median	average	median
Industrial Countries	22.0	20.4	20.9	20.1	21.3	21.0
Latin America	16.0	7.9	16.8	10.8	14.7	10.9
South East Asia	14.1	11.1	23.3	21.1	24.0	23.4

Source: IMF dababase

To analyse the behaviour of private savings during the 1990s further, Table 3 presents data for a sample of individual industrial and developing countries. The table includes data for six developed countries, France, Germany, Italy, Japan, the United Kingdom, and the United States, two newly industrialised countries, Korea and Chinese Taipei, and Latin American countries, including Argentina, Chile, Colombia, Mexico, and Peru . For most countries, these ratios are five-year averages during the early 1990s, with the exceptions noted in the table.

Table 3 indicates that, among the sample countries, the ratio of private savings to GDP is highest for Korea and lowest for Mexico. All the Latin American countries represented in the table have gross savings ratios significantly lower than Italy, Germany, France, Japan, Korea, and Chinese Taipei. For reasons that will be discussed below, savings rates in the United Kingdom and the United States are particularly low.

When private savings rates are decomposed between households and corporations savings contributions, a further conclusion emerges: in contrast to other regions, corporations are the most important source of private savings for most of the Latin American countries represented in Table 3[6]. Correspondingly, household savings in Latin America are relatively low[7].

However, data on corporate savings must be interpreted with some care. Part of the problem with gross savings rates is that capital consumption allowances are included. Because capital consumption allowances are actually included in the price of the good, they are, in an economic sense, a cost of production. For accounting and

Table 3. **Private Savings**
(percentage of GDP and composition)

Countries	France	Germany	Italy	Japan	UK	US	Korea	Chinese Taipei	Argentina	Colombia	Chile	Mexico	Peru
Years	1990-94	1991-95	1990-94	1989-93	1991-95	1991-94	1990-92	1987-91	1990-94	1990-94	1990-94	1990-94	1991-94
Gross Private Savings	20.4	19.6	24.6	26.0	16.1	11.7	28.2	22.2	15.2	11.6	18.4	10.6	13.2
Composition													
Business	50.7	49.3	22.0	46.3	48.5	31.3	38.2	24.8	n.a.	44.1	104.6	70.5	54.3
Household	49.3	50.7	78.0	53.7	51.5	68.7	61.0	75.2	n.a.	55.8	-4.6	29.7	45.7
Total	100.0	100.0	100.0	100.0	100.0	100.0	100.0	100.0	n.a.	100.0	100.0	100.0	100.0

Note: For Chinese Taipei, the ratio is a percentage of GNP.

Source:

France: OECD, Financial Accounts of OECD Countries, France 1980/1995.

Germany: Deutsche Bundesbank, Monthly Report, various issues.

Italy: OECD, National Accounts, 1982-1994.

Japan: Economic Planning Agency, Annual Report on National Accounts, 1995

UK: Office for National Statistics , Economic Trends, various issues.

Korea: The Bank of Korea, Monthly Statistical Bulletin, various issues.

Chinese Taipei: Central Bank of China (Taiwan), Flow of Funds in Taiwan District, 1992.

Latin American Countries: IMF database, Agosín, Crespi and Letelier (1996), Calderón (1996), Gonzales de Olarte, Lévano de Rossi and Lontop (1996).

tax purposes, they are also treated as expenses, but in the national income accounts, they are included as part of gross savings because they are used to fund the equipment replacement element of gross investment. Capital consumption allowances are, therefore, automatically part of gross corporate savings. As a result, if net savings by both households and corporations is low, consumption allowances will be a large portion of gross savings, which will increase the share of corporate savings in total savings. This is the case for the United Kingdom and the United States.

Thus, ideally, we would like to determine whether corporate savings are high, after accounting for depreciation. This, of course, would require measuring net retained earnings of all businesses. Since many countries do not keep such statistics, we approximate business savings behaviour by looking at retained earnings ratios of corporations listed either on the IFC stock exchange index for the individual country or a popular domestic stock exchange index. These data, which are presented in Table 4, indicate that business savings (retained earnings) as a percentage of total earnings have been very high in all the Latin American countries represented in the table. They are also high in Korea, and they have also been, until very recently, extremely high in Chinese Taipei and Japan as well. Retained earnings ratios are low in Germany, the United States and the United Kingdom.

Thus, data from either a macroeconomic source — the national accounts — or a microeconomic source — corporations' earning ratios reported at the stock exchanges — confirm that a main feature of savings pattern behaviour in Latin America is that corporate savings are, by and large, the most important contributor to private savings in the region. This is an additional feature distinguishing savings behaviour in Latin America from both industrial and other developing countries.

Corporate and Household Demand for Liquidity and the Strength of Financial Markets

The Impact of Confidence in the Financial System on the Deployment of Savings

Whether financial institutions that hold marketable securities develop (the often-labelled Anglo-Saxon system) or whether financial institution development is confined mainly to banks and other investment institutions that do not actively trade securities (the often-labelled universal banking models), households will not entrust their savings to these institutions if they do not feel that these institutions will maintain the real value of their accumulated savings. Corporations that save in excess of their immediate funding needs will face the same problem since they, too, must accumulate financial assets. Hence, lack of confidence in the financial system creates a disincentive to save for both households and corporations.

Table 4. Retained Earnings Ratio
(percentages)

Countries	Germany	Japan	United Kingdom	United States	Korea	Chinese Taipei	Argentina	Chile	Colombia	Mexico	Venezuela
1986	n.a.	74.2	n.a.	n.a.	74.0	90.3	97.9	73.1	92.7	97.1	n.a.
1987	n.a.	64.7	n.a.	n.a.	83.7	61.8	93.1	n.a.	90.2	96.8	n.a.
1988	n.a.	71.2	n.a.	n.a.	99.7	99.7	90.9	99.9	99.9	n.a.	n.a.
1989	n.a.	72.6	n.a.	54.2	99.7	99.6	n.a.	99.2	99.5	98.5	n.a.
1990	55.9	82.8	n.a.	44.6	73.5	82.7	n.a.	94.5	90.0	99.9	n.a.
1991	46.4	79.8	n.a.	42.4	78.4	79.0	n.a.	99.8	87.3	97.4	92.3
1992	12.0	71.3	n.a.	26.2	78.6	80.3	58.9	99.9	76.0	n.a.	94.8
1993	29.0	n.a.	n.a.	34.5	79.7	93.5	80.4	93.8	79.4	97.5	94.2
1994	16.8	41.4	21.2	45.7	79.1	17.6	86.7	94.9	91.1	97.3	95.6
1995	37.6	n.a.	n.a.	57.9	n.a.	24.2	n.a.	n.a.	n.a.	n.a.	n.a.

Note: Retained earnings ratio is the percentage of retained earnings relative to total earnings.

n.a.: not available

Source:

Germany: Deutsche Borse

Japan: Nomura Research Institute (1993)

UK and US: Bloomberg Information System

Korea, Chinese Taipei, Argentina, Chile, Colombia, Mexico and Venezuela: IFC database.

While both households and firms can avoid using a financial system in which they have no trust by spending their income on real goods and services, they could also save by exporting capital. In fact, as will be evident from the empirical analysis for Korea and Chinese Taipei presented below, there is some support for the belief that domestic savings rates are positively affected by the ability of households to hold foreign securities, even when the domestic financial system is considered weak.

For households and corporations to build trust in the domestic financial system, they have to perceive an expected positive real rate of return on domestic financial assets on a sustained basis. An environment characterised by highly volatile real interest rates coupled with periods of negative real rates creates a disincentive for domestic savings. As household and corporate confidence in the domestic system grows, they will have incentives to substitute out of domestic expenditures or foreign asset accumulation into holding domestic financial assets. Note, however, that if improved trust in the system is accompanied by an increase in expected real interest rates, the domestic savings rate will be affected by both a substitution and a wealth effect resulting from the expected increase in real interest rates. While the substitution effect will promote a higher domestic savings rate, the wealth effect will induce higher current consumption and, therefore, a decline in the domestic savings rate.

Once confidence in the financial system has been established, the economy can reap numerous economic benefits. For example, financial institutions can convert liabilities issued by non financial firms into securities that more closely meet the needs of households. They can pool securities to permit small investors to achieve more diversification than they could achieve on their own. They can create sophisticated financial products such as annuities or products that provide payoffs in the event of specific contingencies, such as death or prolonged illness.

In addition, financial institutions can improve the performance of non financial firms by placing controls on corporate managers which would not be economically feasible for most individual investors. They can provide a pool of capital to engage in leveraged buyouts of under performing firms. Or, as equity holders, they can influence boards of directors to discipline or replace current management.

Trust in financial markets implies a deepening of financial markets in the sense that economic agents are willing to hold claims on borrowers in the system. This implies that trust in the financial system should encourage domestic private-sector savings, since saving is one method by which financial claims are accumulated.

It must be noted that financial deepening does not necessarily lead to the development of an Anglo Saxon-type financial system with the securitisation of a wide variety of claims on borrowers. Indeed, most deep financial systems in the world are bank-dominated systems. In the event that an Anglo Saxon financial system develops, numerous institutional investors holding marketable securities — such as pension fund managers, mutual fund managers, and, to some extent, life insurance fund managers — create active financial markets. For example, in the United States between 1975 and 1989, pension fund and mutual fund (excluding money market funds) assets grew from 19 per cent of household financial assets to 31 per cent of household financial assets. Over this same period the turnover ratio (the percentage of shares traded to listed shares per day) on the New York Stock Exchange increased from an average of about 25 per cent in the 1970s to about 55 per cent in the 1980s.

How Market Structure and Confidence Affect the Corporate to Household Deposit Ratio

Corporate demand for liquid financial assets is directly linked to the need to maintain working capital for the production process, whereas accumulation of other financial assets is related to the long-term investment decisions of the firm.

At low levels of confidence in the financial system, corporate demand for liquid financial assets provided in the formal markets — largely formed by banks — tends to be more stable than household demand for liquid financial assets because corporations must hold liquidity as part of the production process. For example, medium and large corporations need liquidity to pay the wage bill, including withholding taxes and social insurance contributions and to maintain the ability to adjust inventory levels quickly if sales should exceed expectations. Moreover, low levels of confidence in the financial system are usually associated with an uncertain financial environment. Under such conditions, corporate borrowers must find some means of protecting themselves from the uncertainty of fund availability, especially since, in economies where this type of financial market prevails, most of the corporate sector has limited access to relatively cheap sources of foreign funds. The desire of the corporate sector to ensure access to bank funds under conditions of uncertainty encourages corporations to accumulate liquid bank balances. This fact contributes to the stability of corporate demand for deposits in many developing countries[8].

Of course, households and small firms must also hold liquidity for transaction purposes. But economies in which trust in the financial system is low often have large informal sectors where bank deposits, the primary means of holding liquidity for medium and large corporations, play a much less important role in providing liquidity than in the formal sector. Thus, in economies where the private sector has low confidence in the soundness of the domestic financial markets, the ratio of corporate to household holdings of bank deposits will tend to be high.

While the level of confidence in the financial system affects corporate demand for liquidity, this demand is also affected by other factors, in particular, the structure of financial markets. Empirically, in bank-dominated systems, the lack of diversified and liquid financial markets implies that corporations will be limited in their ability to borrow liquid funds on demand[9]; hence, corporations will need to hold more liquidity than they do under more securitised and liquid financial systems.

The processes by which firms and households manage liquidity in three types of markets is analysed in the following accounting framework. The first market in which economic agents have little confidence in the financial system is bank dominated. The second is a bank-dominated system in which confidence is high, and the third is a securitised financial system.

The two examples in Figure 1 represent two cases in which financial markets are dominated by bank loans and bank deposits rather than marketable instruments. In both these cases, we assume the household sector owns the corporate sector. Figure 1a represents the case in which there is little confidence in the banking sector. In this example, corporations finance liquid asset holdings with retained earnings to minimise the uncertainty of access to credit. Also, in this example, the household sector holds no liquid assets because the firm retains the funds through which the household sector accumulates deposits. Thus, in this example, lack of confidence in the financial sector results in all private sector holdings of liquidity taking place through the corporate sector.

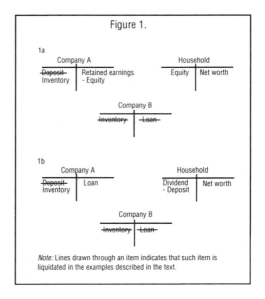

As illustrated in Figure 1a, when a firm (company A) accumulates financial assets, for example, a demand deposit, it does this by retaining earnings, in which case it has a liability to the household sector in the form of equity and a demand deposit as an asset. This demand deposit can then be used to fund a loan to a second firm (company B), which might hold inventory as an asset, as illustrated in Figure 1a.

Another possibility, when there is more confidence in the financial system, is that the firm pays dividends to the household as it has no need to retain all of its earnings. In this case, the household receives a demand deposit as an asset, as illustrated in Figure 1b. However, for company A to hold liquid assets, it must now issue a liability, in this case a loan, to acquire its deposit. In this example, the cost of liquidity is the spread the firm must pay between the cost of borrowing and the return on the deposit[10]. To balance loans and deposits, we again assume that a second firm issues a loan to fund inventory.

In the two cases described above, the corporation with the demand for liquidity can use its bank deposit to purchase inventory if it needs to do so unexpectedly, which is an important reason for holding a liquid asset. The recipient corporation (company B) uses the demand deposit to pay off its loan, which reduces the quantity of loans and deposits in the system.

In the third case, where there is a liquid market for financial assets, the same transaction can occur with fewer financial assets, as illustrated in Figure 2. In this case, the corporation (company A) pays out earnings to the household, so the household has a demand deposit (deposit A) as an asset and an equivalent amount of net worth on the liability side of its balance sheet. Immediately, the household transfers its demand deposit (deposit A) to a money market mutual fund in exchange for a share in the fund. Company B, which is funding inventory with a bank loan funded by deposit A, issues commercial paper to a securities dealer. The dealer funds his inventory with a bank loan, which creates a deposit (deposit B) that the dealer gives to company B in exchange for the commercial paper. Company B then uses this deposit to pay off its bank loan so both bank loan and deposit are extinguished. The dealer then sells the commercial paper to the money market mutual fund, receiving deposit A in return. The dealer then uses deposit A to pay off his loan.

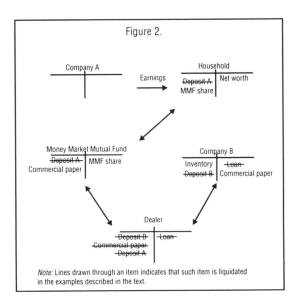

Figure 2.

Note: Lines drawn through an item indicates that such item is liquidated in the examples described in the text.

Company A in this example holds neither financial assets nor liabilities. If company A wants to buy inventory, it issues a marketable security, such as commercial paper, at the time of inventory acquisition. It sells the commercial paper to a dealer who, using a line of credit with a bank, acquires a loan and a demand deposit, which he uses to pay for the commercial paper. Company A then uses the demand deposit to acquire the inventory from the second firm. Company B uses its demand deposit to pay off its maturing commercial paper; hence, it transfers the demand deposit to the account of the money market mutual fund. The money market mutual fund then uses the demand deposit to purchase commercial paper from the dealer. The household never participates in these transactions; during the entire time, it holds a share in a money market mutual fund.

If the settlement system is efficient in the above case, all of these transactions can occur within a single day so no financial institution, other than the money market mutual fund, need hold assets and liabilities overnight. The requirement here is that the banking system be willing to accept promises to deliver funds at the end of the day rather than require the delivery of funds against each transaction. For example, when company A issues commercial paper, it cannot actually receive the delivery of funds to its demand deposit account until the end of the day. The banking system must therefore be willing to let the first firm pay for inventory before it has actually used funds. The banking system is willing to do this if conditions in the money market are such that any bank caught short of funds at the end of the day can be almost completely certain that it can obtain them in the money market.

Hence, a condition for these transactions to occur is a large and liquid money market. Large and liquid money markets require a network of dealers that are willing to perform the functions described above as well as financial institutions, such as money-market mutual funds, that are willing to be active participants in the market for securities. The gain in creating conditions in which these transactions can occur is that the economy saves on the cost of financial intermediation, as illustrated in the second case where the household receives earnings from company A and the company borrows to obtain a deposit (Figure 1b). In the first case, where the firm retains the earnings and holds a deposit, the household must suffer the consequences of illiquidity and therefore must borrow if it wants to purchase real goods or services. Hence the cost in this case is measured by the household's cost of borrowing. In some Latin American countries, this cost can be extremely high.

We conclude that where confidence in the system is low, the financial system will be bank-dominated because no one has confidence in open market instruments, and corporations will hold substantially more liquid assets than households. Where trust in the system is high, but policy decisions prevent liquid markets from developing, corporate liquidity declines relative to household liquidity. In markets where confidence in the system is high and securitised markets are permitted to develop, households will hold almost all the liquidity.

Therefore, based on the above analysis, the following relationship can be established:

$$(C/H)_1 > (C/H)_2 > (C/H)_3$$

Where:

$(C/H)_1$ represents the ratio of corporate to household holdings of liquidity in the case where economic agents do not trust the domestic financial system

$(C/H)_2$ represents the ratio of corporate to household holdings of liquidity in the case where economic agents trust a bank-dominated financial system

$(C/H)_3$ represents the ratio of corporate to household holdings of liquidity in the case where economic agents trust a securitised and liquid financial system.

Empirical Evidence of the Impact of Confidence in the Financial System on Gross Private Savings Ratios

The Corporate to Household Deposit Ratio as a Proxy for Confidence in the Financial System

To evaluate whether the corporate to household deposit ratio can be used as a proxy for confidence in the financial system, we first consider whether the relationship established above holds for a sample of countries where data on corporate and household bank deposits is available.

Table 5 shows data on corporate to household bank deposit ratios for Chile, Mexico and Peru, the only three Latin American countries for which data are available. Consistent with the high financial fragility in Latin America, the ratio of corporate to household bank deposits is extremely high for Mexico and Peru. In Chile, where the financial system is strongest among Latin American countries, this ratio is significantly lower than the other two Latin American countries[11]. However, it is still considerably higher than that experienced in industrial and newly industrialised countries. In France, Germany, Japan, and the newly industrialised countries of Korea and Chinese Taipei, where securitised markets have not yet fully developed, but where confidence in the stability of financial markets is strong, corporate to household deposit ratios are lower than in Latin America[12]. In the United States, where securitised markets are quite prevalent, and Italy, where there is an active short-term government bond market with outstanding paperequal to about 20 per cent of GDP, corporate to household deposit ratios are the lowest among the countries in the sample[13]. In the United Kingdom, where securities markets are also developed, the ratio is low, but slightly above that for Chinese Taipei[14].

Table 5. **Composition of Bank Deposits: Household and Corporate Sectors**

(percentage)

Countries	France	Germany	Italy	Japan	United Kingdom	United States	Korea	Chinese Taipei	Chile	Mexico	Peru
Year	1995	1994	1995	1994	1990	1995	1994	1991	1992-95	1991-94	1994-95
Households	81.3	72.1	90.5	78.0	80.4	92.5	78.0	85.1	62.9	49.7	54.9
Business	18.7	27.9	9.5	22.0	19.6	7.5	22.0	14.9	37.1	50.3	45.1
Total	100.0	100.0	100.0	100.0	100.0	100.0	100.0	100.0	100.0	100.0	100.0
Ratio of corporate to household deposits	23.0	38.0	10.5	28.2	24.4	8.1	28.2	17.5	59.0	101.7	82.2

Note: The data for Chile are the average of year end of 1992, 1993, 1994, and 1995. For Peru, they are the average of Dec. 94, Aug. 95, Jan. 96.

Sources:

France: OECD. Financial Accounts of OECD Countries, France 1980/1995

Germany: Deutsche Bundesbank. Monthly Report

Italy: OECD. Financial Accounts of OECD Countries, Italy 1989/1995

Japan: Economic Planning Agency. Annual Report on National Accounts, 1995

United Kingdom: Flow of Funds

United States: Board of Governors of the Federal Reserve System, Flow of Funds Accounts of the United States, 1996

Korea: The Bank of Korea. Monthly Statistical Bulletin

Chinese Taipei: Central Bank of China (Taiwan), Flow of funds in Taiwan District, 1992

Chile: Superintendencia de Bancos e Instituciones financieras (Chile), Información Financiera, various issues

Mexico: Calderón, Madrid (1996)

Peru: Superintendencia de Banca y Seguros, Información Financiera Mensual (various issues)

Further substantiation that the ratio of corporate to household deposits provides an indicator of confidence in the system is presented in Figure 3, which depicts corporate and household deposits relative to GDP in Mexico for 1991 through 1994. As shown in the figure, in the period preceding the Mexican financial crisis, household deposit holdings fell, relative to GDP, whereas corporate holdings actually increased, probably in an attempt to increase liquidity in a more uncertain environment. Thus, the corporate to household deposit ratio increased in times of financial market distress.

Figure 3. **Mexico: Deposit Holdings by Sector**

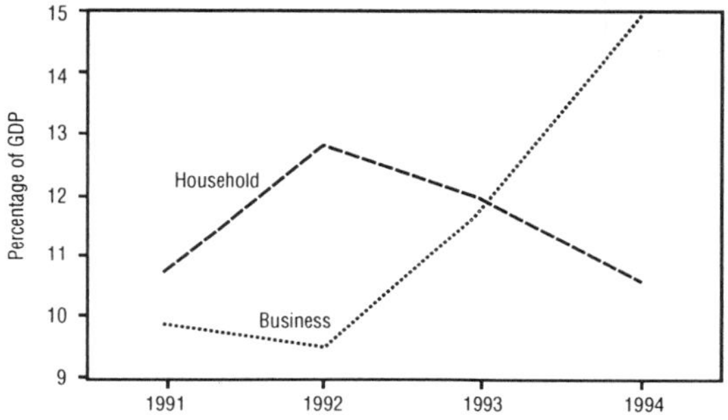

Source: Calderón (1996).

The data presented in Figure 4, which plots the corporate to household deposit ratio against net interest margins at banks for a sample of countries, also suggests that the quality of the financial system is influential in determining the extent to which households are willing to hold bank deposits. Bank spreads are much higher in Latin America than in Germany, Japan, and Korea. While there are numerous factors affecting spreads, including the competitive environment, an important factor is that banks in Latin America provide their customers with protection against liquidity crises, which are more frequent in the volatile economies of the region than in the other economies represented on the figure. This protection in effect gives bank customers assurance of access to a limited supply of credit in a liquidity crisis at an interest rate below that prevailing in the interbank market. In return for this assurance bank customers are willing to supply deposits to the bank at interest rates below the interbank interest rate and to pay a premium for bank credit in periods when credit market conditions are relatively easy[15].

Table 6. **Ratio of Corporate to Household Deposit Holdings and Ratio of Liquid Financial Assets to GDP**
(percentage)

Countries	France	Germany	Italy	Japan	United Kingdom	United States	Korea	Chinese Taipei	Chile	Mexico	Peru
Year	1995	1994	1995	1994	1990	1995	1994	1991	1992-95	1991-94	1994-95
Ratio of Corporate to Household Deposit Holdings	23.0	38.0	10.5	28.2	24.4	8.1	28.2	17.5	59.0	101.7	82.2
Year	1995	1995	1995	1995	1995	1995	1995	1995	1995	1992-94	1995
Ratio of Liquid Financial Assets to GDP	70.9	66.6	65.9	219.5	98.2	76.1	73.5	205.1	35.2	33.5	16.8

Note: Ratios of corporate to household deposit holdings are from Table 5. Liquid assets include checkable deposit, currency, time deposits, savings deposits, money market fund shares, security RPs, foreign deposits, government securities, municipal securities, mutual fund shares, and open market paper.
For Mexico, the number of 1995 is not used because that is a crisis year.
Source: Table 5 and IMF. International Financial Statistics, various years.

Figure 4. **Sectoral Bank Deposits and Interest Rate Spread (percentage)**

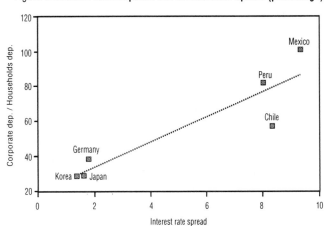

Note: For actual time periods used in calculating these ratios, see Table 5 for sectoral bank deposits. Periods used to calculate interest spreads are as follows: Germany (1987-91), Japan (1990-94), Korea (1991-94), Chile (1992-93), Peru (1994), Mexico (1991-94). For Mexico, interest spread is of the average of two largest Mexican Banks.
Source: See Table 5.

Thus, the width of bank interest rate margins can be viewed as a gauge for the likelihood of a significant lack of liquidity in a financial system. Since such an event can lead to numerous bank failures, this signal becomes a proxy for savers' demand for protection against the consequences of liquidity shortage. In such an event, weak banks may fail, causing some savers to lose the real value of their savings. The probability of liquidity shortage appears to be particularly high in the Latin American countries depicted on the figure[16].

Table 6 displays the ratio of corporate to household deposit holdings against the ratio of liquid financial assets to GDP, which is a traditional measure for financial depth, for the countries in the sample. The table shows a clear inverse correlation between these two variables: the liquid asset to GDP ratios are substantially lower and the corporate to household deposit holdings are substantially higher for Latin American countries than the other countries presented in the table[17]. Thus, the corporate to household deposit ratio as a measure of confidence in the financial system provides a signal about confidence consistent with that provided by the more frequently used concept of financial depth.

Examining the Relationship between Confidence in and Structure of Financial Markets and Private Savings in Industrial Countries

It is well known that the financial systems of the United Kingdom and the United States are more securitised than those in Germany and Japan. This is reflected in the structure of financial assets held by households and the structure of financial assets held by financial institutions. As indicated in Table 7, households in the United Kingdom and the United States hold a much smaller portion of their assets in the form of liabilities of banks than is the case in Germany or Japan. In the United States, the pension fund reserves are the largest single financial asset, and in the United Kingdom the largest financial asset is pension and insurance reserves, items which cannot be separated in the United Kingdom flow of funds. In Germany, households hold primarily bank deposits and bonds issued by banks. In Japan, households hold a much greater portion of their financial assets in insurance reserves and trust account assets than in Germany, although bank deposits are still the primary financial asset[18].

Table 7. **Bank Liability Holdings**
(percentage of household financial assets)

Countries	Germany	Japan	United States	United Kingdom
Year	1994	1994	1994	1990
Percentage of Total Financial Asset Holding	41.4	52.6	18.2	27.3

Source:
Germany : Deutsche Bundesbank, Monthly Report, various issues.
Japan: Bank of Japan, Economic Statistics Annual, 1995.
US: Board of Governors of the Federal Reserve System. *Flow of Funds Accounts of the United States*, 1996.
UK: Flow of Funds.

Institutional investors in the United States hold most of their assets in marketable securities, either bonds or stocks, as indicated in Table 8. The case is similar in the United Kingdom. In contrast, in Japan, life insurance companies and trusts, the most important institutional investors in that market, hold a high percentage of their assets in non marketable loans. Thus, even though Japanese households have a wider array of financial institutions to choose from than German households, this has not resulted in active financial markets as has occurred in the United States and the United Kingdom. The wide variety of financial institutions in Japan has also not led to the development of large and liquid money markets. As indicated in Table 9, the ratio of money market instruments to GDP is over 60 per cent in the United States and less than 20 per cent in Japan.

The differences in financial institution behaviour in the United Kingdom and the United States, on the one hand, and Germany and Japan on the other, should result in non-financial firms in the latter two economies, holding a higher proportion of liquid assets on their balance sheets than non financial firms in the former two

Table 8. **Composition of Institutional Investors' Assets**
(percentage)

Countries	Japan	UK	US
Year	1992	1990	1992
Loans and/or Deposits	45.0	17.6	8.0
Equities	23.0	70.6	35.0
Domestic & Foreign Bonds	32.0	11.8	57.0
Total	100.0	100.0	100.0

Note: Loans include mortgages for both US and Japan. Bonds includes money market instruments for US. Bonds include
both domestic and foreign bonds. US equities are market values, for Japan, equities for bank trusts and securities
investment trust, equities are market value, for insurance companies, equities are lower of market or acquisition cost.
For UK, equities are all UK company securities, which may include some corporate bonds.
Source:
Japan: Bank of Japan, Monthly Economic Statistics.
US: Board of Governors of the Federal Reserve System, *Flow of Funds Accounts of the United States*, 1996.
UK: Flow of Funds.

Table 9. **Money Market Instruments Outstanding**
(percentage of GDP)

Countries	Japan	US
Year	1995	1995
	16.8	64.3

Note: Money market instruments include certificate of deposits, call money, financing bills, bond repos and commercial
paper.
Source:
Japan: Bank of Japan, Economic Statistics Annual, 1995.
US: Board of Governors of the Federal Reserve System, *Flow of Funds Accounts of the United States*, 1996; Federal
Reserve Bulletin, June 1994.

Table 10. **Non-financial Firms' Liquid Asset Holdings**
(percentage)

Countries	Germany	Japan	UK	US	Korea	Chinese Taipei
Year (average)	1994	1989-93	1987	1990-94	1993-94	1991-92
Liquid Asset to Tangible Assets	n.a.	19.4	11.3	9.2	n.a.	n.a.
Liquid Asset to Real Asset Estimate	70.2	37.9	12.7	9.5	58.1	25.0

Note: Liquid assets include checkable deposit, currency, time deposits, savings deposits, money market fund shares, security
RPs, foreign deposits, government securities, municipal securities, mutual fund shares, and open market paper.
n.a.: not available
Source:
Germany: Deutsche Bundesbank, Monthly Report.
Japan: Economic Planning Agency, Annual Report on National Accounts, 1995.
UK: Flow of Funds.
US: Board of Governors of the Federal Reserve System, *Flow of Funds Accounts of the United States*, 1996.
Korea: The Bank of Korea, Monthly Statistical Bulletin.

economies. This is because the US and the British firms should be able to raise funds from diverse sources much more quickly than their German and Japanese counterparts. As indicated in Table 10, by various measures, the evidence is consistent with the reasoning above as well as the framework developed in the previous section. Ideally, we would like to compare liquid assets to tangible assets valued similarly across markets. These figures are available for the United States, the United Kingdom, and Japan. By this measure, Japanese non-financial firms hold substantially more liquid assets than non-financial firms in the other two countries.

Since we do not have tangible asset estimates for Germany, we estimate a proxy value for the real assets of the firm that we can use across all four markets. We take the market value of equities as reported in the flow of funds data for each country plus the book value of other financial liabilities less the reported value of financial assets[19]. By this measure, the liquid asset to real asset ratios are significantly higher in Japan and Germany than they are in the United Kingdom and the United States.

German corporations finance their liquid assets at least partially through borrowing from financial institutions. The evidence for this is provided in Table 4, which presents retained earnings ratios across countries, which shows that German corporations retain less than their United States, United Kingdom and Japanese counterparts. Thus, German firms represent the classical care illustrated in Figure 1b.

In contrast, Japanese firms have, until recently, retained a much higher portion of their income than firms in the other three markets. Financial institutions are the major holders of equity in Japan. The fact that they permitted corporations to retain income indicates that, until recently, they believed that the risk of leaving resources in the hands of non financial corporate managers was low relative to the cost of reintermediating the funds. This view, is, however, beginning to change as the prolonged recession is creating doubts about whether the Japanese corporate system can restructure itself to return to profitability without pressure from financial intermediaries. This has become especially urgent with the realisation that an ageing population needs high financial returns to provide a comfortable retirement.

While corporations have been forced to pay out more of their earnings, Japanese overall private savings rates have remained fairly constant over the last five years. This indicates that households have not lost faith in the stability of the financial system, even though they, through financial intermediaries, are demanding more cash flow from corporations. Part of the reason for this is that the government has stood behind deposits at private banks and offers a government-owned alternative depository institution in the form of the postal savings system, which has grown rapidly in recent years.

As far as the private gross savings to GDP are concerned, Japan saves a much higher portion of GDP than the other three countries, but Germany saves significantly more than either the United Kingdom or the United States. To what extent are the differences in the financial systems across the four countries responsible for this? A recent study on capital market productivity by McKinsey suggests that capital investment made in the United States over the last 20 years has been much more productive than similar investments made in Germany and Japan over the same period. As a result of the higher income on capital, a $1 000 investment in a portfolio of US stocks and bonds in 1974 yielded $5 666 by 1993, after inflation, compared to a $4 139 after inflation yield on a $1 000 investment in German stocks and bonds, and $3 957 yield after inflation on a $1 000 portfolio of Japanese stocks and bonds[20].

Examining the Relationship between Confidence in Financial Markets and Private Savings in Newly Industrialised Asian Countries

A comparison of the recent experiences of Chinese Taipei and Korea provides insights into the role that confidence in the financial system plays in affecting private savings rates. Taipei Chinese households, unlike their Korean counterparts, hold a large portion of their financial assets directly in the form of equities. In the late 1980s, there was an asset boom, both in terms of equity prices and real estate prices and a subsequent collapse in 1991. Taipei Chinese households decreased their savings rate from 20 per cent of GNP to 16 per cent between 1986 and 1991. However, over the same period, household deposit holdings increased from 47 per cent to 50 per cent of household financial assets. By 1992, they had increased to 54 per cent of household financial assets. Most of these deposits were held in the postal savings system and in commercial banks, both of which held substantial assets in claims on foreign reserves. In addition, between 1986 and 1990, government savings remained high, and these funds were invested in foreign reserve assets, which increased household faith that their liquid assets could be converted into foreign currency in a crisis. Thus, by making available savings instruments that would ultimately permit savers to have a claim on foreign assets, the government was able to stem the decline in domestic savings resulting from fears about the value of domestic financial assets.

It should also be noted that the ratio of corporate savings is relatively low in Chinese Taipei (Table 3), despite the fact that retained earnings ratios have, until recently, been quite high (Table 4). This may indicate that the Taipei Chinese financial system may be failing to police how firms use financial resources, which may be another reason why overall private savings ratios in Chinese Taipei have been declining.

Examining the Relationship between Confidence in Financial Markets and Private Savings in Selected Latin American Countries

As we have seen, the ratios of corporate deposit holding to household deposit holding are much higher in Latin America than in any of the other markets discussed so far, reflecting the fact that confidence in financial markets in this region is lower than in the rest of the countries in the sample. This limited confidence should lead to lower overall domestic savings ratios in Latin America than in the other countries discussed above, except where securities markets have been developed extensively and have resulted in very high capital market productivity as is the case for the United

105

Kingdom and the United States. This fact is confirmed in Figure 5, which plots the corporate to household deposit ratio against the gross private savings rate, excluding the United Kingdom and the United States.

An interesting feature from Figure 5 is that Chile looks more similar to Germany than to Mexico and Peru. This is consistent with the fact that Chile has been a pioneer in establishing a stable banking system after a crisis and it has achieved the most developed financial market among Latin American countries. Thus, although Chile has not yet reached the degree of confidence in financial systems attained in industrial countries, it is clearly on its way.

The experiences of the United Kingdom and the United States provide Latin America with another apparent option for dealing with a low savings rate. If it is difficult to increase savings, why not increase the efficiency of savings use by promoting the increased securitisation of financial markets? This might appear to have the added bonus of by-passing a banking system in which investors do not seem to have much faith. The problem with this solution is that, unless financial institutions, including banks, have highly developed credit skills, creation of liquid markets merely provides risky borrowers with the opportunity of taking a larger share of the scarce savings. This fact is well illustrated by the recent experience of Mexico.

In the early 1990s, the central bank of Mexico embarked on a policy of maintaining liquidity in the market for government bills and notes. It agreed to purchase these securities under an agreement to resell from banks facing a deficit in their clearing accounts with the central bank at the end of the day. This guarantee effectively assured banks that they could continuously roll over their repurchase agreements with the central banks. In other words, they were guaranteed the right to run continuous deficits in their payments accounts.

Figure 5. **Sectoral Bank Deposits and Gross Private Savings (percentage)**

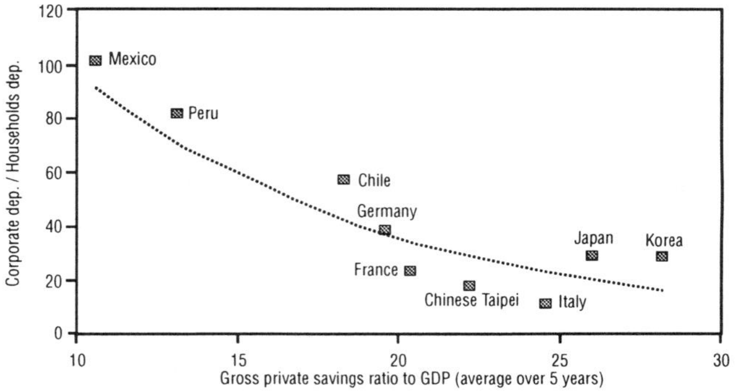

Note: For actual periods, see Table 5 for sectoral bank deposits, Table 3 for gross private savings ratio, respectively. For Chinese Taipei, the ratio relative to GDP is used.
Source: For deposit figures, see Table 5. For gross private savings ratio, see Table 3.

106

This policy had its intended effect. Fluctuations in short-term interest rates were dampened because banks that were short of funds at the end of the day did not have to bid for scarce funds in the interbank market. The market for government securities became more liquid as banks could always count on the central bank to make a market. The unintended consequence of the policy, however, was that risky banks were able to expand their loan portfolios very aggressively because they knew that if borrowers were occasionally late with a payment they could still meet their commitments by borrowing from the central bank through the repo market. In the peso crisis, the cost of attempting to create liquidity before the market is ready for it became obvious.

This experience implies that the Latin American countries should first build the credibility of the banking system and other financial intermediaries before they attempt to build liquid securities markets.

Conclusion

This Chapter complements previous studies aiming at explaining the low private savings rate experienced in Latin America. The major claim in the paper is that the low Latin American private savings rate can be associated with the limited confidence of households and businesses in domestic financial institutions, where the low confidence can be proxied by the observed high ratio of corporate to household holdings of bank deposits.

We have established an accounting framework for analysing the impact of confidence in the financial system and financial market structure on the ratio of corporate to household deposit holding. This analysis suggests that in markets where confidence is low, households will substitute out of liquid financial assets whereas medium and large corporations will not, primarily because the latter have a larger stake in remaining connected to the formal financial sector than the former. Moreover, in the risky environment that characterises financial systems where confidence is low, corporate borrowers must find some means of protecting themselves from the uncertainty of fund availability: the desire of the corporate sector to assure access to bank loans under conditions of uncertainty encourages corporations to accumulate liquid bank balances. Thus, corporate demand for liquid financial assets will increase relative to that of households as confidence deteriorates.

The analysis also shows that the structure of financial markets interacts with confidence in the financial system to determine the corporate to household holdings of liquid assets. In bank-dominated systems, corporate liquidity demand relative to that of households will be higher than in securitised financial systems.

Empirical evidence for the above propositions is developed by analysing experiences across industrialised, newly industrialised, and Latin American countries. The evidence suggests that the ratio of corporate to household holdings of bank deposits is a believable proxy for confidence in the financial system. This evidence is obtained by presenting data showing a positive relationship between interest rate spreads and corporate to household deposit ratio as well as a comparison across countries of the behaviour of corporate and households holdings of bank deposits. An additional result from the analysis is that the ratio of corporate to household holdings of deposits is negatively correlated with more traditional measures of financial depth, such as the ratio of liquid financial assets to GDP.

The evidence also shows a clear negative relationship between private savings rate and the ratio of corporate to household holdings of bank deposits. Indeed, the financial systems of Latin American countries, where private savings rates are lower than in other developing countries and most industrial countries, exhibit the behaviour of bank-dominated, low confidence systems in that corporate to household liquidity ratios are highest among the countries studied.

Our conclusions strengthen the case that policies to improve the quality of financial systems must be aggressively pursued. In Latin America, the first priority must be in creating confidence in the banking system. This is because strong and reliable capital markets cannot be built without a well-functioning banking system that can provide liquidity to financial markets without excessive reliance on liquidity from the central bank. If financial market liquidity is primarily dependent on central bank provision of liquidity, in weak financial systems, investors can easily interpret such support as leading to monetary instability, which, in turn, encourages financial disintermediation.

Notes

1. See, for example Edwards (1995), Gavin, Hausmann and Talvi (1996), and Schmidt-Hebbel and Servén (1995).

2. See for example, Rojas-Suárez and Weisbrod (1996a).

3. After all, in Latin America, fragile financial markets have implied low expected real rates of returns on domestic financial assets on a sustained basis as negative real interest rates in crisis periods have tended to wipe out positive real returns in good times.

4. Even where firms attempt to economise on the use of bank deposits by circulating receivable claims among themselves, they must ultimately convert some of the receivables into bank deposits to pay taxes.

5. For a discussion of saving patterns in different regions of the world, see IMF (1995).

6. While we are not aware of a study that discusses this feature of savings in Latin America at the regional level, individual country studies acknowledge this characteristic. See, for example, Agostin, Crespi and Letelier (1996), Calderón Madrid (1996), Cardenas and Escobar (1996), and Gonzales de Olarte, Lévano de Rossi and Lontop (1996).

7. Data by sector are available for Chile, Mexico, and Peru, in Latin America, as well as for Korea and Chinese Taipei and three industrial countries.

8. Corporations in developing countries usually maintain a relationship with a bank precisely for the reason of retaining access to liquidity. When they borrow, they in fact borrow a bank deposit. To be able to access loans in a liquidity crisis, they must hold balances with their "relationship bank" during normal times. This limits the ability of corporations to substitute out of banks into the informal sector.

9. This empirical observation holds for high-trust systems, such as Germany, as well as developing countries. However, in the former, it is probably the policies of the authorities that prevent the development of markets for immediate funds whereas in the latter it is underlying economic conditions.

10. In many Latin American countries the spread is quite high, encouraging firms in this region to retain earnings to finance liquidity.

11. See Rojas-Suárez and Weisbrod (1995) for indicators of financial market strength in Latin American countries.

12. Notice that "confidence in the financial system" is a relative concept. For example, there can be relatively high confidence in Japan's financial system in spite of the current problems in its banking system because the public expect that the authorities will resolve these difficulties successfully and that holders of bank deposits will not lose the real value of their assets.

13. Italy does not have a commercial paper market, but its liquid government bills market permits corporations to raise liquidity quickly because a lender can easily sell a government bill.

14. The Chinese Taipei data are affected by their high savings ratio and the lack of any other financial instruments other than deposits for households to hold. As will be explained below, the ratio of liquid assets to real assets at Chinese Taipei firms is substantially above this ratio in the United Kingdom, indicating that firms in Chinese Taipei are more worried about maintaining liquidity than their British counterparts.

15. See Rojas-Suárez and Weisbrod (1996b).

16. There are policies that can be instituted to encourage households to accumulate bank deposits even when liquidity crises are frequent. For example, the authorities can hold a store of international reserve assets to assure depositors that they can switch to foreign assets in the event of a crisis.

17. The relatively high (compared to Peru) ratio of liquid financial assets to GDP in Mexico is largely explained by a large presence of government bills. In contrast, in Chile, private assets account for most of the depth of the system.

18. The Italian financial market is an interesting hybrid of a securitised and bank-dominated market. As indicated above, it has a very liquid money market, but it has a very undeveloped institutional investor market. For example, insurance companies, the only major institutional investors, have assets equal to only 10 per cent of the assets held by banks.

19. Financial assets in Japan and Germany include equities held at market value. British and US firms do not hold substantial equities on their balance sheets.

20. See, *Capital Productivity*, McKinsey Global Institute, Washington, D.C., June, 1996. The portfolio yields are quoted from *The Wall Street Journal*, November 25, 1996, p. A18.

Bibliography

AGOSÍN, M., T. CRESPI and L.S. LETELIER (1996), "Explicaciones del Aumento del Ahorro en Chile," Red de Centros de Investigaciones Económica, mimeograph, Inter-American Development Bank, Washington, D.C.

BANK OF JAPAN (1995), *Economic Statistics Annual*, Tokyo, Japan.

BANK OF JAPAN, "Monthly Economic Statistics" (various issues), Tokyo, Japan.

BANK OF KOREA, "Monthly Statistical Bulletin" (various issues), Seoul, Korea.

BOARD OF GOVERNORS OF THE FEDERAL RESERVE SYSTEM (1996), *Flow of Funds Accounts of the United States*, Washington, D.C.

CALDERÓN MADRID, A. (1996), "Determinantes del Ahorro Interno en México: A Qué se debió la Caída en el Ahorro Privado durante los Años previos a la Crisis de 1994"? Red de Centros de Investigaciones Económica, mimeograph, Inter-American Development Bank, Washington, D.C.

CARDENAS, M. and A. ESCOBAR (1996), "Los Determinantes del Ahorro Interno en Columbia: 1925-1994", Red de Centros de Investigaciones Económica, mimeograph, Inter-American Development Bank, Washington, D.C.

CENTRAL BANK OF CHINA (Chinese Taipei) (1992), *Flow of Funds in Taiwan District*, Taipei, Chinese Taipei.

DEUTSCHE BUNDESBANK, "Monthly Report" (various issues), Berlin, Germany.

EDWARDS, S. (1995), "Why are Saving Rates so Different Across Countries? An International Comparative Analysis", NBER Working Paper, No. 5097.

ECONOMIC PLANNING AGENCY OF JAPAN (1995), *Annual Report on National Accounts*, Tokyo, Japan.

GAVIN, M., R. HAUSMANN and E. TALVI (1996), "Saving Behaviour in Latin America: Overview and Policy Issues," mimeograph, Interamerican Development Bank, Washington, D.C.

GONZALES DE OLARTE E., C. LÉVANO DE ROSSI and P. LONTOP (1996), "Determinantes del ahorro interno y ajuste estructural en el Perú, 1990-1995," mimeograph, Red de Centros de Investigaciones Económica, Inter-American Development Bank, Washington, D.C.

INTERNATIONAL FINANCE CORPORATION database.

INTERNATIONAL MONETARY FUND (1995), *World Economic Outlook 1995*, Washington, D.C.

JAPPELLI, T. and M. PAGANO (1994), "Saving, Growth and Liquidity Constraints", *Quarterly Journal of Economics*, Vol. 109, February.

NOMURA RESEARCH INSTITUTE (1993), *Manual of Securities Statistics*, Tokyo.

OFFICE FOR NATIONAL STATISTICS, "Economic Trends" (various issues), London.

OECD, Financial Accounts of OECD Countries, France 1980/1995, Paris.

OECD, Financial Accounts of OECD Countries, Italy 1989/1995, Paris.

OECD, National Accounts 1982-1994, Paris.

ROJAS-SUÁREZ, L. and S. WEISBROD (1995), "Financial Fragilities in Latin America: The 1980s and the 1990s", IMF, Occasional Paper No. 132, Washington D.C., October.

ROJAS-SUÁREZ, L. and S. WEISBROD (1996a), "Banking Crises in Latin America: Experiences and Issues" in *Banking Crises in Latin America*, R. HAUSMANN AND L. ROJAS-SUÁREZ, eds., Inter-American Development Bank, Washington, D.C.

ROJAS-SUÁREZ, L. and S. WEISBROD (1996b), "Central Bank Provision of Liquidity: Its Impact on Bank Asset Quality," World Bank-ADEBA, Washington, D.C.

SCHMIDT-HEBBEL, K., S. WEBB and G. CORSETTI (1992), "Household Savings in Developing Countries", *World Bank Economic Review*, Vol. 6, September.

SCHMIDT-HEBBEL, K. and L. SERVÉN (1995), "Saving in the World: Puzzles and Policies," The World Bank, Washington, D.C.

SUPERINTENDENCIA DE BANCOS E INSTITUCIONES FINANCIERAS (CHILE), "Información Financiera" (various issues), Santiago de Chile, Chile.

SUPERINTENDENCIA DE BANCA Y SEGUROS (PERU), "Información Financiera Mensual" (various issues), Lima, Peru.

A Comment by Bernhard Fischer

The authors are to be congratulated for their courage in relating empirically and in an internationally comparative way private savings by sectors to the status of financial systems.

Measurement Issues Relating to Private Savings by Sectors

A number of measurement problems, besides that of measuring appreciation, may seriously distort calculations of private savings ratios by sectors (Dean, Durand, Fallon, Hoeller, 1990). For example, the household sector includes unincorporated enterprises which consist mainly of firms, small family business and owners of dwellings. The relative importance of unincorporated enterprises varies across countries as does the way they are treated in national-accounting or flow-of-funds statistics. These differences make international comparison difficult. Apart from this, other concerns are the inclusion of purchases of consumer durables in capital rather than current expenditures, the treatment of public and private pension and life insurance schemes as well as the savings by social security funds. While savings by employees in private pension funds is included in household savings, this is not the case for government social security schemes. These different treatments make sectoral savings ratios difficult to interpret for comparison between countries because the relative importance of social security and private schemes varies considerably across the countries included in the sample for the study.

Corresponding adjustments for one sector would have a counterpart in the definition of savings of other sectors or in the definition of household investment. While adjustment would not so much affect the overall national investment or savings balance, they could significantly affect the savings ratios for the household and corporate sector. Another measurement issue, which might be particularly important when comparing and measuring trends in household savings ratios from Latin American countries with those of other countries, is related to the impact of inflation. With persistent inflation, holding losses and gains in monetary assets and liabilities should be treated as current transactions. Inflation adjustment would reduce the level of savings of the lending sectors and increase that of the borrowing sectors. Similar problems arise due to exchange rate movements at least to the extent that a proportion of financial assets and liabilities held by households is denominated in foreign currency.

Income Distribution and Private Savings by Sectors

The basic hypothesis developed by Rojas-Suárez and Weisbrod is that how and to what extent households and corporations save would depend on households' trust in financial institutions. While the degree to which a financial system is used will, of course, depend on the degree of confidence in its institutions and its functioning, the impact of financial systems on the relative share of business savings vis-à-vis household savings is less clear. At least other, and perhaps more important and determinants of this ratio should be included in a model (Masson, Bayoumi, Samiei, 1995). As an alternative hypothesis, one may suggest that the share of corporate savings to household savings is more rigorously influenced by other factors, such as changes in the distribution of income.

Between 1990 and 1993 the share of retained earnings in Germany to the net social product decreased from 5.4 to 1.4 per cent (Table 1). At the same time the share of aggregated private savings decreased at about the same size by 4.7 percentage points from 13.9 to 9.2 per cent of the net social product. In 1990 the share of retained earnings as percentage of total private savings was 39 per cent against 15 per cent in the recession year 1993. Such changes cannot easily be explained by changes in the savings behaviour of private economic agents. Rather they point to the presumption that the evolution of aggregate private savings is heavily influenced by changes in retained earnings.

Kaldor (1962) has provided an explanation for this phenomenon by hypothesising that the aggregate private savings ratio is dependent on changes in the distribution of income. He assumes that entrepreneurs save a higher share of their income than wage earners, which implies that a change of the income distribution to their favour increases savings as a share of the net social product. This may be particularly true with respect to positive changes in profits which most probably can be treated — at least in developed countries — as additional savings (Scherf, 1995). Empirical evidence for Germany supports the view that considerable changes in the distribution of income were accompanied by similar significant variations in the level and structure of the accumulation of private wealth.

In the long run, savings by private households were relatively stable in Germany, only increasing due to precautionary motives in periods of recessions. In contrast, savings by the corporate sector (retained earnings) were relatively volatile, whereas producing enterprises obviously have a dominant influence on the development of corporate savings. Figure 1 suggests that changes in the distribution of income critically determine the size of retained earnings and these in turn the movement of the private savings ratio.

Table 1. **Private Wealth Formation[1] and Income Distribution, Germany**
1970-95

Year	Savings by sectors					Gross income	
	Private savings (a)	Household savings (b)	Corporate[2] savings (c)	(c) as % of (a)	Producing enterprises	Corporate[2] sector	Producing enterprises
1970	15.4	9.0	6.4	41.6	3.8	27.9	23.2
1971	14.3	8.9	5.3	37.1	2.2	26.4	21.6
1972	14.3	9.4	4.9	34.3	2.0	25.9	20.7
1973	13.0	8.8	4.2	32.3	1.9	25.0	19.4
1974	12.9	9.5	3.4	26.4	0.0	23.0	17.3
1975	13.2	10.6	2.7	20.5	0.0	22.7	16.3
1976	12.9	8.7	4.2	32.6	1.8	23.8	18.0
1977	11.4	7.9	3.5	30.7	1.5	23.1	17.8
1978	12.3	7.5	4.8	39.0	3.4	23.8	18.4
1979	12.4	8.0	4.5	36.3	3.1	23.4	18.3
1980	10.7	8.3	2.4	22.4	0.6	21.2	15.8
1981	10.1	9.0	1.1	10.9	-0.9	20.3	14.2
1982	9.6	8.5	1.1	11.5	-1.1	20.2	13.4
1983	10.2	7.0	3.2	31.4	1.5	22.2	15.9
1984	10.1	7.2	2.9	28.7	1.0	23.3	16.8
1985	9.6	7.1	2.5	26.0	0.8	23.8	17.2
1986	12.1	7.6	4.5	37.2	2.3	24.7	18.8
1987	12.4	7.6	4.8	38.7	2.2	24.3	18.6
1988	13.8	7.7	6.0	43.5	2.8	25.3	19.8
1989	12.7	7.5	5.2	40.9	2.7	26.2	19.7
1990	13.9	8.5	5.4	38.8	2.7	26.8	20.4
1991	12.9	8.4	4.4	34.1	1.9	26.1	19.5
1992	11.0	8.1	2.9	26.4	0.7	25.2	18.3
1993	9.2	7.8	1.4	15.2	-0.3	23.7	n.a.
1994[3]	9.5	8.7	0.8	8.5	n.a.	23.8	n.a.
1995[3]	9.6	8.6	1.0	10.4	n.a.	24.8	n.a.

1. As percentage of the net social product.
2. The corporate sector includes producing enterprises, house building and financial sector companies (banks, building societies and insurances).
3. Data for united Germany.
Sources: Statistisches Bundesamt (1996), Scherf (1995) and own calculations.

Financial Sector Structure and Private Savings Behaviour

To what extent is the degree of confidence in a financial system related to the inflationary history of a country? How is the type of relationship between private savings by sectors and the financial system affected by the level and structure of taxes and the degree of interlocking-ownership among banks and firms? Would a more differentiated argumentation be needed if behavioural differences and different barriers of access to financial institutions would be taken into account for small and large firms? What role does the informal financial sector play?

115

These issues may be difficult to settle, both theoretically and empirically, but even if the analyses are restricted to the question of what determines the form in which private savings are held, i.e., as (unproductive) real assets or as financial assets, confidence in the financial sector would only be one stimulus in favour of financial assets. Other incentives and determinants would include the level of real interest rate, the density of bank branches, the degree of urbanisation, and access to credit (Fischer 1986 and 1989).

Figure 1. **Private Savings, Gross Income and Retained Earnings of the Corporate Sector — Germany, 1970-93**

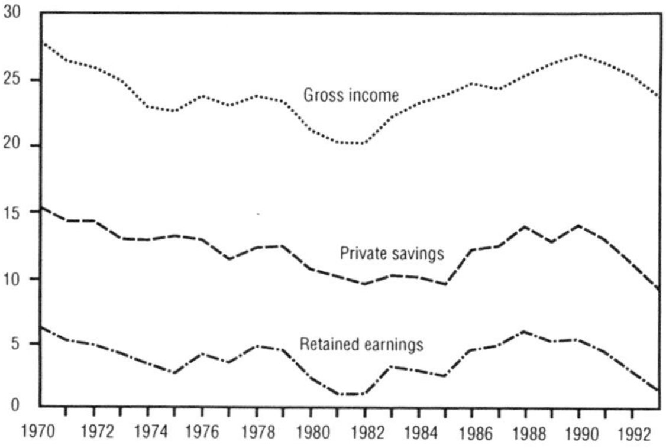

Source: Table 1.

Bibliography

DEAN, A., M. DURAND, J. FALLON and P. HOELLER (1990), "Saving Trends and Behaviour in OECD Countries", *OECD Economic Studies, No. 14*, Paris.

DEMIRGÜÇ-KANT, A. and M. VOJISLAV (1996), "Stock Market Development and Financing Choices of Firms", *The World Bank Economic Review*, Vol. 10, No. 2.

FISCHER, B. (1986), "Sparkapitalbildung in Entwicklungsländern. Engpässe und Reformansätze", *Forschungsberichte des Bundesministeriums für wirtschaftliche Entwicklung*, Vol. 78, Munich.

FISCHER, B. (1989), "Savings Mobilization in Developing Countries: Bottlenecks and Reform Proposals", *Savings and Development*, Vol. 13, No. 11.

KALDOR, N. (1962), "Essays on Value and Distribution", London, Reprint from KALDOR, N., Alternative Theories of Distribution, in *The Review of Economic Studies*, Vol. 32, 1955/56, No. 2.

LINTNER, J. (1956), "Distribution of Income of Corporations among Dividends, Retained Earnings and Taxes", *American Economic Review*, Vol. 46, No. 2.

MASSON, P.R., B. TAMIMI and S. HOSSEIN (1995), "International Evidence on the Determinants of Private Saving", *IMF Working Paper*, WP/95/51, Washington, D.C.

SCHERF, W. (1995), "Die Bedeutung der nicht ausgeschütteten Gewinne für die Koordination von Sparen und Investieren", *Wirtschaft und Gesellschaft*, Vol. 21, No. 4.

A Comment by Stephany Griffith-Jones

This article makes an important contribution to the analysis of the determinants of private savings in Latin America. It convincingly argues that the fragility of Latin America's financial systems has lowered trust in financial markets and discouraged private savings. It also argues that the ratio of corporate savings to household savings — typically high in Latin America, as compared to East Asian and developed countries — is also related to confidence in the financial system.

Rojas-Suárez and Weisbrod have emphasised an important causal link, between financial markets and savings, as well as between financial markets and the composition of savings, and thus make a very interesting contribution to our understanding of the determinants of savings.

In the context of the composition of savings (and their distribution between corporate and household), the authors do not mention tax policy at all, which seems a very important determinant of this distribution. Recent literature on Chile (for example, a recent paper by Agosin *et al.* (1996) argues rather convincingly that the 1984 tax reforms in that country — which implied that if recipients of distributed profits left funds either in the company or invested them in another company, they would not be taxed until they actually withdrew those funds — was a major factor in explaining the significant increase in the level of corporate savings, its share in total savings and its contribution to increase total savings. Similarly Akyuz (1996) in a recent *World Development* article argues that in the East Asian countries, such as South Korea, Taiwan and Japan, fiscal instruments played a very important role in helping supplement corporate profits and in encouraging retentions so as to accelerate capital accumulation. These fiscal incentives included various tax breaks and special depreciation allowances to encourage companies to both retain and invest profits. The scale was important, though diminishing. During the 1950s in Japan, the increase in the balance of tax-free reserves amounted to more than one third of total corporate savings; such policies also played a catalytic role on the banking system, as banks were more willing to lend for investment qualifying for accelerated depreciation.

There are a number of additional links between financial systems and savings which can complement the authors' analysis. Firstly, and probably most important, there is the fact emphasised by Helmut Reisen that the East Asians have promoted savings very effectively by creating special institutions for this purpose. As Stiglitz and Uy (1996) and others have shown, these institutions have attracted many small savers by giving them not just positive real returns but also security, and easy access. The Japanese postal savings system was created in the 19th century, and offered both attractive financial terms and convenient access to small savers. The postal saving banks mobilised huge amounts of saving — up to 25 per cent of national savings in Japan since the 1950s, 20 per cent in Chinese Taipei and 12 per cent in Singapore. In the context of the Rojas-Suárez and Weisbrod paper, it is interesting to highlight that in Japan postal savings were particularly important during periods of financial distress, when confidence in banks fell. Stiglitz and Uy, (*op. cit.*), describe how households shifted very strongly to postal savings during the 1930s as they lost confidence in fragile banks. Less well-known to development economists, but also very relevant, is the very successful experience of savings institutions in Europe, such as the German Sparkassen and the Spanish Cajas de Ahorro in mobilising savings; again an interesting feature of the Spanish Cajas de Ahorro is that they have been more sound than banks.

Similarly, several of the East Asian countries have fully funded rather than pay-as-you-go social security systems. In particular the Singapore Central Provident Fund has made a clear positive contribution to increase Singapore's aggregate savings.

A second important aspect in financial-market development and its link with savings shows an apparently negative initial correlation between liberalisation of consumer credit and mortgage lending with levels of savings. In this context, it is interesting that most East Asian governments reportedly encouraged savings by deliberately preventing mortgage markets and consumer credit instruments from developing (Wade, 1990; Stiglitz and Uy, 1996). This contributed to the sharp increase in savings as a proportion of income.

Japelli and Pagano (1994) provide rather conclusive empirical evidence that for OECD countries restrictions on mortgage availability (and particularly high down-payment ratios) raise household savings rates. Furthermore, as Deaton (1992) and Muellbauer (1994) showed, the existence of a borrowing constraint raises the incentive for precautionary and other savings. Initially, relaxation of credit restrictions diminishes the need for precautionary savings; however, once new credit limits are exhausted, the incentive at the margin for precautionary savings may be restored.

Both the US and the British experiences are very illuminating in that respect. In the British case, the rapid financial liberalisation of credit to households that occurred in the 1980s included liberalisation of restrictions on building societies, for example allowing them to expand their lending without an accompanying property transaction, which increased the attractiveness of credit-financed consumption at low interest rates, as well as the abolition of hire-purchase controls, which led to aggressively marketed new personal credit facilities. As Begg and Griffith-Jones (1996) show, both housing loans and personal credit increased sharply in the United Kingdom, relative to private consumption during the 1980s, and led to a fairly sharp fall in household savings, part of which has recovered in the mid-1990s.

Muellbauer and Murphy (1990) and Muellbauer (1994) provide evidence that an important part of this decline in British household savings was caused by this specific aspect of financial liberalisation. Bayoumi (1993) also finds empirically quite an important link between financial liberalisation and the fall in British household savings. It should be mentioned, for the sake of completeness, that other causes have also been given for explaining falls in household savings, and in particular the belief in a sustainable higher rate of productivity growth linked to the Thatcher economic reforms, which may have led to an upward revision in estimates of permanent income.

There seem to be strong parallels between the British experience of the 1980s and the Mexican experience of the 1990s. Liberalisation of consumer credit — and its very rapid increase — in Mexico clearly contributed to the very rapid fall in household savings, which played a fairly important role in explaining a growing current account deficit (Calderón Madrid, 1996). As in Britain, the perceived growth of permanent income, linked to apparently successful economic reforms and, in the Mexican case, access to NAFTA, played an important role. The literature has argued that even the development of stock markets, which reduce the risk of rate of return variability, may lower precautionary savings. However both in the case of development stock markets and in the case of increased bank lending to enterprises, there is a very important positive effect on growth, related to the fact that through a variety of mechanisms financial intermediation increases the productivity of investment. Thus, an additional question that the authors may wish to pose and try to answer is what developments in financial structures lead to larger increases in the productivity of investment, which may be a more important variable than the level of savings.

One such link (amongst many possible ones) that has been explored in the literature relates again to credit to households. Liquidity-constrained households may buy smaller and cheaper housing, which may re-direct savings away from residential to non-residential investment. De Long and Summers (1991) find that growth is much more strongly correlated with machinery and equipment investment than other components of investments such as residential housing. Thus increasing housing credit of a certain type could not just lower household savings, but lower the average productivity of investment (even though building may have other positive economic effects).

There seem to be also important differences between Anglo-Saxon and German-Japanese models of financial sector, in that the latter, reportedly due to the close connections between banks and companies in Germany, provide more long-term funding, which makes long-term projects more profitable. However, these differences seem to be diminishing somewhat in recent years.

Two final comments. Firstly, the authors argue that savings rates are low in Anglo-Saxon systems, because they offer high rates of return on savings. This is a very interesting point. However, there has been a lot of empirical work on the link between rates of returns and savings both in developed and developing countries and there is no clear consensus about whether steady state elasticities are positive or negative (see Normann and Owens, 1997, for a very good review of the literature). If that is the case, it would seem less likely that higher returns (e.g. on equity markets) would reduce savings ratios. However, there may be need for additional econometric work to test this interesting hypothesis.

Finally, Table 1 and Figures 1 and 2 present data, which complement some of Rojas-Suárez and Weisbrod's very interesting information on distribution of financial assets and which may be helpful to the authors. It is also comforting that, though coming from entirely different sources, these data confirm several of the empirical conclusions of the Rojas-Suárez and Weisbrod paper, such as the far higher preference of US households to invest in equities, and the relatively higher preference by Japanese households to invest in cash and deposits. It should be stressed, however, that analysis of these data — as well as the data in the paper — needs to make a clear distinction between national and financial savings, as the latter may rise without the former increasing.

Table 1. The World: Ownership of Investment Assets

as at year end 1993 ($ billion)

World*	Private Individuals	Public Pension Funds	Private Pension Funds	Charities	Insurance Companies	Total	Collective Investment Schemes
Total Assets Owned	28 858	2 236	4 323	376	6 771	42 566	3 792
Amount Internally Managed	25 183	1 260	1 058	207	6 490	34 198	n.a.
Amount Externally Managed	3 636	976	3 264	256	251	8 383	n.a.
Of Externally Managed:							
Amount Segregated	1 393	781	2 137	211	111	4 633	n.a.
Amount Pooled	2 254	156	1 051	45	116	3 622	n.a.
Amount Externally Managed by:							
Bank Owned Managers	2 014	442	1 515	149	90	4 210	1 534
Insurance Owned Managers	210	157	528	7	23	925	664
Independent Managers	1 424	337	1 146	100	113	3 121	1 694
Of Total Assets, Amount Invested in:							
Cash	12 709	381	216	18	499	13 824	1 110
Domestic Bonds	3 585	857	1 001	85	2 592	8 120	1 152
Domestic Equities	4 840	582	1 659	140	1 292	8 512	910
Foreign Denominated Bonds	470	20	140	4	169	803	190
Foreign Equities	986	88	431	11	241	1 757	351
Other Assets	6 268	308	875	119	1 978	9 550	79

*   These figures are based on a country by country analysis of 18 countries.

In North America	The United States, Canada
In Europe	Austria, Belgium, Denmark, France, Germany, Ireland, Italy, Norway, Spain, Sweden, Switzerland, the Netherlands, the United Kingdom
In the Far East/Pacific	Australia, Hong Kong, Japan

Source: Intersec.

Figure 1. **Financial Asset Intermediation and Ultimate Ownership in the United States**

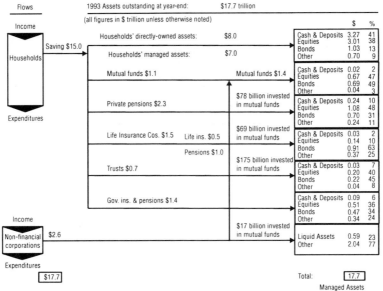

Source: US Federal Reserve Flow of Funds.

Figure 2. **Financial Asset Intermediation and Ultimate Ownership in Japan**

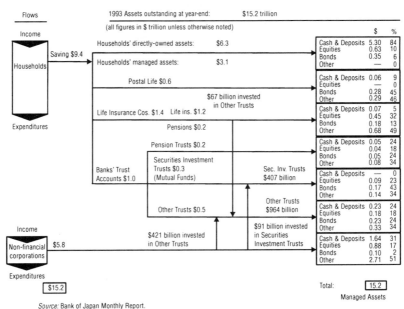

Source: Bank of Japan Monthly Report.

Bibliography

AGOSÍN, M., G. CRESPI and L. LETELIER (1996), "Explaining Chile's Increase in Saving", paper presented at IDB Seminar on *Savings in Latin America,* Bogota, Colombia, June.

AKYUZ, Y. (1996), "The Investment-profits Nexus in East Asian Industrialization", *World Development,* Vol. 24, No. 3.

BAYOUMI, T. (1993), "Financial Deregulation and Household Saving", *Economic Journal,* November, Vol. 103, No. 421.

BEGG, D. and S. GRIFFITH-JONES (1996), "Swinging since the 1960's: Savings in the UK", paper presented at IDB Seminar on *Savings in Latin America,* Bogota, Colombia, June.

CALDERÓN MADRID, A. (1996), "Savings in Mexico", paper presented at IDB Seminar on *Savings in Latin America,* Bogota, Colombia, June.

DE LONG, J.B., J. BRADFORD and L. SUMMERS (1991), "Equipment Investment and Economic Growth", *Quarterly Journal of Economics,* Vol. 106, No. 2.

DEATON, A. (1992), *Understanding Consumption,* Clarendon Press, Oxford.

JAPELLI, T. and M. PAGANO (1994) "Saving, Growth, and Liquidity Constraints", *Quarterly Journal of Economics,* Vol. 109.

MUELLBAUER, J. (1994), "The Assessment Consumption", *Oxford Review of Economic Policy,* Vol. 10, No. 2, Summer.

MUELLBAUER, J. and A. MURPHY (1990), "Is the UK Balance of Payments Sustainable?" *Economic Policy,* Vol. 5, No. 2, October.

NORMANN, G. and J. OWENS (1997), "Tax Effects on Household Savings", in this volume.

STIGLITZ, J.E. and M. UY (1996), "Financial Markets, Public Policy, and the East Asian Miracle", *The World Bank Research Observer,* Vol. 11, No. 2, August.

WADE, R. (1990), *Governing the Market,* Princeton University Press, Princeton, NJ.

Why Low Inequality Spurs Growth: Savings and Investment by the Poor

Nancy Birdsall, Thomas C. Pinckney and Richard H. Sabot

New empirical evidence on the relationship between inequality and growth contradicts an important dimension of the conventional wisdom regarding the nature of the process of transforming low income into high income economies. The conventional wisdom is that high rates of economic growth are likely to be associated with high levels of inequality in the distribution of income. This prediction, made decades ago, was largely based on economic theory. Kuznets (1955) saw rising inequality as the by-product of growth and structural change. As workers shift from a low to a high productivity sector there is a tendency for inequality to increase at first. Kaldor (1978) and — more specifically for developing countries — Galenson and Leibenstein (1955) saw the causality running the other way, from high inequality to rapid growth. If the rich have a higher marginal propensity to save than the poor, greater concentration of income results in higher savings in the aggregate, hence in more rapid capital accumulation and growth.

There is evidence, however, that countries with relatively low levels of inequality in 1960 grew faster over the subsequent three decades than countries in which the distribution of income was more skewed[1]. Rather than being associated with more rapid growth, high levels of inequality appear to be a constraint on growth. Thus, higher levels of inequality help to explain Latin America's slower growth relative to East Asia.

Figure 1 relates percentage growth in GNP for the period 1965 to 1990, and income inequality, as measured by the ratio of the income share of the top and bottom quintiles. Latin American countries are concentrated in the southeast corner, indicating that they experienced slow growth and high inequality, while East Asian countries, having achieved both low inequality and rapid growth, stand alone in the northwest corner. Birdsall, Ross and Sabot (1995) assess econometrically the relationship between inequality and growth, controlling for other determinants of growth. The addition of a measure of inequality, in 1970 or earlier, to the basic Barro function explaining variations in growth rates among 74 countries over the period 1960-89, does not much change the parameter estimates.

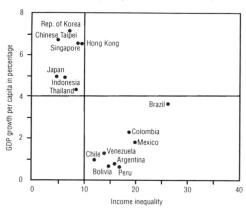

Figure 1. **Income Inequality and Growth of GDP, 1965-90**

Note: Income inequality is the average ratio of the income shares of the richest 20 per cent and the poorest 20 per cent of the population.
Source: Based on World Bank (1993) *The East Asian Miracle: Economic Growth and Public Policy.*

How important is high inequality as a constraint on growth? For this sample of low and middle income countries in 1960, the average annual growth in per capita GDP between 1960 and 1985 was 1.8 per cent. One standard deviation increase in primary and secondary education raises growth rates by 0.62 and 0.34 percentage points respectively. A one standard deviation decrease in the level of income inequality raises the predicted growth rate by 0.32 of a percentage point. Although the impact on growth of a change in inequality is smaller than similar changes in enrolment rates, the effect of reducing inequality is still substantial. *Ceteris paribus*, after 25 years, GDP per capita would be 8.2 per cent higher in a country with low inequality than in a country with inequality one standard deviation higher.

Why are the predictions of the old theory contradicted by the new evidence? Some suggested explanations focus on the political implications of a highly skewed distribution of income. Higher inequality leads to the political alienation of the poor and thence to greater political and economic instability. Instability discourages investment, thereby lowering growth. Alternatively, in a democracy, high inequality leads to popular demands for taxes on the capital of the rich, thereby discouraging investment and lowering growth[2].

We suggest a different explanation for the negative relationship between inequality and growth, one that does not depend on the impact of inequality on the political process. Rather we focus on the microeconomic behaviour of poor households. We describe a set of circumstances that can trigger a savings and investment boom among the poor. The poor are credit constrained, implying that they cannot borrow to finance even those investments that yield extraordinary returns.

128

And their poverty precludes much reduction of consumption as a means of financing investments. However, if the returns to labour are sufficiently high, the poor can intensify their work effort to generate additional income to finance high return investments[3]. Under these circumstances, the marginal propensity to save from this additional income may be exceptionally high — 100 per cent or more.

An outward looking, labour demanding growth strategy, of the sort adopted by the rapidly developing countries of East Asia, can generate the preconditions for a savings and investment boom by the poor. It can yield both high return investment opportunities for the poor and high returns to labour. A boom in savings and investment among the poor can, in turn, simultaneously reduce poverty and income inequality and stimulate growth, thereby helping to explain the growth with equity achieved in East Asia. By contrast, an inward looking, capital intensive growth strategy typical of Latin America may constrain the labour supply, savings and investment of the poor, thereby contributing to both high inequality and low growth.

We develop these ideas below. The next section discusses in more detail our hypotheses regarding high return investment and employment opportunities as determinants of savings by poor, credit-constrained households[4]. We then assess whether the assumptions of the model are realistic. The penultimate section considers the implications of the model for the relationship between inequality and growth, with a focus on human capital investment in Brazil and Korea.

Savings and Investment by the Poor

In high income countries, economists normally distinguish between the determinants of savings and the determinants of investment. Because of financial intermediation, households can borrow to finance current investment that exceeds desired current saving, and can accumulate financial assets in years that desired savings exceed desired investment. Therefore, in permanent income and life-cycle models of savings behaviour, while savings in any one year are influenced by current income — considered exogenous — over the long run households save in productive years to provide income for unproductive years in the future. A typical household first accumulates and then decumulates assets.

Savings behaviour in high-income countries, however, does not typically follow the predictions made by life-cycle and permanent income models (Deaton, 1992a; Carroll, 1994). Precautionary motives and liquidity constraints are gaining more prominence as explanations. In low income countries, where a high proportion of households are multi-generational (Deaton, 1990), life cycle and permanent income models are likely to be even less relevant. Adults expect their children to support them in their old age, as they themselves are supporting their parents. Thus there may be little need for "hump" or retirement savings as a vehicle for transferring income between high and low productivity phases of the life cycle.

In such households, savings serve in part as a buffer against stochastic decreases in income. Deaton (1990) asserts that "such households dissave as often as they save, do not accumulate assets over the long term, and have on average very small asset holdings". Deaton (1990, 1992b) develops a model of this precautionary savings behaviour of low-income, multi-generational households[5]. His model assumes that households cannot borrow[6].

Households may choose to hold precautionary savings in unproductive but liquid assets such as stocks of food, jewellery, and precious metals. When they choose to save in productive assets, however, the return to investment represents an incentive to save over and above the benefits in terms of risk reduction. In the absence of borrowing, household investment must be financed by — and thus can be no greater than — household savings. This implies that the expected returns to investment will be, in effect, the "interest rate" relevant for determining savings (as noted by McKinnon, 1973). It also implies that an increase in the returns to investment will directly increase incentives for saving[7]. Schultz (1964) recognised this in his explanation of the correlation of low observed savings rates and the absence of profitable agricultural investment opportunities.

On the one hand, households can increase the share of present income allocated to savings only with substantial sacrifice. There are few luxuries to cut out of consumption bundles that are already scanty. And the poor are likely to have high rates of time preference given the pressing nature of many of their demands for cash. If the returns to investment are initially low, below the rate of time preference for the poor, then savings will result only from precautionary motives. In many environments the incentives for the poor to invest are in fact low.

On the other hand, consider the impact of an increase in the returns to investment — such as might arise from the development of a new agricultural technology, more favourable agricultural price policies, the introduction of a new crop, an improvement in the quality of local schools, or a rise in the demand for educated labour — on income and savings of the poor. An increase in the returns to investment that raises the rate of return above the rate of time preference will, by definition, be attractive to the poor and will induce some poor households to search for ways of obtaining funds for investment[8].

In the presence of credit constraints, the attractive new investment must be financed without borrowing. There are only two possibilities for a household in this situation: finance the investment by decreasing consumption or finance the investment by increasing work effort and thus income. This latter mechanism is vitally important. Past analyses of savings behaviour by the poor, and the response of the poor to improvements in investment opportunities, have considered income to be exogenous. But a rational household faced with improved investment opportunities that yield returns above the rate of time preference will respond by working harder to finance the investment as long as the marginal returns to additional labour are above zero — Birdsall, Pinckney, and Sabot (1995). Present income, then, is a function of the rate of return to investment.

In effect, the increase in the rate of return to investment increases the marginal utility of money in the initial period for a credit-constrained household. This induces the household to accept a lower level of leisure and a lower level of consumption initially, to allow the investment to take place[9]. The household is trading off a loss in utility in the initial period for a larger gain in utility in the future.

In this case, the marginal savings rate of a poor, credit-constrained household will be greater than one. When investment opportunities improve, all of the increase in income that results from increased labour supply is added to savings; in addition, savings increase by the amount that consumption decreases. This high marginal savings rate can lead to overall savings rates for the poor that are quite large, particularly when measured as a percentage of income prior to the increase in investment opportunities.

The dynamics of this response to improved returns to investment can lead to a virtuous circle as increases in investment and income reinforce each other. The rate of time preference of the poor is likely to decline as their income increases. Other investment opportunities then become attractive, and labour supply, savings and investment will increase in order to match savings to desired investment.

The initial increments to savings and investment triggered by an increase in returns to investment will be positively related to the returns to labour. The marginal productivity of additional labour must be sufficiently large, and decline slowly enough, to allow for an increase in current income from decreased leisure.

Moreover, where returns to investment are already high, increases in the demand for labour, hence in returns to labour, can be another trigger for large increases in savings and investment. If at the margin returns to labour are low or decline rapidly, only slight increases in labour supply will occur. Therefore, nearly all of any increase in savings will result from decreases in current consumption. Given that small declines in consumption of the poor are likely to increase the marginal utility of consumption substantially, where the labour supply response is limited, only small increases in savings are likely to result from improved investment opportunities. This implies that a boom in savings among the poor is unlikely to occur when there are conditions of surplus labour of the sort described by Lewis (1954).

In sum, there are two mechanisms that can lead to high marginal savings rates by poor credit-constrained households: First, when the perceived rate of return to investment increases to the point where it is above the discount rate, poor households will have an incentive to invest, and to decrease consumption and increase income to finance that investment. Second, if the return on investment is sufficiently high, an increase in returns to labour at the margin may lead to increases in labour supply, income, and savings. If both mechanisms are triggered, the total impact on savings is more than additive. A labour- and skill-demanding, agricultural-based, and export-oriented development strategy, such as those strategies adopted in East Asia, may raise returns on both investment and labour, thereby triggering both mechanisms — Birdsall, Ross, and Sabot (1995).

Assessing Key Assumptions

Without credit constraints there will be no boom in savings and investment. If households are able to borrow at an interest rate less than their discount rate, they will finance high return investments by borrowing rather than by decreasing either consumption or leisure. A household that can borrow will respond to an increase in the rate of return to investment, hence in permanent income, by borrowing more. The household will also consume more and work less in the first period[10]. So our story requires that credit constraints be binding.

Poor households do borrow: Deaton (1992b) reports that 25 to 40 per cent of rural households surveyed in the Côte d'Ivoire and Ghana had outstanding loans. In Nigeria, Pakistan, Kenya, and Tanzania, surveys indicate that 65 to 90 per cent of households borrowed at some point during a twelve-month period (Udry, 1993; Alderman and Garcia, 1993; Kimuyu, 1994). However, nearly all of these loans are for short terms, one cropping season or less. The present year's crop is often used as collateral. In East Africa less than one per cent of surveyed households had loans that extended beyond the next harvest (Kimuyu, 1994)[11]. It appears as though borrowing to finance multi-year investments, such as the planting of tree crops or augmenting human capital, is simply not feasible for poor households without collateral[12].

In our story, households can only produce income via self employment or by investing. If anything, taking account of a market in which labour can be purchased or sold strengthens our results. Household labour supply would still depend on the marginal utility of leisure, as well as on the returns to investment, the discount rate and the marginal product of labour. Allowing households to sell labour in a perfect market, with the possibility of negative "sales" if the demand for leisure is high enough, would lead to one important change: the output of the own-produced good would no longer increase in the first period in response to an increase in the returns to investment. However, the basic thrust of our story — that households increase work effort, hence income and savings, in response to an improvement in investment opportunities — still holds. Consumption would still decrease in the first period, but rather than increasing labour in self-employment, households instead would raise income by increasing labour market activity. At the margin, as investment opportunities improve, households will either decrease the amount of labour hired or increase the amount of labour sold so as to obtain the income necessary to finance investments. If the labour market is large, then marginal returns to labour are constant, *increasing* the impact on savings of an improvement in investment opportunities.

An Application

We have suggested that a boom in savings and investment — for example in agriculture and in human capital — by the poor may help explain the association of rapid growth and low inequality in East Asia. Data on savings and investment disaggregated by income are not easily available. However, aggregate data on agricultural growth and productivity, and on educational change, comparing East Asia and Latin America, are consistent with our story. It appears that in East Asia the poor participated through their own investments in the agricultural growth and educational change that fuelled East Asia's economic success — but did not participate in Latin America.

It is commonplace that the agricultural sector included a large portion of poor households in developing countries, especially in the early post-war decades. Thus policies that penalised agriculture almost certainly penalised the poor. Schiff and Valdés (1992) report that countries in East Asia, such as Korea and Malaysia, taxed agriculture (directly and through exchange rate and other policies) much less than countries in Latin America. It is also the case that agricultural production and income grew much more rapidly in East Asia, at more than three times the rate of growth of the agricultural labour force, compared to only 50 per cent greater in Latin America (Turnham, 1993). Obviously, measured increases in total factor productivity in agriculture in East Asia were substantial — an annual rate of 2.2 per cent from 1965-1988. These measured increases may in fact reflect in part increased but unmeasured investments in agriculture by poor smallholder households (Timmer, 1995), and unmeasured increases in labour hours and work effort by households that saw returns to their investments rising as urban workers' consumption demands increased (Fei, Kuo, and Ranis, 1981, document this process for Chinese Taipei).

In short, in East Asia, unlike in Latin America, the poor in the agricultural sector had increasing opportunities for high return investments. These opportunities occurred in a context of rapidly growing labour demand as wages and the labour force in the manufacturing sector expanded rapidly (manufacturing sector employment in Korea increased by 58 per cent from 1975 to 1985). Their savings and investment have not been systematically measured, but surely contributed to the rapid growth of agricultural production.

A similar story can be told about high rates of investment in education, including by the poor, in East Asia. Birdsall, Ross, and Sabot (1995) provide evidence of rates of enrolment in education in East Asia above those predicted for countries at their level of income; high enrolments represented investments by families in the human capital of their children. They also provide evidence that rapid accumulation of human capital both stimulated growth and reduced inequality. In the remainder of this section we show how marked differences between Korea and Brazil in investment in human capital contributed to differences between the countries in growth rates and levels of inequality, and suggest that policies conducive to a boom in savings and investment among the poor contributed to Korea's superior growth rate and its success in reducing inequality.

Regressing secondary school enrolment rates on per capita national income for more than 90 developing countries for the years 1965 and 1987 indicates that Korea was well above the regression line — secondary enrolment rates were higher than predicted for countries at its level of income — while Brazil was well below the line[13]. Where enrolment rates are low children of the poor are the least likely to be enrolled. A corollary of the difference in enrolment rates between Brazil and Korea is a higher rate of investment in human capital by the poor in Korea.

The cross-country growth regression estimated by Birdsall, Ross, and Sabot (1995) can be used to estimate the impact of this difference in enrolment rates on growth. If Korea had had Brazil's 1960 enrolment rates, its growth rate would have been 5.6 per cent rather than 6.1 per cent , resulting in 1985 per capita GDP 11.1 per cent less than Korea actually attained. This estimate only establishes a lower bound for the costs to Brazil of low investment in human capital; for one thing, it assumes that quality of schooling did not decline, with concomitant declines in the economic returns to schooling, which it almost certainly did[14].

Low investment in schooling, especially for the poor, also appears to have prevented any improvement in the highly unequal distribution of income in Brazil. In Korea, with rapid educational expansion in the 1960s and 1970s, the relative abundance of educated workers increased and the scarcity rents which the educated earn were eroded, leading to reductions in the inequality of pay in the 1970s and 1980s. By contrast, in Brazil the absolute increment to the labour force of relatively well educated workers was so small in the 1970s that it did not take much of an increase in the demand for educated workers to offset any wage compression effect of the increase in supply. The educational structure of wages barely changed. The net effect of educational expansion in Brazil over the decade was to increase the log variance of wages by roughly 4 per cent , in marked contrast to the 22 per cent decline that resulted from educational expansion in Korea[15].

Marked differences in educational performance help explain why Korea has had both faster growth and lower inequality than Brazil. But why have enrolment rates, particularly among the poor, been so high (and dropout and repetition rates so low) in Korea? Why have enrolment rates, particularly among the poor, been so low (and dropout and repetition rates so high) in Brazil? The story we have told suggests some hypotheses.

Growth in Korea from 1970 to 1990 was export oriented and labour demanding. Over two decades, wage increases in the manufacturing sector were an estimated 8.7 per cent , while annual increases in wage employment were an extraordinary 18.7 per cent[16].

This employment and wage growth dramatically raised the returns at the margin for the labour of the poor, making it attractive to increase time allocated to work in order to finance high return investments, including investments in the education of children. The labour demanding growth path became increasingly skill-intensive over time, contributing to high expected rates of return to schooling, hence to strong household demand for education. Public policy also ensured high quality schooling even in poor districts, thereby contributing to the high rates of return to investment in schooling. In sum, in Korea there were strong incentives for the poor to invest in their children and to work more to finance that investment. It is our supposition that marginal savings rates among the poor were exceptionally high, as households saved in the form of investing in their children's education. These new savings among relatively poor households, as primary and secondary enrolments rose dramatically over two decades, helped ensure education's contribution to aggregate growth set out above.

By contrast, in Brazil the inward looking growth strategy was not labour demanding and so, for the poor, the returns to additional labour time allocated to work were quite low. Lack of dynamism in the demand for labour and skill held down expected returns to investment in schooling. In addition, school quality for the poor tended to be abysmal. Because of the limited supply of educated workers average returns to investment in schooling were high, but for the poor returns to investment in schooling were low (Birdsall and Sabot, 1996). In sum, in Brazil public policy created incentives for high levels of leisure and low levels of savings among the poor.

Table 1. **Per Capita Income of the Poor and Secondary Enrolment Rates**

Country	Per Capita Income	Income Share, Bottom 20%	Per Capita Income, Bottom 20%	Secondary School Enrolment Rate
Indonesia, 1976	240	6.6	79	21
Kenya, 1976	240	2.6	31	17
Malaysia, 1987	1 810	4.6	416	59
Costa Rica, 1986	1 480	3.3	254	42
Brazil, 1983	1 880	2.4	226	35
Korea, 1976	670	5.7	191	88
Botswana, 1986	840	2.5	115	31
Indonesia, 1987	450	8.8	251	47
Philippines, 1985	580	5.5	160	68

Source: World Development Report, various years.

More generally, our story predicts higher investment in schooling in countries with lower inequality. Where inequality is low, the poor are likely to benefit from high returns to labour and to investment in human capital, and thus to save and invest more, including in education. Table 1 presents data from four sets of countries. Within each set per capita incomes are roughly the same. However, the share of GDP going to the poorest quintile, hence the mean absolute income of the poorest quintile, varies considerably. In all but one case, the country with lower inequality has higher secondary enrolment.

Conclusions

We have told a story about savings for households that cannot borrow, in which an increase in returns to investment can raise savings, income, and labour supply. We have suggested that improvements in investment opportunities and returns to labour — features of a labour demanding growth strategy — can lead to exceptionally high marginal savings rates by the poor. Reductions in poverty and income inequality may result. Low inequality and its corollaries — higher absolute incomes of the poor and higher returns to the poor's labour and investment — can also result in higher aggregate savings and investment rates. The implications of our story are therefore potentially far-reaching: ensuring that the poor face incentives to invest and to work more can result not only in higher incomes for the poor, but also faster growth and lower overall levels of inequality. Our story suggests a microeconomic explanation for the cross-country relationship between low inequality and rapid growth that does not rely on the political benefits of low inequality.

Our analysis is of particular relevance to Latin America. The distribution of income is more unequal in Latin America than in other developing regions, in part because policies have been more biased against the poor. Low inequality combined with high growth in East Asia over three decades suggests that sustained growth requires that the poor contribute to as well as benefit from the development process. Ensuring that the poor have opportunities to contribute to growth in Latin America is thus not a matter of altruism but of enlightened self-interest. The challenge in Latin America is to find ways to reduce inequality and make growth more inclusive, not by growth-inhibiting transfers and regulations, but by improving investment opportunities for the poor and shifting to a more labour demanding growth path. It is important that the poor be beneficiaries of the growth process. Our analysis of savings and investment suggests they can be an engine of growth as well.

Notes

1. For estimates of growth rate functions in which the impact of initial inequality is econometrically assessed for a large number of developing countries while controlling for other determinants of growth, see Birdsall, Ross, and Sabot (1995) and Clarke (1995).

2. See, for example, Alesina and Perotti (1994), Alesina and Rodrik (1994), and Persson and Tabellini (1994).

3. Unlike the labour surplus models that follow Lewis (1954), we assume that marginal returns to labour are greater than zero.

4. The analysis in this section summarises the implications of a formal model developed in Birdsall, Pinckney, and Sabot (1995).

5. Much recent research has investigated the saving and dissaving response of rural households to income shocks. See, for example, Townsend (1995) and Paxson (1992).

6. "At least for some households, borrowing restrictions are real and necessary to explain what we observe." (Deaton, 1990).

7. Where there is financial intermediation, the improvement in incentives to save when expected returns to investment improve is indirect, through increased demand for loanable funds and consequent increases in interest rates.

8. Bruton (1985) argues that search behaviour plays a key role in development. He contends that the impact of a policy change that increases returns to investment by the poor could be greater than the change in marginal conditions suggests, by inducing search for yet more profitable investments.

9. There is no "income effect" of the increase in investment returns on consumption in the first period; with a binding credit constraint, the positive impact on consumption of that increase in returns is realised only in the second period. In each period, the marginal utility of leisure must equal the marginal utility of consumption times the marginal productivity of labour. An increase in the returns to investment induces more work and reduced consumption in period one to finance the investment; labour supply increases and consumption decreases in such a way to maintain the equality.

10. See Shibli (1991) for a discussion of households' borrowing response to improved investment opportunities.

11. See Behrman, Foster, and Rosenzweig (1995) for convincing evidence that the poor in rural Pakistan are credit-constrained even in the short period between planting and harvesting. See also Bhalla (1978), Jacoby (1994), and Rosenzweig and Wolpin (1993) for indirect evidence of the importance of borrowing constraints in developing countries. On the macro level, liquidity constraints are being used increasingly to explain savings behaviour even in rich countries (Deaton 1992a).

12. Income and credit constrain investment in human capital only when expected returns to schooling are high. If these returns are low, an increase in the income of the poor may have little or no impact on investment in schooling. Thus, empirically estimated income elasticities of demand for schooling, as conventionally measured, are of little relevance for assessing the model's assumptions. To test our model the demand equations need to include controls for expected returns to investment.

13. While inequality of access by socio-economic background is higher, inequality of access by gender is nearly as low in Latin America as in East Asia.

14. Public expenditures per eligible school-age child rose more than 350 per cent in Korea between 1970 and 1989, while they rose just 191 per cent in Brazil. The increase in Brazil, combined with declines in administrative efficiency, was insufficient to ensure maintenance of quality as the rapid enrolment increases brought a much poorer pool of students into the system. Completion rates, an indicator of quality, fell in Brazil; in the same period they rose in Korea (Birdsall and Sabot, 1996).

15. Birdsall and Sabot (1996); Knight and Sabot (1990).

16. Banerji, Campos, and Sabot (1994), citing World Bank (1993b) and ILO Yearbook of Labor Statistics (various issues).

Bibliography

ALDERMAN, H. and M. GARCIA (1993), *Poverty, Household Food Security, and Nutrition in Rural Pakistan*. Research Report 96, International Food Policy Research Institute, Washington, D.C.

ALESINA, A. and R. PEROTTI (1994), "The Political Economy of Growth, A Critical Survey of the Recent Literature", *World Bank Economic Review* 8(3), September.

ALESINA, A. and D. RODRIK (1994), "Distributive Politics and Economic Growth", *Quarterly Journal of Economics,* 109, May.

BANERJI, A., E. CAMPOS and R. SABOT (1994), "The Political Economy of Pay and Employment in Developing Countries", processed, World Bank, Washington D.C.

BEHRMAN, J. R., A. FOSTER and M.R. ROSENZWEIG (1995) "Dynamic Savings Decisions in Agricultural Environments with Incomplete Markets", processed, University of Pennsylvania, Philadelphia.

BHALLA, S.S. (1978),"The Role of Sources of Income and Investment Opportunities in Rural Savings", *Journal of Development Economics,* 5.

BIRDSALL, N. and R.H. SABOT (1996), *Opportunities Foregone: Education in Brazil,* Inter-American Development Bank, Washington, D.C.

BIRDSALL, N., T.C. PINCKNEY and R.H. SABOT (1995) "Inequality, Savings, and Growth", *Research Memorandum No. 148*, Williams College Center for Development Economics, Williamstown, MA., November.

BIRDSALL, N., D. ROSS and R. SABOT (1995), "Inequality and Growth Reconsidered: Lessons From East Asia", *World Bank Economic Review* 9:3, September.

BRUTON, H.J. (1985), "The Search for a Development Economics"?, *World Development* 13.

CARROLL, C.D. (1994), "How Does Future Income Affect Current Consumption*"*, *Quarterly Journal of Economics,* 109, February.

CLARKE, G. (1995), "More Evidence on Income Distribution and Growth", *Journal of Development Economics,* 47(2).

DEATON, A. (1992a), *Understanding Consumption,* Clarendon, Oxford.

DEATON, A. (1992b), "Household Saving in LDCs: Credit Markets, Insurance and Welfare", *Scandinavian Journal of Economics,* 94 (2).

DEATON, A. (1990), "Savings in Developing Countries: Theory and Review*",* World Bank *Economic Review,* Special Issue, Proceedings of the First Annual World Bank Conference on Development Economics, 61-96.

FEI, J., S.W.Y. KUO and G. RANIS (1981), *The Taiwan Success Story: Rapid Growth with Improved Distribution in the Republic of China: 1952-1979,* Westview, Boulder, CO.

GALENSON, W. and H. LEIBENSTEIN (1955), "Investment Criteria, Productivity, and Economic Development", *Quarterly Journal of Economics* 80, August.

JACOBY, H.G. (1994), "Borrowing Constraints and Progress through School: Evidence from Peru", *Review of Economics and Statistics* 76, February.

KALDOR, N. (1978) "Capital Accumulation and Economic Growth", in *Further Essays on Economic Theory* (ed.) N. KALDOR, Holmes & Meier Publishers, Inc., New York.

KIMUYU, P.K. (1994), "Credit and Financial Markets", in "Policy and Rural Development: Two Communities in East Africa", (ed.) T.C. PINCKNEY, Williams College, Center for Development Economics, Williamstown, MA.

KNIGHT, J. and R. SABOT (1990), *Education, Productivity, and Inequality.* Oxford University Press, New York.

KUZNETS, S. (1955), "Economic Growth and Income Inequality", *American Economic Review* 45:1, March, 1-28.

LEWIS, W.A. (1954), "Economic Development with Unlimited Supplies of Labour", *The Manchester School* 22.

MCKINNON, R.L. (1973), *Money and Capital in Economic Development.* The Brookings Institution, Washington, D.C.

PARK, Y.-B., D. ROSS and R. SABOT (1992), "Educational Expansion and the Inequality of Pay in Brazil and Korea", processed, World Bank, Washington, D.C.

PAXSON, C.H. (1992), "Using Weather Variability to Estimate the Response of Savings to Transitory Income in Thailand", *American Economic Review* 82.

PERSSON, T. and G. TABELLINI (1994), "Is Inequality Harmful for Growth?", *American Economic Review* 84 (3), June.

ROSENZWEIG, M.R. and K.I. WOLPIN (1993), "Credit Market Constraints, Consumption Smoothing, and the Accumulation of Durable Production Assets in Low-Income Countries: Investment in Bullocks in India", *Journal of Political Economy* 101 (2).

SCHIFF, M. and A. VALDES (1992), *The Political Economy of Agricultural Pricing Policy, Volume 4: A Synthesis of the Economics in Developing Countries,* A World Bank Comparative Study, The Johns Hopkins University Press, Baltimore and London.

SCHULTZ, T.W. (1964), *Transforming Traditional Agriculture,* Yale University Press, New Haven and London.

SHIBLI, M.A. (1991), *Investment Opportunities, Household Savings, and the Rates of Return on Investment: A Case Study of the Green Revolution in Bangladesh,* University Press of America, Lanham, MD.

TIMMER, C.P. (1995), "Getting Agriculture Moving: Do Markets Provide the Right Signals?" *Food Policy* 20 (5), October.

TOWNSEND, R.M. (1995), "Consumption Insurance: An Evaluation of Risk-Bearing Systems in Low-Income Economies", *Journal of Economic Perspectives* 9.

TURNHAM , D. (1993), *Employment and Development: A New Review of Evidence,* OECD Development Centre, Paris.

UDRY, C. (1993), "Credit Markets in Northern Nigeria: Credit as Insurance in a Rural Economy", in *The Economics of Rural Organization: Theory, Practice, and Policy.* (eds.) K. HOFF, A. BRAVERMAN and J.E. STIGLITZ, Oxford University Press, Oxford.

A Comment by François Bourguignon

Birdsall, Pinckney and Sabot present an interesting hypothesis to explain a possible positive link between the degree of income equality in a country and its rate of growth.

The basic argument in the paper may be summarised as follows. Credit-constrained rural households in developing countries have a higher marginal propensity to save when presented with enhanced investment opportunities than those who could borrow in a near-perfect credit market. This is reinforced by their possibility of supplying more labour to their own farms or, possibly, to the local labour market. A virtuous circle may then develop, with faster growth and lower time discount rates generating new investment opportunities and an increased desire to seize them.

Labour-intensive, agricultural and export-oriented development strategies of the type chosen in East Asia are precisely able to trigger such a virtuous circle. By contrast, inward looking strategies of the type applied in Brazil and more generally in Latin America did not provide higher returns either to the investments made or the labour supplied by the poor.

In addition, the virtuous circle of increased savings and investments by the poor requires a reasonably egalitarian income distribution ensuring that the returns to labour will be high enough for additional work to allow significantly increased savings. This is again a big difference between East Asia and Latin America and may explain the low level of investment by the poor in new agricultural technologies or in education in the latter region over the last two decades or so.

This looks like a nice story, but in fact its interpretation is not totally clear. In particular, the role of inequality in the paper seem somewhat ambiguous. There already are well known models which tie income inequality and growth together through the imperfection of the credit market. As argued in Banerjee and Newman (1993), credit-market imperfections prevent the poor from undertaking risky investment projects which have substantial fixed cost. Standard moral-hazard or adverse selection phenomena imply that some minimum wealth is required by formal or informal lenders from agents who want to borrow the amount necessary to seize the investment opportunities. Under these conditions, it is clear that redistributing wealth from very rich agents — who do not have to borrow to invest — to poor agents just below the

143

minimum wealth constraint should increase the number of projects undertaken and therefore the rate of growth in the economy. An argument of this type is also applied by Galor and Zeira (1993) to investments in the schooling of children.

The implicit mechanism linking inequality, savings and growth in the present paper does not seem to be of this sort. It is simply suggested implicitly that, other things being equal, the return to the labour of the poor will be higher in a more egalitarian society, so that the poor in such a society are more likely to generate the savings required to seize investment opportunities open to them through their labour. Actually, what is required is that the potential earnings rate faced by the poor be high enough so as to be an incentive to work more, to save and to invest. Strictly speaking, this is not directly related to the degree of inequality of the actual distribution of earnings or income, but rather to that of potential earnings, that is the distribution which would be observed if everybody were working full time, and to the existence of spare time, or more exactly market time, among the poor. So, the link with the observed distribution of income has still to be established formally, and the authors may be right in mentioning that this link will depend on the way the rural labour market actually works.

There may be some contradiction between this argument and the fact that investment in education — to which the authors refer at length as an application of their theoretical framework — will be most likely when returns are high, that is when the difference between the earnings rates of poor and non-poor is large enough and, therefore, the distribution of income sufficiently unequal! The authors are right in pointing out that secondary school enrolment rates tend to be higher, *ceteris paribus*, in more egalitarian countries but their theoretical interpretation of this evidence is not fully convincing. (It is interesting to note that Deininger and Squire (1996) find that this relationship might in fact go through land ownership, which they suggest might be in support of some of the models alluded to above in which wealth is the ultimate determinant of investment).

If the role of inequality in their argument is not totally clear, the authors are certainly right in pointing out that different development strategies in East Asia and in Latin America have generated differences in investment opportunities for the poor which may have had incidence on both the growth rate and the distribution of income in the two regions. However, they may be a little hasty in dismissing all political economy links between income inequality and growth. Generalising the argument found about the redistribution system in Alesina and Rodrik (1994), Persson and Tabellini (1994) and Bertola (1993) to the choice of a development strategy does not seem unjustified. After all, the distributional implications of an export-oriented agriculture-based strategy are certainly quite different from those of inward-looking and import-substitution development . Through political economy mechanisms, the initial distribution of income may determine the extent of redistributive taxation as in the existing models in the literature — as well as the choice of a development strategy.

The only problem is that political economy models of the type developed by Grossman and Helpman (1994), where government decisions result from various interest groups competing in lobbying activity or even bribery, might be more appropriate than the standard median voter and majority voting framework to explain such decisions. In any case, the issue of whether the initial distribution of income has played a role in the choice of a development strategy in East Asia and Latin America is worth serious thought.

Getting into more technical aspects of the paper, two general points need to be made. First, the case for credit-constrained households' having a very specific saving and labour-supply behaviour may be somewhat overstated. The story told in the paper would not be that different if households were facing an apparently perfect credit market where the rate of return on savings would be subject to a permanent upward shock. If the intertemporal elasticity of substitution in the standard dynamic model of consumption is larger than unity, then it is well known that present consumption is a decreasing function of the rate of return on savings. Adding labour in this framework is not a problem. For a given wage rate, leisure should be proportional to consumption, so that an increase in the rate of interest should indeed lead to both a drop in current consumption and an increase in labour supply, which are precisely the effects emphasised in the paper. What is more, one may even prove that the change in labour supply due to the change in the rate of return on wealth will be higher, the higher the wage rate. This is not to suggest that the hypothesis of a perfect credit market would be justified for poor people in developing countries, but simply that one does not really need to use a very sophisticated rationing model to make the basic point in the paper on the behaviour of households facing an increase in investment opportunities or, equivalently, an increase in the rate of return of their potential savings.

Second, the empirical evidence in favour of the association between growth and inequality may not be as strong as that suggested by the authors. There are many cross-sectional studies which do not find any significant statistical link between the distribution of income and the rate of growth, Deininger and Squire (1996), for example. Despite Clarke (1995) for example, the existing evidence is certainly not very robust.

The relationship between schooling and inequality would seem to be a little stronger, and the existence emphasised in the paper of a virtuous circle linking investment in education, income equality and growth might not have to be discarded. However, the nature of the causality linking secondary school enrolment rates and the degree of equality in society has still to be elucidated. Is it the case that egalitarian countries tend to invest more in education, or that more education tends to produce more egalitarian societies, or still that both variables are essentially endogenous? Likewise, the ambiguous statistical link between human capital accumulation and growth has repeatedly been emphasised.

145

There is a wider gap between savings and growth than is often assumed. The gap may be still bigger between inequality and savings or inequality and growth. It is interesting that we have totally changed our mind in comparison to the 1970s when the relationship between income distribution, savings and growth was essentially the Kaldorian story. Unfortunately, abandoning an illusion is not necessarily equivalent to revealing the truth.

Bibliography

ALESINA, A. and D. RODRIK (1994), "Distributive Politics and Economic Growth", *Quarterly Journal of Economics*, Vol. 104.

BANERJEE, A. and A. NEWMAN (1993), "Occupational Choice and the Process of Development", *Journal of Political Economy*, Vol. 101.

BERTOLA, G. (1993), "Factor Shares and Savings in Endogenous Growth", *American Economic Review*, Vol. 83(5).

CLARKE, G. (1995), "More Evidence on Income Distribution and Growth", *Journal of Development Economics,* Vol. 47, No. 2, August.

DEININGER, K. and L. SQUIRE (1996), *New Ways of Looking at Old Issues: Inequality and Growth*, mimeo, World Bank, Washington, D.C.

GALOR, O. and J. ZEIRA (1993), "Income Distribution and Macroeconomics", *Review of Economic Studies*, Vol. 60.

GROSSMAN, G. and E. HELPMAN (1994), "Protection for Sale", *American Economic Review*, Vol. 84.

PERSSON, T. and G. TABELLINI (1994), "Is Inequality Harmful to Growth", *American Economic Review*, Vol. 84.

Fiscal Policy and Private Saving in Latin America in Good Times and Bad

Michael Gavin and Roberto Perotti

Latin America's relatively low and, recently, declining rates of national saving have prompted calls for a policy response. Among the more frequently floated responses is a proposal that fiscal policy be oriented toward the achievement of higher rates of national saving through the apparently straightforward mechanism of generating larger public-sector savings. The hope is that higher public savings will translate into higher total domestic saving, which will be channelled into growth-promoting domestic investment.

It has long been recognised that an increase in public saving may lead to a reduction in private saving, which would reduce or even eliminate the impact of the higher public saving on total domestic saving. The logic is compelling: fiscal surpluses today mean lower debt service in the future, and unless the public sector is expected to consume all of the saving, this lower debt service creates the expectation of lower taxes in the future. If the private sector is clever enough to realise this and, importantly, it has the requisite access to financing, it will respond by reducing the current rate of saving.

This private-sector response to higher public saving has two implications. First, as a matter of long-run development policy, public saving will be less effective in raising total domestic saving than it would have been with myopic or constrained private savers who either do not or cannot incorporate the public sector's intertemporal budget constraint into their own planning. Second, as a matter of short-run macroeconomic management, the private-sector response renders transitory fiscal adjustments less effective in affecting transitory or cyclical fluctuations in domestic aggregate demand, because the impact of the fiscal policy on aggregate demand is substantially offset by a countervailing change in private spending[1]. As we shall discuss below, fiscal policy has tended to be pro-cyclical in Latin America, at least during economic downturns. To the extent that private savers offset the demand effects of these destabilising fiscal policies, they have reduced their economic costs.

How important is this private offsetting of changes in public saving? Barro (1974) laid out conditions under which a tax-induced rise in public saving would lead to a completely offsetting private response, and much of the subsequent literature was devoted to examining the plausibility of these assumptions, and of testing the hypothesis of full "Ricardian neutrality"[2]. For policy purposes, however, this literature was to a large extent beside the point, for the relevant question is not whether the private sector fully offsets changes in public saving, but, instead, whether there is any offsetting at all, and, if so, how large it appears to be.

A number of recent empirical studies of saving in industrial and developing countries alike have examined this, among other questions[3]. While the literature is in many respects immature, and important data and statistical problems remain to be sorted out satisfactorily[4], most studies point toward an important negative relationship between private and public saving, which has generally been given the causal interpretation that public saving "crowds out" private saving to a significant degree, though not entirely. Estimates of the Ricardian "offset coefficient" vary across studies, but both zero and unity can generally be rejected, and estimates tend to cluster in the range of 0.40 to 0.60, suggesting that for every dollar by which public saving is increased, private saving tends to fall by 40 to 60 cents.

For some commentators, this means that the glass is half full[5]. While recognising that higher public saving will be offset in part by lower private saving, they emphasise that the offset will not be complete, and promote a long-run policy of higher public saving in order to raise national saving and, one may hope, domestic investment. For others, the glass is half empty[6]. While accepting that the offset will not be complete, they argue that it is likely to be high enough to render a policy of raising national saving through higher public saving to be excessively costly, in light of the many legitimate and pressing demands for public spending, and of the distortions that would be generated by large increases in taxes. They argue that fiscal policy should be oriented towards ensuring the solvency of the public sector, so that fiscal policy can become a force to promote macroeconomic stability, rather than a source of instability, but that once this has been achieved there is little to be gained by increasing public sector surpluses even further.

Our contribution to this debate is as follows: we argue that existing measures of the Ricardian "offset coefficient" are flawed because they fail to take account of the differing interaction between public and private saving that we should expect to see in Latin America during "good times" and "bad times". This difference, which is rooted in the existence of more severely binding borrowing constraints during "bad times" than are present during "good times", means that the ability of the private sector to offset changes in public saving will be lower in "bad times" than in "good times".

Drawing upon recent work[7], we first present some key facts on fiscal outcomes in Latin America, documenting that fiscal policy has been pro-cyclical in the region, and (in sharp contrast to the industrial economies) that this pro-cyclicality has been most pronounced in economic downturns. We argue that the pro-cyclicality results from the fact that during bad times the public sector loses the access to financing that would be required to pursue a countercyclical fiscal policy. We reason that this curtailment of market access is likely to be felt by the private sector, as well, and that this should, in turn, lead to lower "offset coefficients" during bad times than would be observed during good times. We then present empirical evidence that the difference is both economically and statistically important in Latin America, and conclude with some observations on the policy implications of our findings.

Fiscal Policy is Pro-cyclical in Latin America

While the fundamental problems facing fiscal policy makers in Latin America and industrial economies are in most respects similar, fiscal outcomes have been very different. These differences are in several dimensions, but arguably the most striking is the sharp discrepancy between the cyclical behaviour of fiscal outcomes in the two regions. Table 1 summarises some evidence on this. The table reports the results of estimating equation (1):

$$ S_{i,t} - S_{i,t-1} = \alpha_0 + \alpha_1 \hat{Y}_{i,t} + \alpha_2 \hat{\tau}_{i,t} + \alpha_3 S_{i,t-1} + \varepsilon_i, \qquad (1) $$

which relates the change in the fiscal surplus country i in year t, measured as a percentage of GDP, to the contemporaneous rate of real GDP growth, the percentage change in the terms of trade, and the lagged fiscal surplus[8]. The purpose of the exercise is to characterise the typical fiscal response to changes in macroeconomic conditions, recognising that the estimated coefficients will reflect both the strictly endogenous responses of the budget to the new macroeconomic environment — automatic stabilisers — and whatever discretionary policy responses have been typical of the region during the sample period.

In columns 1 to 3 of Table 1 we present estimates of equation (1) for the industrial economies and Latin America separately, over the 1970-1994 period[9]. (Unless otherwise noted in the table, all regressions also include time and country dummy variables.) The first entry of column 1 indicates that, in the industrial economies, the fiscal surplus tends to increase when the rate of economic growth is high, pointing toward a counter-cyclical fiscal response to output shocks that is strong in both statistical and economic terms. (Counter-cyclical is used here in the Keynesian sense of a positive, stabilising association between the fiscal surplus and real output.) In the short run, about 20 cents of every additional dollar of increased real income is saved in the form of a higher budget surplus, reflecting some combination of automatic stabilizers and discretionary policy actions . Income shocks due to variations in the terms of trade are also reflected in higher fiscal surplus. None of this is very surprising.

The story is very different in Latin America. As the first entries of columns 2 and 3 suggest, in Latin America there has been a very weak relationship between real output and the fiscal balance; the point estimate is about a fifth the size of the response observed in the industrial economies, suggesting that only about 5 cents of every dollar of increased income finds its way into an increased fiscal surplus, and the estimated coefficient is statistically insignificantly different from zero. (Column 3 summarises the same regression as does column 2, except that in column 3 we have excluded all observations in which the rate of inflation was higher than 100 per cent. The main reason for doing this is that during periods of very high inflation the measurement of budgetary aggregates becomes problematic, and the data are subject to large measurement errors. Excluding these high-inflation observations has very little effect on the point estimates, but it increases substantially the precision with which they are estimated. We consider the regressions that drop high-inflation observations preferable.)

Table 1. **The Cyclical Response of the Overall Fiscal Balance – Good times and Bad**

	(1) Indust	(2) Latam	(3) Latam	(4) Indus	(5) Latam	(6) Latam
GDP growth	.1949	.0489	.0429	–	–	–
	(4.56)	(1.15)	(1.06)			
GDP growth, good times	–	–	–	.0988	.0931	.1165
				(2.12)	(1.46)	(2.14)
GDP growth, bad times	–	–	–	.6599	-.0114	-.0921
				(5.93)	(-0.15)	(-1.17)
Terms of trade (% change)	.0359	.0178	.0186	.0322	.0186	.0199
	(2.31)	(1.60)	(2.06)	(2.13)	(1.66)	(2.22)
Lagged fiscal surplus (% GDP)	-.1584	-.4118	-.4547	-.1683	-.4182	-.4626
	(-4.45)	(-7.36)	(-7.71)	(-4.85)	(-7.42)	(-7.88)
Adjusted R^2	.2583	.1792	.2182	.2979	.1725	.2290
Degrees of freedom	342	258	213	341	257	212
F test of H_0: coeff 2 = coeff 3	–	–	–	20.32	0.87	3.98
				[0.000]	[0.351]	[0.047]
Country dummies included	yes	yes	yes	yes	yes	yes
Time dummies included	yes	yes	yes	yes	yes	yes
Excl. high-inflation observations	no	no	yes	no	no	yes

Note: The dependent variable is the change in ratio of the overall fiscal surplus to GDP. Numbers in parentheses are t-statistics. Numbers in square brackets are significance levels of the corresponding F-test.

This approximately acyclical response of the financial balances in Latin America does not result from fiscal structures that insulate the budget from macroeconomic developments. On the contrary: because of the region's reliance upon non-tax income and other indirect taxes, revenues are substantially more volatile and sensitive to macroeconomic developments in Latin America[10]. The difference in cyclical behaviour instead results from the very different behaviour of expenditure in Latin America and the industrial countries. Total expenditure is roughly unaffected by the cycle in the industrial countries, with countercyclical transfer payments roughly offsetting some degree of pro-cyclicality in government purchases of goods and services, while both transfers and government purchases are highly pro-cyclical in Latin America. Note that, if one believes that the balanced budget multiplier is positive, this behaviour means that instead of being roughly acyclical, fiscal policy is pro-cyclical in Latin America.

It bears emphasis that this behaviour is at odds with both neoclassical (distortion-smoothing) and Keynesian prescriptions for optimal fiscal policymaking[11]. The neo-classical approach would advocate maintaining rough constancy of tax rates and thus the generation of budget surpluses in good times to avoid the need for costly increases in tax rates or inefficient cuts in expenditure during bad times. The Keynesian approach would promote much the same result with the aim of stabilising aggregate demand. This apparently sub-optimal behaviour cries out for an explanation. We provide one below.

In addition to the different cyclical responses, the regression results summarised in columns 1 and 3 highlight another important difference between fiscal outcomes in Latin America and the industrial economies. The coefficients on the lagged fiscal surplus provide an indication of how rapidly fiscal deficits and surpluses tend to be eliminated over time, with a larger negative number indicating that imbalances tend to vanish more rapidly. Our estimates suggest that deficits are, in fact, substantially less persistent in Latin America than they are in the industrial countries. One interpretation of this is that Latin America is well endowed with particularly conservative fiscal policy makers who abhor fiscal deficits, unlike their more reckless counterparts in the North. We have no direct evidence against this interpretation, but find another more plausible. We interpret the lower persistence of fiscal deficits in Latin America as evidence that the financial markets that are called upon to finance fiscal deficits are substantially less forgiving of imbalances in Latin America, and frequently force policymakers into rapid and occasionally disruptive fiscal adjustments[12].

Pro-cyclicality is Especially Strong in Bad Macroeconomic Times

This pro-cyclicality of fiscal policy is bad enough, but if one looks a little closer the picture gets even less attractive. Not only has Latin American fiscal policy been pro-cyclical on average, it has been particularly so in bad macroeconomic times, when a stabilising response would have been most valuable, and when in fact fiscal policy is particularly stabilising in the industrial countries.

Evidence for this is presented in columns 4 to 6 of Table 1, above, where we present estimates of the typical fiscal response to output shocks, this time distinguishing between "good times" and "bad times". In this exercise, "bad" times are years in which a country's real output growth is at least one standard deviation below the average rate of growth over the 1970-94 period, and good times are all other years[13]. In the industrial economies, the fiscal response to output growth is very different in the two regimes. There is a statistically significant but relatively minor tendency for the budget surplus to increase with output in good times; as column 4 indicates, about 10 cents of every dollar of higher real GDP finds its way into the budget surplus. However, in the industrial countries the fiscal response to changes in real GDP is much stronger in bad times, when for every dollar of decline in real GDP the budget deficit increases by nearly 66 cents[14].

This paints a picture of a region in which downturns are economically and/or politically more costly than upturns, and in which the fiscal response is accordingly stronger. Implicit in this picture is the presumption that industrial-economy governments will be able to finance the deficits required to run a countercyclical fiscal policy during downturns. We commonly take this for granted in the industrial economies, but it bears mention here because it cannot be taken for granted in Latin America.

In Latin America, too, there are important asymmetries between good times and bad, but they are the opposite of those that characterise the industrial economies. During good times, the fiscal response to output shocks is similar to that observed in the industrial economies; about ten cents of every dollar of higher income finds its way into a higher budget surplus[15]. However, in bad times a *decline* in real GDP is associated with an *increase* in the budget surplus of nearly 10 cents for every dollar of lost income[16]. Because a neutral policy of roughly constant tax rates and real spending would lead to the emergence of fiscal deficits during bad times, this finding implies, of course, a major discretionary fiscal contraction during economic downturns.

The pro-cyclicality of Latin American fiscal policy is even more evident if one focuses on "deep" recessions, which we define as recessions in which the cumulative decline in real GDP is at least 1.5 per cent (industrial economies) or 4 per cent (Latin America). Figure 1, taken from Gavin, Hausmann, Perotti and Talvi (1996), plots the cumulative change in real GDP during each recession next to the cumulative change in the fiscal surplus, measured as a percentage of GDP.

In the industrial economies, in virtually all recessions the budget surplus moves in near lock step with the decline in GDP. In those economies the average decline in real GDP during "deep" recessions was 3.3 percentage points, and the average decline in the fiscal surplus was 3.0 percentage points of GDP. Nothing similar is seen in Latin American recessions, where the cumulative decline in real GDP averages nearly 11 per cent, and on average the fiscal balance moved toward *surplus* by nearly 2 percentage points of GDP[17]. This would obviously have required a very major discretionary fiscal contraction.

Pro-cyclicality is Associated with Loss of Market Access in Bad Times

What explains the pro-cyclical tendencies of Latin American fiscal policy during bad times? It cannot be ignorance by Latin America's policymakers of the virtues of running fiscal deficits during bad times — this is as natural as falling off a log. We

Figure 1.

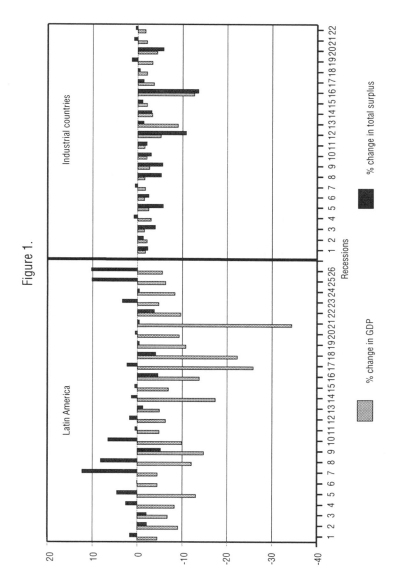

suggest, instead, that the observed pro-cyclicality of fiscal policy has to do with a loss of market access during bad times, which makes it impossible, or extraordinarily expensive, to finance the deficits that would be implied by a countercyclical policy. The experiences of Argentina and Mexico during 1995 and 1996 provide an illuminating case in point. Both countries fell into deep recession after the "Tequila" shock of December 1994. But rather than permit fiscal deficits to increase, both countries have implemented strongly contractionary policies of tax increases and cuts in public spending, which can only have amplified the painful recessions experienced in both countries. The reason for these actions was a sharp reduction in both countries' capacity to finance even moderate fiscal deficits, and the need to reassure international investors that the recessions would not lead to large fiscal deficits, with the aim of avoiding further loss of confidence and even more drastically curtailed access to financial markets.

The idea that Latin American fiscal policy has been shaped to an important degree by tightly binding borrowing constraints during bad times is supported by the behaviour of the inflation tax, a fiscal resource of last, desperate resort in most countries. In the industrial economies, the inflation tax rate[18] is weakly but positively correlated with real GDP growth and the lagged fiscal surplus, which would be consistent with a Phillips curve, and inconsistent with the idea that large budget deficits tend to be followed by bursts of inflation. (See Table 2.)

In Latin America, the picture is very different. Inflation is highly negatively correlated with output growth, suggesting that inflation tends to increase strongly during bad macroeconomic times. Inflation is also strongly negatively correlated with the lagged fiscal surplus, suggesting that large fiscal imbalances have often led to increases in the inflation tax, and that inflation is in this sense a fiscal phenomenon in a way that is not evident in the industrial economies.

Table 2. **The Cyclical Response of the Inflation Tax Rate**

	GDP growth	Lagged inflation tax	Lagged surplus (% GDP)	Adjusted R^2	Number of obs.	see
Industrial economies	.0732 (1.25)		.1358 (3.06)	-.020	448	.028
Latin America	-.6078 (4.28)		-.4938 (-2.59)	.078	280	.106
Industrial economies	.0296 (0.52)	-.2072 (-6.42)	.1156 (2.72)	.068	448	.027
Latin America	-.7704 (-6.20)	-.3294 (-9.45)	-1.0675 (-6.08)	.308	280	.092

Note: Dependent variables: change in the CPI inflation-tax rate. All regressions include country dummy variables.

We have presented three pieces of evidence on the behaviour of fiscal policy in Latin America that suggest the importance of borrowing constraints during bad macroeconomic times: *i)* periods of low output growth typically elicit a contractionary fiscal response, which is consistent with the idea that governments lose the market access required to finance deficits during bad times; *ii)* the speed with which fiscal deficits vanish in Latin America is higher than is typical of industrial economies, suggesting, again, that financial markets frequently force Latin American governments into more rapid fiscal adjustments; and *iii)* inflation tends to rise sharply during periods of low economic growth, which is most easily understood as a consequence of a loss of access to noninflationary finance during bad times. There is more to be said about the underlying causes and the consequences of this "precarious creditworthiness", but it would take us away from the main subject of this paper, which is the relationship between private and public saving in Latin America.

Public and Private Saving in Good Times and Bad

What are the implications of this pattern of fiscal behaviour for the relationship between private and public saving? As mentioned above, one of the conditions required to observe a substantial private response to an increase in public saving is that financial markets permit the private sector to engage in the borrowing that may be required for at least some consumers to reduce their saving rate. We would thus expect the "Ricardian offset coefficient" to be higher in times and in places where borrowing constraints are relaxed, and lower where financial markets are imperfect and borrowing constraints bind tightly.

We presented evidence above that Latin American governments often find themselves suddenly without access to the financial markets that they need to finance deficits, or, put differently, become subject to more tightly binding borrowing constraints, during bad times. While we have no direct evidence for the position of private borrowers, it seems highly plausible that the private sector is no better placed than is the public sector, and, as with the public sector, that the borrowing constraints that face the private sector become more severe in bad macroeconomic times[19].

If so, this suggests that there will be systematic differences in the ability of the private sector to offset changes in public saving in good times and bad times. In bad times, when borrowing constraints are binding, the private sector might like to offset an increase in public saving by dissaving, but they will find themselves unable to finance the required (private) deficits. In good times, on the other hand, offsetting the change in public saving is likely to be much easier for most of the private sector, either because it requires no borrowing, but merely a reduction in a positive rate of financial saving, or because if borrowing is required, the markets will be there to make it possible. Thus, the Ricardian "offset coefficient" is likely to be higher (in absolute value) in good times, and lower in bad times[20]. Estimates of the impact of public saving on private saving that do not account for this difference in regime will underestimate the "offset coefficient" that applies to normal or good times, while overestimating the coefficient that applies in bad times.

We draw out some policy implications of this below, but first ask whether there is any evidence for the hypothesised difference in the effects of public saving in good and bad times. We work with a simple version of the framework that is often adopted in empirical studies of saving, beginning with variants of the following equation:

$$\left(S_{i,t}^{p} - S_{i,t-1}^{p}\right) = \alpha_0 + \alpha_1 \hat{Y}_{i,t} + \alpha_2 \hat{\tau}_{i,t} + \alpha_3 \left(S_{i,t}^{g} - S_{i,t-1}^{g}\right) + \alpha_4 T_{i,t}^{\pi} + \alpha_5 S_{i,t-1}^{p} + \varepsilon_{i,t} \qquad (2)$$

which attempts to explain the change in the ratio of private saving to GDP in country i during year t with real GDP growth, the growth rate of the terms of trade, the change in the ratio of public saving to GDP, an estimate of inflation tax revenue as a share of GDP, and the lagged private saving rate[21].

Growth in real GDP and in the terms of trade are expected to increase the saving rate, to the extent that changes tend to be interpreted as being at least partly temporary. Increases in public saving are expected to reduce private saving, for the reasons that we have discussed above. The appearance of inflation tax revenue is essentially a measurement issue. Conventional measures of saving do not subtract from private income, or add to public income, the transfer of real resources that is generated by the inflation tax on high powered money[22].

Table 3 presents the results of estimating variants of this equation on the same panels of data from industrial and Latin American countries that were used above. The measures of private and public saving are from the International Monetary Fund's *World Economic Outlook* database, inflation tax revenue was computed using data from the *International Financial Statistics,* and the other data are as in the previous work.

The first two coefficients reported in columns 1 and 2 suggest that, in both regions, growth in real GDP and in the terms of trade are associated with increases in the rate of private saving, although in Latin America the impact of GDP growth is weak in both economic and statistical terms. In both regions there is also strong evidence of a negative relationship between public saving and private saving, with an estimated "offset coefficients" of about .63 in Latin America and .73 in the industrial economies.

In subsequent columns of Table 3 we allow the estimated impact on private saving of GDP growth and changes in the rate of public saving to depend upon the regime in which the economy finds itself, with "good time" and "bad time" regimes defined as above. In the industrial economies, the estimated impact on private saving of changes in public saving does not depend upon whether the the economy is in the "good times" or the "bad times" regime, and is in the .70-.75 range in both cases. This is consistent with the idea that access to financial markets does not abruptly vanish in the industrial economies during bad times, and that private borrowing constraints do not suddenly intensify.

Table 3. **Private and Public Saving – Good Times and Bad**

	(1) Indust	(2) Latam	(3) Indust	(4) Latam	(5) Latam
GDP growth	.2580 (6.61)	.0913 (1.08)	–	–	–
GDP growth, good times	–	–	.1975 (4.42)	.2575 (2.03)	.3343 (3.03)
GDP growth, bad times	–	–	.4495 (4.37)	-.0714 (-0.44)	-.0806 (-0.53)
Terms of trade (% change)	.0728 (5.46)	.0499 (2.26)	.0727 (5.49)	.0546 (2.47)	.0593 (3.05)
Change in public saving rate	-.7253 (-13.89)	-.6288 (-5.74)	–	–	–
Change in public saving, good times	–	–	-.7581 (-12.90)	-.7726 (-5.01)	-.8103 (-5.70)
Change in public saving, bad times	–	–	-.6779 (-7.43)	-.3695 (-2.43)	-.3800 (-2.58)
Inflation tax (% of GDP)	.3290 (0.67)	.5631 (3.10)	.4217 (0.86)	.8125 (3.76)	.9117 (4.45)
Lagged private saving (%GDP)	-.1870 (-5.81)	-.2155 (-5.49)	-.1803 (-5.64)	-.3593 (-6.84)	-.3553 (-7.50)
Adjusted R²	.4578	.3002	.4676	.3285	.3320
Degrees of freedom	316	204	314	192	
F test of H$_0$: coeff 2 = coeff 3	–	–	3.711 [0.055]	2.060 [0.153]	
F test of H$_0$: coeff 6 = coeff 7	–	–	0.611 [0.435]	3.536 [0.062]	214
Country dummies included	yes	yes	yes	yes	3.711 [0.055]
Time dummies included	yes	yes	yes	yes	no

Note: The dependent variable is the change in ratio of private saving to GDP. Numbers in parentheses are t-statistics. Numbers in square brackets are significance levels of the corresponding F-test.

In Latin America the estimated "offset coefficient" is during good times roughly the same as in the industrial countries. During bad times, however, the estimated "offset coefficient" falls to only 0.37, less than half the size of the coefficient estimated for good times[23]. This is consistent with the idea that, in Latin America, borrowing constraints reduce the ability of the private sector to offset changes in public saving during bad times.

The response of private saving to output shocks is also consistent with this idea. During good times in Latin America, output shocks are associated with an increase in the rate of private saving, which is consistent with consumption-smoothing savers if the output shocks are at least partly transitory. The same is true of the industrial economies, and indeed the estimated impact of GDP growth on saving during "good times" is roughly the same in the two regions. In bad times, however, the behaviour of private Latin American and industrial-country savers diverges. During bad times in Latin America, the saving rate is insensitive to real GDP growth, while there is a very large impact on the rate of private saving during bad times in the industrial countries. Our interpretation of this result is that, while the Latin American private sector might like to protect their level of consumption by lowering their rate of saving during recessions, many consumers find themselves unable to secure the financing of the implied private deficits.

Some Policy Implications

The key result of the preceding section was that, in Latin America, the Ricardian "offset coefficient" is much lower in bad macroeconomic times that it is in normal, or good times. (In the industrial economies, where the sudden curtailment of access to financial markets is not a feature of economic downturns, we did not expect to see a major difference between "bad" and "good" times, and we did not in fact see one.) During bad times, our estimated "offset coefficient" was about 0.4, toward the lower end of the range of estimates to be found in the existing literature. During good times, the estimated coefficient was about 0.8, at the high end of the range of existing estimates.

This suggests to us that existing empirical work, which does not distinguish between bad times and good times, is coming up with estimates that are an average of the different coefficients that apply to the "good times" and "bad times" in their sample. They thus underestimate the "offset coefficient" that applies in normal, or good times, and that would be relevant for thinking about a long-run policy of attempting to raise national saving by raising public saving and, in doing so, they understate the economic costs of the proposed policy.

Our point estimate of the "offset coefficient" that applies during normal times suggests that raising national saving by one percentage point would require an increase in fiscal surplus of a full 5 percentage points. In the typical Latin American country, tax revenue accounts for less than 15 per cent of GDP; if Brazil is excluded, the average is 13 per cent of GDP[24]. Thus, to increase national saving by one percentage point of GDP, the tax burden would have to be increased by over one-third. This would be one thing if the region's low rate of tax collection reflected low tax rates, which could be raised without introducing major, growth-impeding economic distortions, but this is not the case. Tax collections are low as a result of large informal sectors and other factors, and despite the existence of tax rates that are in many cases at or above industrial-country levels, and that in many cases already create major distortions. There is a very real danger that attempts to raise national saving by increasing these taxes will result in a supply-side driven "paradox of thrift", in which adverse effects on economic activity and thus private saving dominate the effects of higher public saving. This is true even under the rather optimistic assumption that the large surpluses do not generate strong pressures for increased public spending[25].

While the Ricardian "offset coefficient" that applies to good times may have been underestimated by previous studies, our analysis also suggests that the coefficient that applies to bad times has been *overestimated* in the existing literature. An implication is that, during bad times, the capacity of the private sector to "undo" the effects of changes in fiscal balances is much attenuated which, in turn, means that the pro-cyclical behaviour of fiscal policy during downturns that has unfortunately been typical in the region has been highly destabilising for countries in the region. This finding sheds further light on previous findings that fiscal instability is an important source of macroeconomic volatility in Latin America[26]. It is by contributing to this macroeconomic volatility that fiscal policy has almost certainly done its most severe damage to economic growth, saving and investment in the region, and it is by removing itself as a source of instablity that fiscal policy can most effectively promote economic growth and, thereby, saving.

The only way to prevent the destabilising outcome is to improve public sector creditworthiness, so that governments will not find themselves without access to financial markets when they need it most. This means trying to improve the efficiency of tax systems, to create enough "fiscal slack" to reassure investors that the government has the capacity to accommodate adverse shocks, thus reducing the danger that they will head for the exits at the first sign of trouble. It means strengthening budgetary institutions, to raise the likelihood that the fiscal surpluses that emerge in good times will be used to retire public debt, not to plant the seeds of the next fiscal crisis by expanding hard-to-reverse spending programmes. It is likely to mean higher public saving than has been observed in most countries of the region during much of the past several decades. By promoting public solvency and thereby reducing the likelihood that fiscal policy will be a destabilising force, these higher public surpluses are likely to make a major contribution to economic development in the region, whatever their direct effects on national saving.

Notes

1. This statement is only true when the change in fiscal policy involves changes in taxes or transfer payments. Even in a world of full Ricardian equivalence, transitory changes in government investment or consumption spending would affect domestic demand and national saving.

2. See for example Bernheim (1987).

3. See for example Corbo and Schmidt-Hebbel (1991), Edwards (1995). A number of such studies are reviewed in Schmidt-Hebbel, Servén and Solimano (1994).

4. Available data on private and public saving are flawed in many ways, often failing for example to account for economically relevant but conventionally unmeasured taxes such as the inflation tax on high-powered money, and improperly treating the inflationary component of public interest payments as real income for the private sector and a real expenditure of the public sector. The major statistical problems are the potential endogeneity of public saving to "shocks" in private saving, and troublesome fact that theory points toward the importance of expected future as well as contemporaneous budgetary variables. Some studies use an instrumental variables procedure to cope with the potential endogeneity of public saving, but it is not always clear that the proposed instruments are valid. It might also be argued that most existing studies fail to take sufficient account of the difference between changes in government taxes and consumption.

5. See, for example, Edwards (1995) and Schmidt-Hebbel, Servén and Solimano (1994).

6. See, for example, Gavin, Hausmann, and Talvi (this volume).

7. See Gavin, Hausmann, Perotti and Talvi (1996).

8. Except for inclusion of the change in the terms of trade as an explanatory variable and our distinction between behaviour during good and bad times, this regression is essentially the same as the analysis carried out by Bayoumi and Eichengreen (1995) for US states. The fiscal data are from the IMF's *Government Financial Statistics,* after some cross-checking and updating from other sources, and refer to that publication's definition of the consolidated central government (budgetary central government, plus social security funds). National accounts data for industrial economies and Latin America are from the OECD and the IDB's Economic and Social Database, respectively. Data on the terms of trade are from the World Bank.

9. Twenty-one industrial countries are included in the analysis: Austria, Belgium, Canada, Denmark, France, Germany, Great Britain, Italy, the Netherlands, Norway, Sweden, Switzerland, the United States, Japan, Finland, Iceland, Greece, Ireland, Portugal, Spain and Australia. The 14 Latin American economies included in the analysis are Argentina, Bolivia, Brazil, Chile, Colombia, Costa Rica, the Dominican Republic, Ecuador, Mexico,

Panama, Paraguay, Peru, Uruguay, and Venezuela. Some industrial countries and a number of Latin American countries were missing data for some years of the sample period.

10. See Gavin, Hausmann, Perotti and Talvi (1996) for a lengthier discussion. The elasticity of real fiscal revenue with respect to real output is estimated at about 0.9 in the industrial economies, and 1.25 in Latin America.

11. If shocks to real GDP were much more persistent in Latin America than they are in the industrial economies, then the insensitivity of fiscal balances to GDP shocks could be explained on neoclassical grounds. In background work for Gavin, Hausmann, Perotti and Talvi (1996), we explored this issue and found that, taking the regions as a whole, the dynamic properties of output and the terms of trade were similar in Latin America and the industrial economies.

12. As we emphasise below, this "precarious creditworthiness" is not an exogenous feature of the Latin American macroeconomic environment, but is instead the result of fiscal management that has not been sufficiently attentive to the demands placed on policy by the region's volatile macroeconomic environment. See Gavin, Hausmann, Perotti and Talvi (1996) .

13. Similar results are obtained if one defines "bad" times as periods when output growth is negative.

14. The difference between the estimated impact of GDP growth in good times and bad is statistically significant at any conventional confidence level.

15. See column 6 of Table 1 which drops high-inflation observations and is our preferred specification. The point estimates reported in column 5, which includes high-inflation observations, are similar to these, but they are estimated with substantially lower precision.

16. This point estimate is not statistically significantly different from zero. It is significantly different from the estimated positive impact of GDP shocks on the fiscal surplus during "good times" at the 5 per cent confidence level.

17. This point estimate of the average change in the surplus is statistically significantly different from zero at the 7 per cent, but not the 5 per cent level of confidence.

18. The inflation tax rate is the rate of inflation divided by one plus the rate of inflation, and it measures the proportional loss in the real value of non-interest bearing monetary wealth over a given period of time.

18. The recent experiences in Argentina and Mexico provide some evidence on this. When the governments of those countries lost access to international financial markets, so did the private sectors. Access was restored to both private and public sectors at more or less the same time.

20. A number of recent and influential papers have recently argued that the macroeconomic consequences of changes in fiscal policy depends upon prevailing budgetary and macroeconomic conditions. Giavazzi and Pagano (1990, 1995) argued that the impact of fiscal consolidations on private demand depends upon whether the initial budgetary stance is untenable or not. When it is, a fiscal consolidation can have "non-Keynesian"

expansionary effects, by increasing confidence. Perotti (1996) also argues that the impact of fiscal policy on private consumption demand depends upon whether or not there is "fiscal distress", as measured by high ratios of public debt to GDP or a recent history of very rapid accumulation of public debt. Bertola and Drazen (1993) provide a theoretical model of these effects. Here we focus on a different mechanism through which the impact of fiscal policy becomes regime-dependent, and emphasise the role of macroeconomic, as opposed to fiscal, "good times" and "bad times".

21. Equation (2) is a parsimonious version of a commonly-encountered specification in the empirical literature on saving, see e.g. Corbo and Schmidt-Hebbel (1991) and Edwards (1995), except that we estimate in first differences, and include time and country dummies, while excluding demographic and similar variables.

22. The adjustment was made by Ernesto Talvi for Gavin, Talvi and Hausmann (1996). It is often large in Latin America, but only seldom so in the industrial economies. The inflation tax is not the only, or even the most important measurement problem created by inflation. Of arguably more empirical significance is the inflationary component of nominal interest payments on public debt, which are conventionally but improperly considered real income of the private sector and expenditure of the public sector. We lacked the data required to adjust for this.

23. The difference in the point estimates is statistically significant at the 6 per cent confidence level if time dummies are included in the regression, and at the 4 per cent level if time dummies are not included.

24. These numbers refer to the central government; in several countries the general government is substantially larger. However, it is the central government upon which the task of macroeconomic management largely falls, and toward which proposals to increase fiscal surpluses are typically directed.

25. See Talvi and Végh (1996).

26. Gavin and Hausmann (1996) present evidence that fiscal volatility is an important source of volatility in real output in Latin America, and through its effects on monetary outcomes, an important source of volatility in the real exchange rate. There is a substantial and growing body of evidence that volatility in real output, the real exchange rate, and measures of fiscal and monetary policy themselves have reduced investment and lowered economic growth in many developing economies. On the links between volatility and growth see, for example, Aizenman and Marion (1993) on policy volatility, Ramey and Ramey (1995) on the volatility of real output, and Inter-American Development Bank (1995) on volatility in the terms of trade, the real exchange rate and policy. Inter-American Development Bank (1995) summarises a number of related papers.

Bibliography

AIZENMAN, J. and N. MARION (1993), "Policy Uncertainty, Persistence, and Growth", *Journal of Development Economics,* 145:163.

BARRO, R. (1974), "Are Government Bonds Net Wealth?", *Journal of Political Economy,* 82.

BAYOUMI, T. and B. EICHENGREEN (1995), "Restraining Yourself: Fiscal Rules and Stabilization", *IMF Staff Papers,* 42(1).

BERNHEIM, B.D. (1987), "Ricardian Equivalence: An Evaluation of Theory and Evidence", *NBER Macroeconomic Annual: 1987,* MIT Press, Cambridge MA .

BERTOLA, G. and A. DRAZEN (1993), "Trigger Points and Budget Cuts: Explaining the Effects of Fiscal Austerity", *American Economic Review,* 83.

CORBO, V. and K. SCHMIDT-HEBBEL (1991), "Public Policies and Saving in Developing Countries", *Journal of Development Economics,* 36.

EASTERLY, W., C. RODRÍGUEZ, and K. SCHMIDT-HEBBEL (1994), *Public Sector Deficits and Macroeconomic Performance,* Oxford University Press, Oxford.

EDWARDS, S. (1995), "Why are Saving Rates so Different Across Countries? An International Comparative Analysis", NBER Working Paper No. 5097.

GAVIN, M. and R. HAUSMANN (1996), "Sources of Volatility in Developing Economies", mimeo, Inter-American Development Bank, Washington, D.C.

GAVIN, M., R. HAUSMANN and E. TALVI (1996), "Saving in Latin America: Evidence and Policy Issues", this volume.

GAVIN, M., R. HAUSMANN, R. PEROTTI and E. TALVI (1996), "Managing Fiscal Policy in Latin America: Volatility, Procyclicality and Limited Creditworthiness", Working Paper No. 326, Office of the Chief Economist, Inter-American Development Bank, Washington, D.C.

GIAVAZZI, F. and M. PAGANO (1990), "Can Severe Fiscal Adjustments be Expansionary?", in O. BLANCHARD and S. FISCHER (eds.) *NBER Macroeconomic Annual,* MIT Press, Cambridge, MA.

GIAVAZZI, F. and M. PAGANO (1995), "Non-Keynesian Effects of Fiscal Policy Changes: International Evidence and the Swedish Experience", mimeo, University of Bocconi.

HAUSMANN, R. and H. REISEN (1996), *Securing Stability and Growth in Latin America: Policy Issues and Prospects for Shock-Prone Economies,* Inter-American Development Bank and the OECD Development Centre, Paris.

HONOHAN, P. (1995), "The Impact of Financial and Fiscal Policies on Saving", mimeo, Economic and Social Research Institute, Dublin.

INTER-AMERICAN DEVELOPMENT BANK (1995), "Overcoming Volatility in Latin America", in *Economic and Social Progress in Latin America: 1995 Report,* Johns Hopkins University Press for the Inter-American Development Bank, Baltimore.

MORANDÉ, F. (1996), "Savings in Chile: What Went Right?", Working Paper No. 322, Office of the Chief Economist, Inter-American Development Bank, Washington, D.C.

PEROTTI, R. (1996), "Fiscal Policy When Things Go Badly", mimeo, Columbia University.

RAMEY, G. and V. RAMEY (1995), "Cross-Country Evidence on the Link Between Volatility and Growth", *American Economic Review,* 85(5).

SCHMIDT-HEBBEL, K., L. SERVÉN and A. SOLIMANO (1994), "Saving, Investment and Growth in Developing Countries: An Overview", mimeo, World Bank, Washington, D.C.

TALVI, E. and C. VÉGH (1996), "Can Optimal Fiscal Policy be Procyclical?", mimeo, Inter-American Development Bank?,Washington, D.C.

A Comment by Guillermo Perry

Technicalities

The Specification of Models

The structure of equation 1 makes it is difficult to interpret the results. A possible alternative would be to use a dynamic adjustment model, as follows:

S_t^* = desired fiscal surplus at time t

S_t = actual fiscal surplus at time t

y_t = GDP growth rate at time t

T_t = change in terms of trade at time t

$S_t^* = a0 + a1\, y_t + a2\, T_t$ desired fiscal surplus

$S_t - S_{t-1} = b\, (S_t^* - S_{t-1}) + u_t$ gradual adjustment to the desired level

Substituting for S_t^*, we obtain

$S_t - S_{t-1} = b\, a0 + b\, a1\, y_t + b\, a2\, T_t - b\, S_{t-1} + u_t$

Therefore, when comparing "bad" and "good" times, the coefficient of the rate of growth of income can be interpreted as the product of two coefficients (one associated with the desired adjustment in the fiscal balance and the other with the speed by which the economy moves from the current fiscal balance to the desired fiscal balance). Thus the coefficient of y_t may be different in "good" and "bad" times either because $a1$ has changed or because b has changed. However, if b has changed, the coefficients of the other variables also will have changed. Under this interpretation, the correct way of testing for the difference between in Table 1 would be to allow for **different coefficients for GDP growth** *and* **for the other variables (the terms of trade and the lagged fiscal surplus)**. If the authors' interpretation is correct, we would in fact expect that the adjustment in bad times *(b)* is faster, due to lack of access to credit. However, the authors make the coefficient of the other variables the same in both "good" and "bad" times, which may lead to biased estimates of the coefficient of GDP growth.

The explanation for the regressions presented in Table 2 is that under certain circumstances governments rely on inflation tax revenue to finance their expenditures. This would suggest that the regression should be estimated using the inflation tax *revenue* (inflation tax rate times unremunerated public sector liabilities, usually the monetary base), rather than the inflation tax *rate* (which is the specification used by the authors).

The authors justify including inflation tax revenue as an additional explanatory variable in equation (2) because "conventional measures of saving do not subtract from private income, or add to public income, the transfer of real resources that is generated by the inflation tax on high powered money." This measurement problem is real. However, **the "correct" way to proceed is to adjust the measures of public and private saving, instead of including inflation tax revenue as an additional variable** (which is what the authors do). These two procedures are not equivalent, and thus the results of the estimation will most likely change (although it is not possible to say in which direction) if the "correct" procedure is used.

Estimation Techniques

The estimation of the equations as simple regressions presents several problems:

i) possible joint endogeneity (e.g. fiscal surplus determines growth;

ii) omitted variable bias (e.g. economic reform explains both growth rates and fiscal surplus);

iii) country dummies should not be included during the first differentiation of the model.

A better approach would be to use an error-correction model, i.e. to establish long-run relationships and the speed of adjustment from short-run shocks. This would be the correct way to handle the underlying dynamic structure of the model.

Interpretation and Policy Implications

Assuming that results will still hold once the technical problems have been corrected, it is worth discussing alternative interpretations.

As the authors mention, one way of interpreting the results is that (during the period they studied) economic policy makers in Latin America became more conservative than in OECD countries: it does not matter if times are good or bad, they are always in the business of increasing the fiscal surplus. Such an interpretation, and the results, suggests a trend, rather than different responses to the cycle.

In fact, there may be a missed factor that explains the trend: initial conditions (e.g. the size of public debt *vis-à-vis* revenues or primary surplus) which required a large adjustment that is only possible in a long period of time.

The interpretation of the difficulties in accessing credit in bad times is quite plausible, but it should be tested either directly or indirectly. One could either use a proxy such as spreads or make a comparison with the behaviour of other developing countries that, in principle, would be subject to the same restriction.

In any case, the discussion assumes that borrowing constraints are fully exogenous. They could be due to high levels of public debt *vis-à-vis* revenues or primary surplus (in bad times nobody wants to finance an already overburdened government). In this case, we are back to the lack of consideration of initial conditions which may explain the observed behaviour.

It is also possible that the poor management in "good times" (low saving, high current account deficits) lead to more vulnerable economies in bad times. In such a case, however, the policy recommendation is the same: save more in good times, to be able to dissave (both from accumulated saving and improved creditworthiness) in bad times.

The suggested interpretation implies that the authors believe that both government officials and private agents are myopic: if they know that they will be cut off from credit in bad times, why don't they save more in good times? At least with respect to private agents, it is inconsistent to assume perfect foresight and rational expectations, to expect full or high Ricardian offset and, at the same time, myopic behaviour in the good times.

An additional point on Ricardian offset. At times the paper confuses public surplus (eq. 1) with public savings (eq. 2). An increase in public surplus due to investment cuts, does not have to be matched by decreased private saving as there was no change in public saving, and the investment cut may be correctly perceived as temporary. So from the results of Table 1 it does not follow that public saving increases in bad times, as implied by the authors.

169

The policy recommendation in the end is the same as was criticised at the outset: pursue public saving, at least in good times. Certainly, the rationale offered is different: it is not to increase total saving, but to circumvent financial restrictions in bad times so as to get less output volatility. But then what happened to the authors' arguments about the high cost and political difficulties of achieving a high public surplus in Latin America, especially when they estimate that the offset coefficient is quite high in good times?

A Comment by Luigi Spaventa

Gavin and Perotti compare the cyclical behaviour of fiscal policies and the response of private saving to changes in the government's budget balance in Latin American countries and in industrial countries during the 1970-94 period. Their novel and valuable contribution is to make a distinction between "bad times" (years in which a country's growth rate was at least one standard deviation below the period's average) and "good times" (all other years).

In their first scenario, fiscal policies are countercyclical in industrial countries but appear to be procyclical in Latin America. In an equation explaining the change in the fiscal surplus (as a ratio of the GDP) the coefficient of the growth rate[1] is fairly high (0.2) in industrial countries but close to zero in Latin America for the period as a whole. The contrast is more dramatic when separate estimates are made for good and bad times. In good times fiscal policy is similar in the two groups, with surpluses increasing by 10 per cent of the rise in income. In bad times, however, industrial countries let their fiscal surplus decrease by some 66 per cent of the fall in the GDP, while in Latin America the surplus *increases* by 10 per cent, clear evidence of procyclical fiscal policies.

The second scenario concerns the response of private saving to GDP growth and to changes in public saving[2]. Taking the whole period, changes in public saving are offset to a considerable extent, but not wholly, by opposing changes in private saving in both regions, with an offset coefficient of 0.73 in industrial countries and 0.63 in Latin America[3]. Again, the picture changes when bad times are considered separately. While the coefficient remains roughly the same for industrial countries, in Latin America it becomes less than half in bad times compared to good times. Unlike in the industrial countries, moreover, private saving is insensitive to GDP changes in bad times. The two situations together produce a gloomy picture. In Latin America there are no private (consumption smoothing) or public stabilisers at work during a recession; worse, fiscal policies are procyclical and their perverse effect is offset only to a very limited extent by the behaviour of private saving.

Both situations arise from stringent borrowing constraints in bad times[4] which compel the public sector to cut deficits and prevent the private sector from financing the desired level of consumption.

The analytical implication of these findings is that estimates of average coefficients that disregard the cyclical situation are likely to be misleading when borrowing constraints become tighter during recessions. The policy conclusions are: attempting to boost national saving by increasing the fiscal surplus would be too costly in view of the relatively high value of the offset coefficient in normal times; and the destabilising mix of procyclical fiscal policies and low offset coefficients during recessions can be avoided if the public sector gains access to markets in bad times. To increase the public sector's creditworthiness, budgetary institutions must be strengthened in order to make a better use of surpluses in good times and reassure investors in bad times.

The picture presented by the authors with their two equations leaves some gaps.

Consider the first finding, which is in a way the more puzzling. The logical sequence of events unfolding during bad times appears to be the same in industrial and in Latin American countries alike: fiscal policy changes are viewed as a *response* to a recession, the difference being in the *sign* of that response. The authors tell us that Latin American countries, unlike industrial countries, are not allowed to let automatic stabilisers do their job and are compelled to offset recessionary effects with discretionary procyclical measures. Latin American countries do more than that. During recessions they endeavour to *reduce* the deficit as a ratio to GDP and, even more, in absolute terms[5]. Why? Are borrowing constraints for the public sector so severe in a recession that an unchanged deficit ratio (and hence a lower deficit in absolute terms and a lower structural deficit), let alone a higher deficit, cannot be financed? The question is legitimate, because those constraints seem to be less stringent for the private sector. In bad times the private saving ratio, though insensitive to a decline in GDP, does not rise with it. Moreover, if public saving rises in bad times, private saving falls, with an offset coefficient which, though small, is significant and has the expected sign. Are Latin-American policy makers *more royalist than the king*? Unlikely, as the authors themselves point out.

One is tempted to consider a different possibility, namely that bad times may not always be the same in industrial countries as in Latin America. Recessions in the former are usually an episode in the business cycle, though external shocks or domestic policies may coincide to influence their duration and intensity. However, a fair number of major recessions in Latin America appear to be associated with full-fledged financial crises, often accompanied by currency crises. It is well-documented that banking crises in Latin America are usually preceded by lending and consumption booms that take place during phases of financial deregulation and unsustainable macroeconomic expansion, often characterised by appreciating real exchange rates and large current account deficits[6]. Gavin and Hausmann (1996) observe that most banking crises occur after a phase of accelerated growth has given way to "a general deterioration of the macroeconomic environment". Growth rapidly slows down before the crisis, "after which the recession deepens for several years".

When there is a concurrent financial and/or currency crisis, expansion does not end with a gentle downturn of the real economy but leads to acute financial distress. It is plausible that in these cases fiscal (and monetary) policies are tightened to stem the crisis and their outcome is likely to be a deeper recession. It is not surprising that a recession is associated with discretionary fiscal restriction, but it is the latter that causes the former rather than being an anomalous reaction to it. When deficits are reduced as a result of a deliberate policy change made under the pressure of a financial crisis, it may be misleading and also conceal the connection between financial fragility and macroeconomic volatility to use a scenario in which adopting contractionary policies during a recession is dictated only by an abrupt loss of access to markets.

This is not to say that borrowing constraints do not matter. Typically, when the crunch comes, current account deficits become unsustainable and capital outflows make it difficult for the government to finance its borrowing, so that both must be curtailed with restrictive policies. However, again those policies are the result of a deliberate choice, while it is not obvious that the public sector's borrowing constraints would be so stringent if the recession had not occurred in an economy beset by a financial crisis. On the other hand, episodes of deliberately restrictive fiscal policies in a recessionary environment are not uncommon in industrial countries in the aftermath of currency crises. Recent examples are Italy and Sweden in 1992-93 after the collapse of the European Monetary System.

The case of Mexico after 1995, cited by the authors as an "illuminating" example of the procyclical fiscal policy in Latin America, could instead be considered an example of the sequence discussed here: first a financial crisis, then restrictive policies and finally recession. Moreover, that crisis was preceded by familiar phenomena: a rapidly appreciating real exchange rate, a growing current account deficit, financial deepening and deregulation, a credit boom and a rapid rise of domestic liquid assets, and, as a result, the system's increasing financial vulnerability[7]. The contagion effects of the "Tequila shock" were not confined to Latin American countries like Argentina. The resulting "flight to quality" also affected the peripheral European economies, as witnessed by the remarkable increase in the yield spreads of their currencies with respect to the German mark.

The distinction between good and bad times is an interesting and fruitful insight. However, as has been mentioned, if bad times are not all alike, it may be desirable to control for the possible variety of causes. One way to extend the analysis may be to introduce an index of financial fragility as an independent variable when explaining fiscal policy reactions. Two possibilities are the ratio of short-term to total external debt (which is far more variable than total debt ratios in Latin American countries) and, considering that bank deposits are contingent government liabilities, the ratio of domestic liquid assets to foreign assets.

Turning to the behaviour of private saving, the authors find that in Latin America they are insensitive to a decline in GDP in bad times, which is solid evidence that liquidity constraints there prevent consumption smoothing during recessions, unlike in industrial countries. However, the results on offset coefficients between public and private saving are less easy to comprehend.

First, the independent variable in the second equation is not the public (more precisely government) surplus, but public saving[8], i.e. the surplus *plus* public investment. Leaving aside problems of measurement and this variable's meaning, it is possible that the behaviour of public saving may not replicate that of the fiscal surplus. If the latter's increase is due only, or mainly, to a cut in public capital expenditure, public saving remains unchanged, or changes less than the surplus. In principle, if public investment is cut by more than the fall in revenue during a recession, there could be a *larger* surplus and *lower* public saving, in which case a lower value of the offset coefficient, as found by the authors, would be more favourable than a higher value in a recession. As it was not mentioned how public saving changes with the fiscal surplus, there is a missing link between the first equation showing the procyclicality of fiscal policies in Latin America and the equation for private saving's behaviour. From this point of view, a regression of private saving with respect to overall surplus *and* government expenditure, or with respect to government consumption and government investment, may have been more informative[9].

Even assuming that public saving closely follows the fiscal surplus, in bad times a high value of the offset coefficient in industrial countries and a low value in Latin America does not make it possible to draw conclusions about the relative stringency of borrowing constraints in the two regions. In a recession the fiscal surplus falls considerably in industrial countries while it increases somewhat in Latin America, according to the first equation. Assuming the same pattern for public saving in bad times, the independent effect of fiscal policy (neglecting that of other variables) leads to an *increase* in private saving in industrial countries and a decrease (much smaller in absolute value) in Latin America. Hence, a high value of the offset coefficient in industrial countries, in itself, is not evidence that "access to financial markets does not abruptly vanish" in those countries during bad times.

Finally, the values of the offset coefficient and the coefficient of GDP growth are both remarkably high in good times in Latin America, not only in comparison with bad times, but also with respect to industrial countries. As already noted, if good times in Latin America are characterised by financial liberalisation and credit booms in which existing liquidity constraints are relaxed, financial variables are possibly relevant. Estimating the determinants of private saving in a panel of eleven industrial countries and 25 developing countries, Edwards (1995) finds that the coefficients of two of these variables — the money/GDP ratio as a proxy for financial depth and the share of private credit in total domestic credit — are significantly positive and that these coefficients are much lower in Latin America. In other studies, financial liberalisation and the inflow of foreign funds are often found to have a negative, albeit short-term, effect on domestic private saving in developing countries[10]. In light of a frequent association of macroeconomic expansion with foreign capital inflows and credit booms in Latin America, the authors' novel distinction between good and bad times may turn out to be of particular significance if financial indicators are considered in the private saving equation.

Policy suggestions should address not only the ways to enhance the public sector's creditworthiness. Strengthening budgetary institutions is a good thing in itself, but is not a direct remedy for the financial fragility which is often at the root of a crisis and which is a cause of volatility of both output and policies. Mexico was not pursuing a reckless fiscal policy before the collapse. Between 1990 and 1994, its average borrowing requirements and its debt ratio were below Maastricht criteria. If a major cause of financial crises, and hence to some extent the "bad times" that follow, is "financial liberalisation before the supervisory and regulatory system has been strengthened sufficiently to manage prudently the new risks involved" (Goldstein and Turner (1996), p. 56), one is inclined to agree with the conclusions by Gavin, Hausmann and Talvi elsewhere in this volume. It is necessary "to institute a conservative bank supervisory system that enforces appropriate capital-adequacy standards and ... to adjust monetary policy to forestall ... credit booms ... Failing to do so leaves the economy open to periodic macroeconomic and financial crises that have too often interrupted Latin American growth and development".

Notes

1. The other explanatory variables are the change in the terms of trade and the lagged fiscal surplus.

2. The other variables in their equation are the change in the terms of trade, the inflation tax revenue and the lagged private saving ratio.

3. This result is strikingly similar to those obtained by Masson, Bayoumi and Samiei (1996) for a sample of 21 industrialised countries and one of 40 developing countries, with offset coefficients of respectively 0.66 and 0.61. However, the similarity may be deceptive. In Masson *et al.*, the explanatory variable is not public saving but the budget surplus; amongst the developing countries the offset coefficient is near unity for high income countries but very low (0.35) for middle income countries, a category which includes most Latin American countries; and the other explanatory variables for the behaviour of private saving are different from those in Gavin and Perotti.

4. The importance of liquidity constraints in developing countries was explicitly tested by Haque and Montiel (1989).

5. Beside the negative sign of the estimated coefficient for GDP growth in bad times, the authors report that in deep recessions a cumulative GDP contraction of 11 per cent is associated with a decreased deficit of 2 points of GDP.

6. See Gavin and Hausmann (1996); Goldstein and Turner (1996); Gavin, Hausmann and Talvi, this volume; and Reisen, this volume.

7. See Sachs, Tornell and Velasco (1996).

8. As done in Edwards (1995).

9. As done by Bayoumi *et al.* (1996).

10. Financial liberalisation and the inflow of foreign saving are often found to have a negative, albeit relatively short-run, effect on saving in developing countries and therefore allow dissaving to occur in good times.

Bibliography

EDWARDS, S. (1995), "Why are Saving Rates so Different Across Countries? An International Comparative Analysis", National Bureau of Economic Research, *Working Paper Series*, Working Paper No. 5097, April.

GAVIN, M. and R. HAUSMANN (1996), "The Roots of Banking Crises: The Macroeconomic Context", in R. HAUSMANN AND L. ROJAS-SUÁREZ (eds.), *Banking Crises in Latin America*, Inter-American Development Bank and The Johns Hopkins University Press, Washington, D.C.

GAVIN, M., R. HAUSMANN and E. TALVI (1997), "Saving Behaviour in Latin America: Overview and Policy Issues", this volume.

GOLDSTEIN, M. and P. TURNER (1996), "Banking Crises and Emerging Economies: Origins and Policy Options", Bank for International Settlements, *Economic Papers*, No. 46, October.

HAQUE, N.U. and P. MONTIEL (1989), "Consumption in Developing Countries: Tests for Liquidity Constraints and Finite Horizons", *The Review of Economics and Statistics*, 71 (3).

INTERNATIONAL MONETARY FUND (1995), *World Economic Outlook*, Washington, D.C.

MASSON, P.R., T. BAYOUMI and H. SAMIEI (1996), "International Evidence on the Determinants of Private Saving", CEPR, *Discussion Paper Series*, No. 1368, March.

REISEN, H. (1997), "The Limits of Foreign Savings", this volume.

SACHS, J., A. TORNELL and A. VELASCO (1996), "The Collapse of the Mexican Peso: What Have We Learned?", *Economic Policy*, 22, April.

Tax Effects on Household Saving: Evidence from OECD Member Countries

Göran Normann and Jeffrey Owens

Savings during the 1980s fell from their levels in the previous two decades by substantial amounts. This fall in savings was general across almost all the OECD area, regardless of whether the economies originally had very high or low savings ratios. The fall in savings, however, reflects to a substantial extent a fall in public sector savings in many countries. Indeed, in many countries private sector savings were higher in the 1980s than in earlier periods. Nevertheless, looking simply at household savings, there does seem to have been some decline from the levels of the 1970s.

These broad trends are based on a definition of savings which is not precisely the same as an economic definition of savings, and in certain respects national savings figures are misleading. Changes in asset values (either because of inflation or because of changes in their real values) are not fully reflected in national accounts. Depreciation of physical assets is not allowed for. Education spending is treated as consumption, whereas some at least may be investment in human capital. Consumer durables are treated differently in national accounts according to whether they are bought by households or companies. However, whilst these deficiencies in the definition of savings may make individual figures subject to widely different interpretations, it is unlikely that they affect the general trend in savings ratios, and it is this which has been causing concern.

Principal determinants of household savings are likely to be demographic factors, the stock of wealth, saving for retirement, and saving in order to leave a bequest to offspring. Other factors in theory are the rate of return on savings, financial market liberalisation, and the provision of public and compulsory private pensions.

Of particular relevance for an assessment of the impact of taxation on savings is that there is clearly no consensus over whether a higher rate of return to saving increases saving in aggregate or reduces it, although in the case of particular tax schemes aimed at encouraging saving (especially for retirement), if total household saving has in fact increased, this may be due more to factors such as advertising and increased public awareness rather than the effect of the tax concessions on the rate of return.

A major concern is the effect of taxation on the composition of household savings. A principal aim of governments has been tax neutrality. The *allocation* of savings between different assets is one area where the absence of such neutrality can cause substantial changes in the type of savings instruments chosen. Even were governments attempting to achieve tax neutrality as relates to the *level* of savings, it would not be obvious what such a tax system would look like, as taxes on labour income mean that a zero rate of tax is not necessarily neutral. Achievement of either sort of neutrality is complicated by the effects of inflation and the difficulty of defining capital income in a way sufficiently differentiated from labour income in certain circumstances.

Various systems of taxing capital income have been proposed. On the one hand there is the idea of taxing all income accruing to an individual, leading to proposals for a Comprehensive Income Tax. This has traditionally been contrasted with an Expenditure Tax, which allows savings to be taken from tax-free income, only to be taxed when income from the savings is consumed. However, in fact two other systems of taxation are often proposed — the Tax-free Savings Accounts (which have similar economic effects to an Expenditure Tax, but allow savings out of already-taxed income, exempting the return) and Flat-Rate Taxation, which taxes the return to capital income at a standard rate.

Assessing the balance of advantage between the ideal systems is not simple, and in practice all countries operate hybrid systems. The Flat Rate Tax and the Comprehensive Income Tax raise problems of taxing unrealised capital gains. An Expenditure Tax and Tax-free Savings Accounts raise issues concerning equity (the rich have more capital income than the poor), and the Expenditure Tax front-loads the public sector revenue loss. Tax-free Savings Accounts raise problems in distinguishing between capital and labour income.

Empirical evidence indicates that savings are indeed very sensitive to different rates of taxation on different instruments. Evidence on the ability to use the tax system to encourage aggregate saving is much less clear-cut, with the revenue cost of special schemes often substantially offsetting any gains in the overall level of savings.

Recent Trends in Savings in OECD Countries

Savings ratios within the OECD fell sharply in the 1980s, to a rate significantly lower than in the 1970s and 1960s This prompted official concern for a variety of reasons. In some countries, the decline in the savings ratio was accompanied by a worsening of the external position of the economy. This reflects the close relationship between national saving and the current account of the balance of payments, which can be defined as the difference between national income and national expenditure.

Real interest rates in the 1980s were persistently higher than in the past, perhaps reflecting a shortfall in saving in comparison to investment. To the extent that high real interest rates continue, many investments which would have been profitable if interest rates had remained at their previous rate cease to be viable. In the 1990s, large demands on the world supply of savings may be made by Central and Eastern European countries, and by countries previously part of the USSR. In addition, the Latin American debt position is less troublesome than for most of the 1980s raising the possibility of resumed capital flows to countries which have recently been net savers. Net saving in the Dynamic Asian Economies is likely to fall as these countries enter a more mature stage of economic development.

Demographic trends suggest a sharp increase in the number of elderly people in many OECD countries over the next few decades. Many countries have state-funded health services and sometimes extensive public pension schemes which are pay-as-you-go financed rather than being fully funded. There is some concern about whether savings are sufficient to pay for this demographic change.

Table 1 gives savings ratios averaged for each of the last three decades for OECD member countries and the corresponding figures for 1990-1994. Two features stand out. First, the enormous variation in national savings rates remained virtually unchanged since the 1960s. In the 1960s, savings ranged from 14.9 per cent (Turkey) and 17.2 per cent of GDP (Ireland) at the lower end to 30.1 per cent (Switzerland) and 34.4 per cent (Japan). In the early 1990s, the ratios ranged from 13.3 per cent (United Kingdom) to 33.2 per cent (Japan). The increasing integration of global markets during this period seems not to have led to a convergence of levels of national savings.

Secondly, and in contrast to the previous point, global trends in savings behaviour seem until very recently to have been more universal. Gross national savings in the 1980s as a percentage of GDP were 3 percentage points lower than in either the 1960s or the 1970s. National saving increased over this period in only three countries (Norway, Portugal and Turkey). In several countries (including many European countries and Australia), falls in excess of four percentage points were recorded. This decline in the savings ratio was accompanied by a slightly smaller decline in investment ratios, moving the OECD as a whole from a position of being a net capital exporter to being a capital importer from the rest of the world.

Experience in the 1990s (although the data may yet be revised) has been very mixed. Comparing average national saving in 1990-94 to the averages of the 1980s, most countries have seen yet further dramatic falls, but a minority have seen significant increases (Austria, Belgium, Denmark, Ireland, Japan, Netherlands, Portugal, Switzerland and Turkey).

However, these general trends in the overall national rates of savings hide large changes in the development of savings in particular sectors of the economy. National savings are the sum of public and private savings, and private savings themselves can be broken down into their corporate and household component.

Table 1. **Gross Saving as Percentage of GDP**

Average in:	1960s	1970s	1980s	1990-94
Australia				
National of which	24.4	23.7	20.1	16.4
Public	3.9	2.7	1.8	-0.5
Household	11.3	13.1	10.5	7.9
Corporate	9.3	7.9	7.8	9
Austria				
National	27.6	27.8	24.1	25.4
Public	7.1	6.2	2.7	1.6
Household	5.4	6.2	6.4	8.4
Corporate	15.1	15.5	15.1	15.4
Belgium				
National of which	22.6	23.2	16.5	21.2
Public		0.4	-5.8	-4.4
Household		14.7	12.6	14.8
Corporate		8.1	9.6	10.7
Canada				
National of which	21.5	22.4	20.1	14.7
Public	3.6	2.7	-1.3	-3.5
Household	7.6	10.2	11.8	9.8
Corporate	10.3	9.5	9.6	8.5
Denmark				
National of which	23.3	20.8	14.8	17.3
Public		5.3	0.3	-0.6
Household			1.4	3.7
Corporate			11.6	14.2
Finland				
National of which	25.2	26.3	23.7	16.0
Public	7.3	8.9	7.2	0.3
Household	6.4	7.2	7.4	8
Corporate	11.6	10.2	9.1	7.7
France				
National of which	26.3	25.9	20.4	19.9
Public		3.6	1.4	-0.3
Household		13.8	10.3	9.5
Corporate		8.5	8.7	10.7
Germany •				
National of which	27.3	24.4	22.4	22.2
Public	6.2	3.9	2	1.1
Household	7	8.9	8.1	8.2
Corporate	14.1	11.7	12.4	13
Greece				
National of which	19.6	26.5	17.8	15.1
Public	4	2.4	-6.9	-10.3
Household	9.5	16.4	15.9	16.8
Corporate				
Iceland				
National of which	26.3	25.3	17.6	15.4
Public			6.1	2.8
Household				
Corporate				
Ireland				
National of which	17.2	19.4	15.4	19.6
Public			-3.5	-0.9
Household				
Corporate			19.3	20.4

Table 1 (concluded). **Gross Saving as Percentage of GDP**

Average in:	1960s	1970s	1980s	1990-94
Italy				
National of which	28.2	26.0	21.8	18.4
Public			-6.4	-6.2
Household			21.7	19.2
Corporate			6.5	5.4
Japan				
National of which	34.4	35.3	31.7	33.2
Public	6.2	4.8	4.9	7.7
Household	13.4	18.2	15.3	13.2
Corporate	14.9	12.3	11.5	12.4
Netherlands				
National of which	27.7	25.0	23.1	24.4
Public		2	-0.3	-0.6
Household		8	10.1	11.6
Corporate				13.4
New Zealand				
National of which	21.1	21.9	19.2	17.2
Public				
Household				
Corporate				
Norway				
National of which	27.1	26.3	26.9	24.5
Public	6.4	7.8	8.4	4.4
Household		4.6	3.9	4.3
Corporate			14.6	15.1
Portugal				
National of which	24.5	27.4	24.7	25.2
Public			-0.8	
Household			15.7	
Corporate			9.5	
Spain				
National of which	24.6	25.4	20.9	19.9
Public			0.4	-0.3
Household			7.1	7.8
Corporate			12.7	12.4
Sweden				
National of which	24.0	21.1	17.3	14.5
Public			2.1	-1.9
Household			3.3	6.1
Corporate			12	10.3
Switzerland				
National of which	30.1	29.7	29.9	30.6
Public	4.6	4	3.8	0.6
Household	8.1	9.2	9.5	13.7
Corporate	17.1	15.9	15.8	15.9
Turkey				
National of which	14.9	18.1	20.6	21.0
Public				
Household				
Corporate				
United Kingdom				
National of which	18.5	18.0	16.6	13.3
Public	3.6	2.6	0.5	-1.7
Household	5.9	6.2	6.2	7.1
Corporate	9.1	9.2	9.8	8
United States				
National of which	20.0	19.8	17.8	15.4
Public	1.9	0.4	-1.9	-2.9
Household	9.3	10.8	10.6	9
Corporate	8.8	8.6	9.1	9.1

Source: OECD, *National Accounts of OECD Countries*, various years.

Table 1 shows that in Austria, Belgium, Canada, Greece, Switzerland, the United Kingdom and the United States, more than all the decline in national savings since the 1960s can be accounted for by a decline in public sector savings. In other words, the decline in national savings in these countries conceals a growth in savings by the private sector. Indeed, taking the private sector as a whole, savings as a proportion of GDP *increased* in all countries where information was available other than Australia, Finland, Germany and Japan between the 1960s and 1980s. The situation in the 1980s as compared to the 1970s is less clear-cut, with large falls in private sector savings being recorded in France and Japan, but rises in other countries (e.g. Canada).

Looking in more detail at the components of private sector saving, in most countries where information was available, household savings as a percentage of GDP *increased* between the 1960s and 1980s, often by significant amounts (4.2 percentage points in Canada, 6.4 percentage points in Greece), Australia is an exception with a 0.8 percentage point decline. Worries about levels of household savings are clearly not based on comparisons with the 1960s, but rather with the 1970s since when in nearly all the large OECD countries and many of the smaller ones, the savings ratio fell. This fall was particularly marked in the latter half of the 1980s and in the early 1990s there have been further significant falls in Canada, France, Japan and the United States. However in some other countries the household savings ratio has been increasing strikingly since the 1980s (Austria, Belgium, Denmark, Finland, Greece, the Netherlands, Norway, Spain, Sweden, Switzerland and the United Kingdom).

However, as Table 1 also shows, in many OECD economies the corporate sector is a more important source of savings than is the household sector. Internally generated funds have accounted for a greater proportion of GDP than savings by the household sector in Austria, Denmark, Finland, Germany, the Netherlands, Norway, Spain, Sweden, Switzerland and the United Kingdom.

These separate components of savings are not independent of one another. If companies retain earnings for investment rather than paying out dividends, then households might reasonably conclude that they are saving indirectly (the value of their shares, pension rights, investment trusts, bonuses from life insurance, etc., will increase) and so may save a lower proportion of the income they do receive. It is therefore not surprising to find that comparing the 1980s to the 1970s, corporate sector savings have increased whereas household savings have decreased, or vice versa, in most of the countries where a split is available.

More controversially, there may also be a link between public sector saving (or dis-saving) and the private sector. If the government borrows funds, it will have a greater debt repayment burden in the future. This in turn will (eventually) have to be paid out of higher tax receipts. Anticipating these higher future tax payments, households may smooth their disposable income by saving whilst tax rates remain low. Hence it might be anticipated that the greater are borrowings by the public sector, the greater will be savings by the private sector.

In summary, in the 1980s savings ratios fell significantly below their 1970s levels. However, that change reflects to a very large extent changes in public sector saving. Private sector saving, if anything, increased, although in many cases household savings fell from their rates of the 1970s. Countries' experiences in the early 1990s have been very mixed, with both dramatic increases and falls in household and national saving since the 1980s.

The Definition of Savings

A significant problem with looking at the aggregate national or sectoral savings positions, based on standard national accounts procedures, is that these measures do not closely respond to the economic definition of savings. "Redefining" to the national accounts' definitions can lead to very large divergences from official savings rates; for example, the US savings rate could be anywhere between near zero and four times the national accounts' measure depending on which of the many proposed alterations are adopted (Cullison, 1990). This section briefly discusses aspects of national accounts figures, which may give a less misleading picture of patterns of savings.

The usual economic definition of income is that of Hicks — the maximum value that some economic agent can consume during a given period, and still expect to be as well off at the end of a period as he was at the beginning. To the extent that this amount is greater than that actually consumed, there is saving. In national accounts treatments, by contrast, savings are receipts minus disbursements. This latter measure can be altered in various ways to more closely conform with the former.

Assets change in value. These changes are clearly income (either positive or negative) in the economic sense, but not necessarily in the national accounts definitions. For example, supposing there is inflation, nominal interest payments are included fully as a component of income, but the erosion of the real value of financial assets and gains on debt are not accounted for. The current income of financial asset holders (debtors) will therefore be greater than (less than) their properly defined economic income. When the debtor is the government, this is known as "seignorage" and can result in significant improvements to public sector balance sheets. Clearly, for an economy as a whole, if foreign assets and liabilities are ignored, then every debtor has a creditor, so aggregate saving will be unchanged, but the sectoral composition will be altered. For instance, an OECD study by Elmeskov *et al.* (1991) found that the private saving ratio for Italy during the 1980s was 28.4 per cent of GDP without the adjustment, but 22.2 per cent with the adjustment. In contrast, in Finland and Norway, the adjustment would have increased the apparent private sector saving by around 1 percentage point.

Real changes (i.e. not just reflecting general price changes) in the value of assets may also not be reflected in national accounts, but may have had a significant impact on observed private sector savings behaviour during the recent past. When assets increase in value, Hicksian income is increased, and so economic agents may reduce more visible forms of saving on the basis that their stock of wealth is nevertheless increasing. In particular, the substantial changes in house and equity prices have been thought to have had some effect on the savings behaviour of those holding such assets.

Education spending is treated as consumption in national accounts, but it is probable that some of this spending is investment in human capital with an economic return. Given that education spending accounts for several per cent of GDP, any reclassification of spending to be investment rather than consumption would significantly affect savings ratios. Reclassification simply of higher education to be investment rather than consumption would increase the national savings ratio by between 0.5 and 2 percentage points in most cases. Reclassification of all education spending as saving would increase the savings ratio by 4-5 percentage points in most counties. However, given the relative stability of spending on education as a share of GDP in most countries this would not alter significantly the trend in savings one way or the other.

A similar problem arises with spending on consumer durables. If a firm purchases a consumer durable, this is classified in national accounts as an investment, as the "services" from the investment can be sold in the future to give an income (the owner and the customer of the services generally being one and the same firm). If a private consumer purchased a consumer durable, this would be treated as consumption. Reclassifying such spending as investment could add anywhere between 2.3 percentage points (Japan) to over 8 percentage points (Canada) to national savings ratios.

A related problem is R&D spending; again, this is generally not counted as an investment but as an intermediate stage of production. Reclassifying as investment would add one or two percentage points to the savings ratio (depending on the treatment of military R&D), although the effects on the trend are unchanged.

The final, frequently talked about adjustment to the national accounts concept of savings is to take more account of depreciation of physical assets (which in the Hicksian framework would be entered as negative income). This change, contrary to most of the others, would reduce the measured amount of national savings. The net savings ratio could be 10 percentage points below that of the gross figure.

In sum, there are good reasons to believe that the standard, gross measures of savings based on national accounts, could be misleading in that they are a long way from an economic definition of saving. Nevertheless, few of the adjustments outlined above would be expected to affect the *trend* in savings, either national or by sector, and it is the trend that has been causing most policy concern in OECD countries.

The Main Motives for Household Savings

Public sector savings are determined by the difference between government income and government expenditure, and the determinants of these are widely known. Savings by corporations are dependent on their rate of profit and the demands of shareholders for dividends. We, however, are concerned with the taxation of *household* savings. Certainly, taxation can affect the level of savings by corporations. However, the links between taxation and corporate savings have been found obscure and difficult to evaluate, requiring a detailed assessment of corporate income taxation. But explaining the motivations of individuals which determine household savings is also not simple.

Saving represents a decision not to consume current income and there are four major motives which may lead to such a decision:

Life-cycle saving. Households build up their assets to finance consumption after retirement when current earned income is reduced or even becomes zero. More generally they save when income is above their expected long-run sustainable consumption level, and dissave when it is below this level.

Precautionary saving. Saving is seen as a way of allowing for uncertainty about future developments. A household may wish to hold assets to meet possible emergencies, such as unemployment or sickness.

Saving for bequest. Households save to build up assets to bequeath to subsequent generations.

Purchasing "lumpy" assets. Some purchases (e.g. of a car) are "lumpy" and many require that households accumulate funds in advance of the purchase.

Obviously, these motives are not mutually exclusive, and saving decisions will generally be influenced by more than one of them. Rational saving decisions will be based on some kind of optimising behaviour by which the levels and composition of saving are chosen so as to equalise the marginal benefits of alternative uses of income. In practice, there continues to be considerable uncertainty as to how to explain and to predict household saving levels.

Life-cycle Saving

Saving for retirement forms the basis of "Life Cycle Hypothesis" models of household consumption behaviour. Models based on this approach generate the time-profile of consumption over the economic lifetime of the household, the underlying assumption being that the household maximises its utility from the intertemporal consumption stream, subject to an available resource constraint. This suggests that at any time the discounted present value of all future consumption equals the sum of present net wealth plus the discounted present value of all future earned income. The main features of the model are that a household accumulates wealth during the pre-retirement period by consuming less than its disposable income. Wealth reaches its maximum at retirement age, following which it is gradually decreased to finance current consumption. This implies that saving is positive during the pre-retirement phase of the household life cycle and negative thereafter, averaging zero over the entire life span if net bequests made and received are zero. The time-profile of household consumption, and thereby saving, will also depend on various factors, among which the market interest rate, the individual's rate of time preference and degree of risk-aversion, and the functioning of capital markets are considered to be the most important. The household saving ratio during the earning period of the life cycle will also be strongly affected by the length of the retirement span relative to the income earning period. Thus, both the expected life time and the retirement age should be important determinants of individual saving behaviour if this theory is valid.

The Bequest Motive

Households may accumulate wealth beyond the levels required to finance retirement consumption if they desire to pass on to future generations a part of their accumulated wealth. As is the case with most saving determinants, a bequest motive changes the size of the saving ratio only in an economy expanding due to population growth, productivity growth or both, otherwise the bequest motive would simply lead to the transfer of a constant level of assets from one generation to the next, with no effect on the overall saving ratio. In a growing economy, the bequest requires positive lifetime saving of each generation to guarantee heirs a constant ratio of inherited wealth to initial income. The quantitative impact of the bequest motive on the household saving ratio depends on the interest rate and the size of the bequest. While intergenerational gifts or bequests are indeed common, it is not clear whether they originate from the desire to leave bequests or from the fact that due to the uncertainty about the date of death there may have been unspent retirement and precautionary savings. Also, it has been suggested by Horioka (1984) and Hayashi (1986) that bequest may be seen as a form of private annuity, under which the elderly receive care from their children in return for a bequest on death. This would be consistent with the life cycle hypothesis of saving.

Precautionary Saving

Uncertainty pervades the decisions of households. They have no way of knowing their future income sources, date of death or trends in interest rates. Households will be concerned to smooth out the effects of such unforeseen events as unemployment and illness. While there is little disagreement that uncertainty increases the demand for precautionary assets and thereby saving, it is difficult to quantify this relationship. There are no operational quantitative measures of uncertainty, and objectively it is difficult to judge the extent to which precautionary saving contributes to the observed overall level of saving.

Purchase of Lumpy Consumer Items

The purchase of lumpy consumer items is often preceded by an accumulation of savings. While such saving is most common with respect to consumer durable purchases, it can, of course, also occur for current consumption expenditure, such as vacations. For the period in which the planned expenditure materialises, the household will reduce saving correspondingly. This type of saving is due to the imperfect matching of income receipts and consumption expenditure. An alternative way of acquiring consumer durables would be to buy the item first (for example, by accumulating net liabilities), making the necessary saving later in the form of gradual debt repayment.

Major Empirical Determinants of the Household Saving Rate

The life-cycle hypothesis for consumption, at least when combined with the bequest motive and developments in the stock of wealth, is the most widely discussed explanation of the level of saving. According to this hypothesis, the rate of saving depends on *a)* the rate of growth in per capita income, *b)* the stock of wealth, *c)* demographic characteristics, and *d)* the strength of the bequest motive. The predictions of such a theory are as follows.

In a situation of *no growth in income or population*, the capital stock may simply be maintained, with the dissaving of those in retirement offset by the saving of those still working. If the population is *growing*, net saving is needed to maintain the capital/labour ratio. The relation between *income growth* and the saving rate is positive. *Wealth* also affects the level of saving. Where wealth is large relative to income, there is less need for additional saving to provide for retirement or for bequests. Wealth has a negative effect on the saving rate. *Demography* also has a major influence on the level of saving. Higher dependency ratios, reflecting a larger share of the population that is too old or too young to work, contribute to a lower saving rate. Expected longer life will result in more saving by those in the work force, and rising dependency ratios. A fall in the size of families results in a drop in dependency ratios. In addition, other basic changes, such as the share of women in the workforce, may affect the saving rate by reducing volatility and uncertainty in family incomes.

Other possible determinants of the level of savings are the income distribution, public and private pensions, inflation, the availability of consumer credit and the real rate of return to savings. In analysing the impact of taxation on savings the last factor is of particular interest and will therefore be the focus of the following subsection.

The Real Rate of Return and Saving

A higher rate of return decreases the present cost of purchasing a dollar of future consumption, making it attractive to substitute future for present consumption; thus to save more. In addition, the higher return means that future earnings should be discounted at a higher rate, with a resultant fall in the value of human capital. This too should result in increased saving. However, it is also true that in order to achieve a given level of consumption in the future, it is no longer necessary to save as much. It is possible to save less now and consume more, both in the present and in the future. This income effect causes a fall in saving. Given the theoretical ambiguity, whether or not saving is interest elastic is a matter of empirical analysis. Furthermore, given that the real rate of return can be altered by taxation, the appropriateness of measures designed to promote savings by lowering the tax rate is theoretically ambiguous.

Gylfason (1993) provides a very useful review of empirical studies published since 1967, about half of which found significant positive estimates of the interest elasticity of savings. Boskin (1978) found an interest elasticity estimate of 0.4, indicating that saving may change dramatically with a change in interest rate, and that large welfare losses may be created by taxes that discourage capital accumulation by sharply reducing the after-tax rate of return. Summers (1981), noting that a higher rate of return would reduce the present value of human wealth and thus discourage consumption and encourage saving, estimated interest elasticities for saving that were as high as 3.7. Gylfason (1981) supported Boskin's findings, estimating the interest elasticity of saving at 0.3. Makin (1987) estimated an interest elasticity of saving of 0.39 for the United States; much higher than his earlier estimate of 0.1. And although no interest elasticity is directly estimated, Bovenberg and Evans (1990) found that higher real after-tax interest rates for 1980-88 may have caused the private saving rate in the United States to have been 1.5 percentage points higher than if the real after-tax rate had remained at its 1970s average level.

All of the foregoing estimates are for the United States. A study which estimated consumption functions for eight industrial countries, including the United States, found "unambiguously that after-tax interest rates, either real or nominal depending on the country, have a very significant negative effect on private consumption". In a Canadian study on saving and taxation (Beach et al., 1988) it was found that the most sophisticated equations and those with the best fit showed an interest elasticity of about 0.5 to 0.6. They estimated the sensitivity of consumption to changes in the after-tax interest rates for ten different age cohorts. As explanatory variables, their model included the after-tax interest rate, a measure of the extent to which age was below 72, a variable for human capital and one for "other assets". The total effect on consumption of a change in the after-tax interest rate is determined by the sum of the effect on the marginal propensity to consume (MPC) out of wealth and the effect on the discounted value of human capital. They found that increases in the after-tax interest rate led to a higher MPC, and thus higher consumption for all age cohorts; an offsetting effect was the decrease in the discounted value of human capital that accompanied a higher interest rate. The effect of higher interest rates on the discounted value of human capital is much larger for those who are young. The result is that the younger cohorts spend less and save more when the interest rates rise, and the older cohorts save less. The overall result for the economy depends on the relative importance of the different cohorts.

As the Canadian study indicates, elasticities are likely to vary through time and between countries due to demographic factors. Who gets the higher rate of return clearly is relevant in terms of the effect on saving. Another example of this is Gravelle's (1989) observation for the United States that "(s)ince the tax savings of IRA's are more directed toward the younger savers and tax savings from capital gains are more directed toward the older holders of capital, such life cycle models would tend to find IRA's to have a larger effect on saving than capital gains tax incentives of similar magnitude".

Moreover, several studies have suggested much lower elasticities, and even suggested that a higher rate of return might reduce savings. Weber (1970), using United States time-series data, considered the effects of interest rates on consumption. He presents no numerical estimates of the interest elasticity of saving, but concludes that "when the rate of interest increases, consumers have an opportunity to maintain the same level of consumption in the future with less saving today. Consequently, they increase current consumption in response to the interest rate increase." In a subsequent study, Weber (1975) confirmed his earlier findings that an increase in interest rates would increase consumer expenditures. Howrey and Hymans (1978), in a direct challenge to Boskin's results, found no significant interest rate effect and "no strong evidence that (personal cash) saving can be manipulated by policy aimed at changing the after-tax rate of return to saving".

Friend and Hasbrouck (1983), using United States' quarterly time-series data from 1952 to 1980, obtained results suggesting, if anything, that increases in the real rate of return were more likely to increase consumption and reduce saving. Evans (1983) found that when intergenerational transfers (i.e. bequests) were allowed for, the interest elasticity of saving might well be negative instead of positive, in direct challenge to Summers's (1981) results. Using time-series analysis, Hendershott and Peek (1985) reported that the "real after-tax interest rate....does not have a direct influence on the saving ratio". This conclusion was reinforced by Montgomery (1986) who, using quarterly time-series data from 1953 to 1982, found that the effect of the real after-tax rate of return on saving was small. And Baum (1988) arrived at a similar conclusion that "real interest rates have a small and statistically insignificant direct impact on consumption-saving decisions". Makin's (1986) estimate of the interest elasticity of saving for Japan was also small and insignificant at 0.02.

The most influential recent article on intertemporal consumption is Hall (1988), who found that after correcting for methodological problems in previous studies, the estimated intertemporal elasticity of consumption is not significantly different from zero, implying that the rate of return and hence the tax rate has no impact on aggregate savings.

In sum "one cannot be sure whether steady-state savings elasticities are positive or negative" (Stewart, 1988). Skinner and Feenberg (1989) have written that "The general consensus in the literature is that positive interest elasticity estimates, either of consumption or saving, are fragile and fleeting", but they also find that "regressions restricted to the 1980s show a significant correlation between consumption and saving and the after-tax rate of return".

The lack of any clear conclusions on an issue of such importance for policy-making is disappointing. It is, however, perhaps unsurprising. The studies referred to above considered different countries, and different time periods. Given the theoretical ambiguity over the direction of any effect resulting from a change in the real rate of return, it would be a coincidence if different countries had, for example, exactly comparable demographic profiles, and within a country this profile will change. In addition, estimation of savings behaviour is complicated by poor data within each country and non-comparable data across countries, and major difficulties in estimation techniques. A lack of clear conclusions does not, therefore, imply that there is no effect on the rate of savings following a change in the real rate of return, simply that it has not yet been clearly isolated. In addition, it should be emphasised that the studies referred to were of *aggregate* savings; the following section reviews evidence on whether different rates of return on different assets has an effect on the composition of savings, and looks more explicitly at studies which attempt to identify the effects of tax measures on household savings.

The Effects of Taxation on the Level of Saving

Canada has long permitted individuals to deduct contributions to individual Registered Retirement Savings Plans (RRSPs) (although the limit on the deductions has been changed from time to time). More recently, the United States, through its Individual Retirement Accounts (IRAs), has permitted similar deductions. The effect on aggregate saving has been considered in each of the countries, and the existence of RRSPs in Canada during the 1970s, and prior to IRAs in the United States, allows consideration of the extent to which RRSPs contributed to a higher level of private saving in Canada than in the United States.

Jump (1982) examined the effect of the investment income exclusion (C$1 000 a year) as well as the RRSP deductions on the rate of saving in Canada. He concluded that the effect of these incentives was not at the margin for most people — individuals who had investment income in excess of C$1 000 and who saved more than the RRSP limit. Therefore, he concluded that the incentive would effectively be a lump-sum transfer that would not encourage saving at the margin. The main effect would be the conversion of other forms of saving into RRSPs. Jump observed that such incentives required the government to set higher tax rates, and accordingly "may actually have perverse effects insofar as they have been financed by increases in distortionary taxes .... The tax incentives may actually have caused a decline in measured personal saving in Canada". Contrary to this analysis, though, evidence from taxation statistics for 1991 shows that only 28 per cent of pension plan and RRSP contributors contribute to within C$250 of their deduction limit. In addition, a large majority of individuals, even among those in higher-income groups, is able to earn a better rate of return by paying down mortgage and/or consumer debt instead of saving in these plans, since interest on this debt is not deductible in Canada.

In contrast to Jump's conclusions, Carroll and Summers (1987) in a series of regressions designed to explain the difference in saving rates between the United States and Canada, found that "in essentially all of our regression specifications the coefficient for the level of sheltered savings was significantly positive". Thus, sheltering some forms of saving appears to encourage total saving. However, Carroll and Summers note that even if "two-thirds of RRSP saving would not have been done had there been no RRSP program, then RRSPs can directly account for at most a third of the increase in Canadian personal saving". It seems highly unlikely that anything close to two-thirds of RRSP funds reflects a net increase in saving, although recent work by Venti and Wise does suggest that the increasing trend in saving through RRSPs, even before more generous rules introduced from 1990, has been effective in increasing total household saving in Canada during the 1980s.

The difference in the private saving rate between Canada and the United States has caught the attention of others, who have likewise concluded that higher after-tax rates of return, in part due to RRSPs, may well be part of the explanation. Bosworth (1984) wrote that "(the) strongest international evidence that rates of return may affect saving emerges from the comparison of Canada and the United States — two countries with similar economic institutions and social values — during the 1970s". Beach, Boadway, and Bruce (1988) also conclude that "the divergence of Canadian savings rates from those in the United States may well be explained by (favorable) Canadian tax policies toward saving".

Early findings of the effect of IRAs on household saving in the United States were positive (Hubbard, 1984). Venti and Wise (1987), using survey data, were subsequently able to examine the impact of IRAs on household saving in greater detail. Their results, which are striking, raise questions about the wisdom of capping IRAs in the 1986 Tax Reform Act. They conclude that "increasing the IRA limits would lead to substantial increases in tax-deferred saving... The weight of evidence suggest that very little of the increase would be offset by reduction in other financial assets, possible 10-20 percent, maybe less. Our estimates suggest that 45-55 per cent of the IRA increase would be funded by reduction in consumption, and 35 per cent by reduced taxes". While acknowledging that the issue is still open to debate, Feenberg and Skinner (1989) "strongly confirm" the earlier studies that IRAs have increased household saving.

Serious doubt is cast on Venti and Wise's findings in a number of subsequent studies. Gravelle (1989) finds their results implausible in light of the dramatic impact on what has been a historically very stable United States saving rate. A more recent piece of work by Gale and Scholtz (as reported in Burman, Cordes, and Ozanne,

1990), found that "an increase in the IRA contribution limit (in 1985) would have reduced other savings by about 93 cents for every dollar invested in IRAs. Since the resultant tax reductions would be worth an additional 37 cents, net consumption would actually rise by 30 cents for every additional dollar contributed to IRAs". And in surveying the evidence Kotlikoff (1983) has observed that "the only clear fact about household consumption and IRAs is that household consumption as a share of NNP increased precisely during the period that the use of IRAs expanded".

However, such schemes may have an indirect effect on savings. In the United States and Canada, financial institutions have had an incentive to advertise the benefits of saving through IRAs and RRSPs, raising public awareness about the importance of saving for retirement. This may be a significant, if unmeasured, element affecting the total level of saving.

The extent to which schemes which offer a tax-free savings account approach have contributed to higher household saving remains unclear. The earlier observations made above concerning the exclusion of investment income in Canada must be kept in mind — to be effective the exclusion or lower tax rate must apply at the *margin*. Some studies on saving in Japan, in particular, have commented on the effect of tax-free saving on total saving, but in general offer little evidence to suggest that the treatment of savings accounts in Japan has been a significant factor contributing to the high level of saving in that country. Shibuya (1987, 1988) constructed a variable called the "tax-exemption ratio" in an attempt to measure the impact of tax-exempt saving. He concluded that tax exemptions on interest income have only a minimal effect on saving in Japan. Horioka (1984), finding that other factors adequately explained the different saving rates between Japan and the United States, concluded that tax incentives account for little of the difference between the two countries. These conclusions are consistent with that of Hayashi (1986) who found "no strong evidence for a high interest elasticity of saving or for the effectiveness of the tax incentives for saving" (p. 197). Although each individual in Japan was exempt from tax on the interest on savings equal to £103 571 in 1989, Horioka (1990) concludes that the abolition of the tax breaks on saving is likely to be a "portfolio effect rather than a decline in the level of the overall household saving rate".

A final piece of evidence of the effect of taxation on savings is summarised in Table 2. Interest payments on home purchase of a principal residence are tax deductible in most OECD countries, but many countries extend that deduction to cover purchase of secondary residences, and general consumer purchases. Even where deductions are limited to cover particular purchases, borrowing is "fungible" and may be used in ways other than intended in legislation. Tanzi (1992) crudely classifies countries into those with liberal legislation on interest deductibility and those with more restrictive legislation. He then looks at net household saving as a percentage of household income for the two groups of countries. "The expectation is that the countries that provide the more generous treatment of interest expenses will have lower household saving rates. The saving behaviour of households in these two groups of countries is remarkably in line with the expectation. There was an enormous difference in the saving rates of the two groups." As he goes on to note, in the presence of an integrated global capital market, the different treatment of interest deductions in the tax systems must be promoting major flows of capital across countries, reflecting not real differential in the productivity of investment but simply the influence of tax systems.

Table 2. **Net Household Savings**
(as a percentage of disposable household income)

	1985	1987	1988	1989	1990
Countries with most generous treatment of interest deductions					
Finland	3.9	1.8	-1.7	0.0	1.4
Netherlands	2.0	2.1	2.5	3.8	6.5
Norway	-2.5	-6.1	-2.4	0.9	1.9
Spain	8.4	7.5	8.6	7.6	8.4
Sweden	1.8	-3.4	-5.1	-5.1	-0.2
United States	4.5	3.0	4.3	4.7	4.6
Average	3.0	0.6	1.0	2.0	3.7
Countries with least generous treatment of interest deductions					
Australia	7.7	6.4	6.5	6.9	6.0
Belgium	8.3	11.8	13.1	14.4	14.3
Canada	13.3	9.4	10.0	11.0	10.9
France	14.0	10.8	11.4	11.6	11.8
Germany	11.5	12.7	12.7	12.6	13.4
Italy	18.0	15.4	15.4	14.4	15.1
Japan	15.6	14.7	14.3	14.2	14.3
United Kingdom	9.7	6.5	5.2	6.5	8.6
Average	12.3	11.0	11.1	11.4	11.8

Source: Tanzi (1992)

Neutrality and the Tax Treatment of Household Savings

Taxation may affect the level of savings by the household sector but as examined above, there is no clear evidence that in fact it does so. It may also affect the composition of savings — the particular forms in which households save — which is considered in the remaining sections.

Tax neutrality has been the driving force behind tax reforms across the OECD over the past decade. Yet in the field of savings taxation, it is not readily apparent as to what exactly is a neutral tax treatment, and it is even less clear that it is readily achievable. This section therefore discusses concepts of tax neutrality as regards savings and savings instruments.

In the next section, idealised tax systems are assessed against the possible dimensions of neutrality outlined in the present section. Apart from the well-known cases of *Comprehensive Income Tax* and *Expenditure Tax* treatments, this section also considers two other possibilities, used to a lesser or greater extent in OECD countries — the *Tax-free Savings vehicles*, and the *Flat Rate Tax* on investment income. Tax neutrality is not the only possible influence on tax policy, so this section also considers the claims of fairness and equity, and administrative simplicity, in relation to possible tax structures.

The final section summarises the empirical evidence for the effects of tax on the composition of household savings.

Tax neutrality is usually taken to mean that the tax system should not influence economic decisions made by economic agents. There are two ways in which the tax treatment of savings might be assessed for its neutrality or otherwise: in its effects on the *allocation* and on the *level* of savings.

Tax Neutrality and the Allocation of Savings

In certain areas of taxation, the absence of complete tax neutrality may be accepted as doing little harm. There may be a limited number of decisions which may be altered to reflect the tax situation rather than the underlying economic and commercial realities. Nevertheless, the majority of individuals and companies will behave much the same regardless of the tax treatment. The reason for the limited response is often the absence of close substitutes.

Different forms of savings are often very close substitutes, typically differing in only three ways: risk, rate of return, and term. These three attributes of different savings instruments themselves are closely related: an instrument which invests household savings in risky assets must offer a higher expected rate of return than on safe assets to induce households to save in that form; instruments which cannot be realised until long into the future (life insurance, personal pensions) will have to offer a higher expected return than a sight-deposit account.

As different savings instruments are such close substitutes, different tax treatments of different forms of saving are likely to have a large impact on the portfolio decisions of households — the decisions as to which savings instruments to invest in. Evidence for this hypothesis is summarised below.

Allocational neutrality in the domain of savings taxation is difficult to achieve. One reason for this is that the return on savings is often not taxed once, but twice or even more times. Individuals who save often take the reasonable view that they do not have the expertise, nor the volume of savings, to invest their funds in an appropriate way. They therefore invest via intermediaries, who in turn allocate funds to different economic activities which earn a return on the investment, and pay the return back along the chain to the original saver.

In some cases saving does not involve intermediation, and the investment and savings decisions are identical. The clearest example is an investment in one's own home. But in most cases the savings and investment decisions are taken separately.

Allocational neutrality requires that the choice of savings instrument be independent of tax. Tax here includes not just taxes on the final return to individuals (the interest paid on bank deposits, the pensions or insurance paid out to policy-holders) but also taxes on wealth and capital and those taxes paid by professional investors, and the taxes paid on the productive investments to which the savings are ultimately allocated.

An implication is that full neutrality of savings taxation cannot be achieved without full neutrality in the taxation of, for example, corporate income. If at the corporate level firms have a tax incentive to use debt rather than equity, then full neutrality in the taxation of savings could only be achieved if a relatively greater tax on interest payments at the personal level offset the incentive to use debt at the corporate level, for all possible providers of funds (savers). It was noted in a previous OECD report (1991) that no OECD tax system achieved this neutrality, but since 1992 Norway taxes savings at both the corporate and household level at the same rate. At the corporate level there is in principle no tax incentive to use debt finance rather than equity, since in assessing the tax on received dividends credit is given for tax paid by the company on distributed profits, which is at the same rate as on retained profits. Furthermore, capital gains on shares stemming from retained earnings are not taxed, so that no double taxation on retentions occurs.

Even when problems at the corporate level are ignored — or, rather, treated as a dimension of the problem of tax neutrality which is beyond the scope of this chapter — the difficulties of achieving allocational neutrality remain substantial. When the return to assets can be provided in different ways, all the different sorts of return must be taxed in such a way that the overall tax is the same as on other possible assets. The obvious difficulties arise when comparing returns which come in the form of capital gains with those which come in the form of dividends or interest payments, but one might also add the taxation of imputed income from owner occupation, and (especially for small businesses) the possibility that the return on savings is sufficiently "fungible" that proprietors can take the return as earnings which are taxed as income from labour.

An argument sometimes put forward is that certain types of tax non-neutralities in the taxation of savings are unimportant. If life assurance is favoured over personal pensions, why should this matter? The managers of each fund would invest the money in certain assets which would earn a return; in the absence of any forced segmentation (such as a requirement that the managers of one asset fund invest in a certain type of asset which does not apply to managers of any other type of fund), the real economy is unaffected by changes in the tax instrument through which funds are channelled to it.

This argument rests on a belief that savers are indifferent towards the savings instrument, being interested only in the expected return and the associated risk. However, this is unlikely to be so; savings instruments also differ in liquidity (the return to life assurance and pensions only being realisable under certain conditions), and in any case the risk taken by savers who buy a small number of different equities on their own account to fund retirement is greater than when the risk is shared through a fund. Savers might reasonably prefer one form of saving to another; any tax differences which induce them to save through a non-optimal instrument are then causing genuine welfare losses.

In addition, tax differences may cause inefficiencies in the real economy. If institutional saving is tax-privileged over personal saving, possible benefits from shareholder involvement with their companies may be lost. A relative tax benefit may not be passed on to savers in the form of higher returns, but instead may be appropriated by managers of funds in the form of fees which can be charged, leaving the instrument no more attractive than other saving instruments.

Tax Neutrality and the Levels of Savings

The other aspect of tax neutrality which is of relevance for savings taxation is whether taxation influences the level of savings. As indicated above it is possible that there are externalities related to saving which may justify governments seeking to promote more savings than would occur in the absence of intervention.

At the personal level, as described above, savings can be seen primarily (but not solely) as a decision relating to the distribution of consumption over the lifetime of the saver. Arguments have been made that any taxation of savings distorts this decision, and that tax neutrality requires zero rates of tax on savings. In fact, as discussed below, this view is too simplistic. In any case, even were it true, there is no *a priori* reason to expect that an exemption from tax would necessarily increase the level of savings in an economy. Just like other factors affecting the rate of return on savings, taxation has both a substitution effect (tax reduces the amount of future consumption that can be bought by withholding consumption now, so making saving less attractive) and an income effect (in order to be able to consume a given amount in the future, individuals must be prepared to sacrifice more consumption now, so making more saving necessary).

As already noted, any presumption in favour of no taxation on savings on theoretical grounds is far more complex than the above argument. If taxes on the return to savings were the *only* taxes in an economy, then abolishing them would indeed unambiguously promote tax neutrality. In fact, there are other taxes. It is possible that taxes on savings *promote* overall tax neutrality to the extent that they offset the distortions caused by other taxes (in particular, taxes on labour income). Labour supply and savings decisions are not independent.

198

A choice about the allocation of consumption over a lifetime is hardly likely to be separate from a choice as to how much income to earn over that lifetime. When deciding how much to save, an individual will need to weigh up how much labour income he will have in each period, in order to decide how much to save when labour income is high (during periods of full-time employment) so as to provide a capital income to consume when labour income is low (for example, during retirement). But this decision on how much to work is in turn affected by the comparison of the marginal return on an extra unit of labour effort with the marginal value of leisure, and the marginal return to work is influenced by the marginal tax rate on labour income. Hence, given that the amount of labour income earned by an individual is not necessarily optimal (in the sense that a different amount might be chosen were there no tax distortions in this part of the tax system) then tax "neutrality" becomes exceedingly difficult to define, depending on saving behaviour, the links between saving and labour supply, the return to savings and the structure of other taxes.

Complications in Tax Neutrality

Achievement of either sort of tax neutrality is complicated by the effects of inflation and becomes particularly difficult when the distinction between capital and labour income is not clear cut.

A tax system can be said to be "inflation-neutral" if the real post-tax returns to savers are not distorted by changes in the general price level. This requires a tax system to take account of the effects of inflation. There are several ways in which the tax system may fail to do so, the clearest example being the problem of taxing capital gains. Failure to index capital gains for inflation can lead to inflated tax bills; on the other hand, as capital gains are only taxed on realisation, the tax bill can be deferred. Another area where inflation is often not taken into account is the tax treatment of interest received (usually taxed on the gross return) and interest paid (often deductible for the full and not just the real amount). Further problems arise when some parts of tax systems are indexed but others are not.

Taxation of savings becomes particularly difficult when the possibility of remunerating employees in the form of capital income rather than labour income is available. Clearly, such possibilities are at their greatest when considering the owners of small businesses, who can choose whether to pay a return in the form of dividends, capital gains, or wages. Countries have developed special rules (close company legislation, administrative splitting of business income into labour and capital components) in order to cope with this possibility. However, the problem arises elsewhere in the economy, where it becomes less a problem of the taxation of savings, and much more a problem of tax avoidance — for example, instead of paying high level employees and managers a wage or salary, they might be given stock options allowing a return through capital gains or dividends. Clearly, for either small businesses or senior managers, any difference between the taxation of labour income and of capital income could give an incentive for tax avoidance. Consideration of the appropriate level of taxation on capital income cannot be separated from consideration of other parts of the tax system.

A further dimension of tax neutrality is the international allocation of savings. With integrated caital markets, savings taxation based on where the saver lives might affect the amount of savings in that country, but will have no effect on the amount of investment, this being determined by (amongst other things) the rate of corporate taxation. If taxation of savings was predominantly by the source country (e.g. though withholding taxes) then capital mobility would equate post-tax returns, so savings taxation would also influence domestic investment. What evidence there is suggests that whilst capital markets may be less integrated than might initially be thought, they are nevertheless sufficiently integrated for the open economy model to be reasonable. The tax situation is complex; most countries would like to tax worldwide capital income, but may find it difficult to do so. The tax treatment of portfolio foreign source income is currently (1996) under study by the Committee on Fiscal Affairs of the OECD.

Alternative Approaches to Savings Taxation

Theoretical discussion of the tax treatment of savings has traditionally taken the form of contrasting the tax treatment under a "Comprehensive Income Tax" (CIT) with that under an "Expenditure Tax" (ET). In fact, few countries even come close to either idealised form (although they may on balance give something approaching one of these tax regimes more often than the other), and there are in any case two other types of tax treatment of savings which are used to some extent and which have attractions: "Tax Free Savings Accounts" and a "Flat Rate Tax on Investment Income". Most countries have a mixture of these different sorts of tax treatments in operation on different sorts of savings instruments.

This section does not discuss the advantages and disadvantages of having a diversity of tax treatments, but rather compares the situation if countries were to decide to try to follow one or other of the different approaches with various possible aims of tax policy. In addition, it assesses the possible systems for taxing savings against the two other factors which have a powerful influence on tax policy: administrative simplicity and equity or fairness.

Before considering the detailed merits and demerits of these different possible approaches, the basic principles motivating the taxation of interest can be summarised as follows:

— according to the ET and Tax-Free Savings Accounts principles, capital income is not taxed;

— according to the CIT principles, capital income is taxed at the same rate as labour income;

— according to the Flat Rate Tax concept, capital income is taxed at a single, positive rate determined independently of tax rates on labour income.

A Comprehensive Income Tax

The Haig-Simons definition of income is that it is "the algebraic sum of *i)* the market value of rights exercised in consumption and *ii)* the change in the value of the store of property rights between the beginning and end of the period in question". Income consists of wages, interest receipts, dividends, rents and capital gains. A CIT aims to tax all the different sorts of income equally. If the tax has a progressive schedule, then this involves adding all the different income sources together, and taxing them as a whole.

If achieved, the CIT should achieve one form of allocational efficiency — treating all income sources equally necessarily involves taxing all returns on savings at the same rate It is, however, implausible that a CIT could be fully realised, because the administrative requirements are prohibitive.

Consider first unintermediated savings (such as housing). To achieve full neutrality, capital gains must be taxed on an accruals basis. Hence every year, housing (and other durable assets) would have to be valued so that any change in value could be included in the tax base. Aside from the practical difficulties of undertaking such widespread valuation of unsold assets, it is clear that accruals taxation would leave many households with liquidity problems — they could be forced to realise their gains (sell their houses) in order to pay the tax on the gains.

These sorts of problems get even more difficult when intermediated savings are considered. All the gain in the value of assets held by pension funds, investment funds, life assurance companies, and corporations, would have to be attributed to the individuals to whom the gain will (ultimately) accrue, so that they can be taxed appropriately.

In fact, for corporate income such a system is theoretically not impossible, requiring full integration of corporate and personal tax. All corporate income (regardless of whether it was paid out in dividends, interest payments or capital gains) would be assigned to shareholders and taxed accordingly. No tax would be charged at the corporate level, or if one were charged, it would have to be fully imputed to individuals (the implied imputation would therefore be much more extensive than what are currently termed imputation systems in OECD countries and which are limited to dividend payments).

For other forms of intermediated savings, it is not always obvious as to what part of any increase in the value of funds under management of the intermediaries should be allocated to individuals (for example, consider defined-benefit pension plans).

The problems of using CIT to promote allocational neutrality are further underlined when the difficulties of coping with inflation are considered. In theory, indexing appropriate parts of the tax system could ensure that only real gains are taxed. In practice, the administrative costs of indexing such a large number of financial flows (not just interest payments but also interest receipts, etc.) and stocks of assets may be prohibitive. In contrast, CIT does have the attraction that, in making no distinction between capital income and labour income, there are no problems at the borderline of the two.

In the absence of inflation the administration of a CIT would be probably less complex than an expenditure tax, even after taking account of the fact that in principle all assets would need to be revalued each year to take any accruing changes in value (real capital gains or losses) into account in the tax base. All income is taxed, regardless of the source. There are far fewer borderline cases which need to be policed such as for small businesses or the remuneration of senior managers. But if there is inflation, the relative administrative simplicity of a CIT is rather compromised, as it would in principle require indexing provisions for a large number of assets.

As for the level of savings, contrary to what might be expected at a simplistic level of analysis, it is impossible to say whether distortions caused by a CIT lead, as is sometimes claimed, to a decrease in the level of savings. Even were it shown to be true that in a particular economy at a particular time a CIT was distortionary, it would not be possible to say whether the distortion increased or reduced saving.

The principal attraction of a CIT for many is that it makes it easier to achieve distributional objectives. Not only would people with different sources of income but the same total income pay the same amount of tax (horizontal equity), but in that it taxes investment income (accruing mainly to the rich) as well as labour income, a progressive tax schedule should ensure that the rich pay more than the poor (vertical equity). However, it should be noted that while this is true from the perspective of a single period, in the absence of lifetime averaging before applying the appropriate schedule of tax rates, it will not generally be true that two taxpayers with the same present value of lifetime income will receive the same tax treatment, because their lifetime tax liabilities will vary with their patterns of income, spending and saving.

An Expenditure Tax

Under an ET, the tax base is not what is earned, but what is spent. Savings are not taxed at all. If, however, individuals spend more than is earned or received in capital income in a period, then they are taxed on this larger amount. Obviously, since "savings" are tax exempt, some definition of savings is necessary. This is conventionally envisaged as taking the form of "registering" certain assets as being savings, so enabling the documentation necessary for exemption.

As all savings are exempted, allocational neutrality, at least for registered unintermediated savings, is assured. For intermediated savings, the tax system should clearly exempt the intermediaries from tax. This does not necessarily imply that corporation tax is incompatible with an expenditure tax treatment. However, it does imply that the effective tax rate on marginal investments should be zero, and this requires a corporation tax rather different from any which actually exists, namely, a cash-flow corporation tax, a completely neutral profits-based tax, or a similar system.

Given that taxes on labour income exist, there can be no presumption that an ET is necessarily neutral as to the level of savings. A problem with the ET is that an expectation of changes in tax rates can also give strong incentives to change savings behaviour. For example, suppose that there is a belief that the government will increase taxes in the future. Saving now reduces tax at the current (lower) tax rate, but the return will be taxed at the future (higher) tax rate. There is an incentive to defer saving until the higher tax rates apply to the deduction from the tax base, as well as to the return.

One of the strongest arguments in favour of an expenditure tax is that it is naturally inflation neutral —- the effective tax rate is zero, so the size of the nominal gain is irrelevant. It can be run on a cash-flow basis, taxing all receipts minus savings, with both denoted in nominal returns.

An ET can also cope with the difficulty of defining capital and labour income. If returns to unincorporated businesses are taxed on a cash-flow basis, there is no distinction between the return on equity capital, economic rent and labour income. However, no country has ever introduced such a cash-flow tax. Administrative difficulties will arise if one country attempts to introduce an ET unilaterally (for example, it would be necessary to renegotiate double tax treaties) but more importantly, there may be significant macroeconomic disruption, in the short term at least.

It is sometimes argued that an ET is administratively cumbersome. In a situation where there is no inflation, it is certainly true that an ET requires an extra level of administration as compared to a CIT. It is necessary to ensure that all income which is saved is not taxed. The manner in which it is normally envisaged that this could be done is by the creation of a listing of "registered assets". The tax base would be total income, as under a CIT, but all purchases of such assets (including bank accounts, pension rights, etc.) could be accompanied by documentation which when presented to the tax authorities gives rise to a tax deduction. Income minus saving in registered assets leaving household expenditure, the ET tax base is achieved, but without explicitly requiring information on household expenditure, which would clearly be administratively impossible. Nevertheless, this does imply an extra administrative burden on revenue authorities, savers and managers of the registered assets.

A further potential source of administrative burden is at the borderline between capital and labour. There would be problems in taxing small businesses if, for whatever reason, a cash-flow tax on business income was not also introduced. However, the apparent administrative advantage of a CIT over an ET in the absence of inflation is much reduced or even reversed in its presence. The practical impossibility of a pure CIT in inflationary conditions can be contrasted with the fact that an ET is entirely inflation-neutral — no provisions need to be introduced to ensure an ET treatment of savings when there is inflation which would not be introduced in its absence.

The strongest objections to an ET are related to its ability to achieve equity. An ET is equitable to the extent that those who consume more than others will pay more tax. To the extent that expenditure is a useful measure of economic well-being, an ET is fair. The problem is that expenditure is likely to be significantly below income for high income groups and may potentially be above income for low income groups. Given the same tax rates, a CIT may be more progressive than an ET, but this is rather misleading since in comparing a CIT and an ET there is no good reason to apply the same tax rates.

However, this characterisation of ET as not being equitable is not necessarily correct. In the first place, if individuals are not net savers over their lifetime (as would be suggested by the most simple life-cycle hypotheses of saving), then a *lifetime* ET would have a very similar impact to a *lifetime* CIT. To the extent that expenditure is actually a better indicator of permanent income than income itself (as individuals will adapt consumption to reflect their long term income prospects, and not just their immediate income), a single period ET (i.e. without averaging) could even be seen as fairer than the corresponding single period CIT, because taxation of lifetime income is better approximated by the ET.

For example, consider a poor person who has a once in a lifetime bonus, such as a lump-sum payment on retirement which is taxable. This could take him into a higher tax bracket in a CIT, in the absence of any averaging arrangements, whereas if he spread the consumption resulting from the bonus over several years, this might be avoided under an ET. (In practice many countries with progressive CIT based systems do have averaging arrangements of an *ad hoc* nature, to deal with such cases.) However, this argument supposes either that such an individual cannot migrate (at least, not without paying emigration taxes) or that all countries used similar tax systems. Since most individuals are net savers over their working lives, they could reduce taxes by migrating from an ET country to a CIT country at retirement, or more generally, export registered assets and sell them free of tax.

Meade (1978) discussed several elaborate solutions to deal with this problem, none of which seems very feasible in times of free movement of capital and individuals between countries. Clearly this could present a particular problem in the case of retired pensioners, who are no longer tied to a particular country by their employment, although the possibility exists already in so far as expenditure tax treatment is afforded to pension plans and individuals can migrate to tax havens when they retire. Some do; but the absence of wholesale migration on retirement indicates that factors other than taxation motivate decisions on country of residence.

Tax-free Savings Accounts

The aim of tax-free savings accounts is essentially similar to that of an expenditure tax; to exempt from tax the return on savings. However, whereas the expenditure tax does this by allowing savers to save out of untaxed income with the return being added to taxable income, with a tax-free savings account new savings must be out of post-tax income, but the return is not taxed. As with expenditure taxes, tax-free savings accounts essentially require a definition of registered assets, the return on which will be tax-free.

Tax-free savings accounts are capable of achieving neutrality in the allocation of savings under essentially the same conditions as for a proportional expenditure tax — providing the range of registered assets covers all possible forms of savings. Again, as with the expenditure tax, a neutral tax treatment of intermediated savings requires that there is no tax at the margin at the intermediate level. Similarly, as with the expenditure tax, tax-free savings accounts are inflation-neutral. There is no need for capital gains taxation and no issues of indexing for inflation are raised, because there is no tax levied on the return.

The equity considerations applying to tax-free savings accounts are complicated. Different people with the same income but some with more income from savings than others will pay different amounts of tax, nor will the amount of tax paid be related to consumption in any systematic way. This may be seen as inequitable. Perhaps even more unsatisfactory is the implication that the very well-off with large amounts of capital income and with high consumption levels may not pay any tax. The justification would have to be that they had already paid tax on the savings beforehand. This raises obvious transitional difficulties — how would untaxed inherited wealth be treated?

A key difference between tax-free savings accounts and an expenditure tax is that whereas anticipated changes in the tax rate can substantially affect the incentive to save in the latter case, this is not true in the former. Tax is paid when income is received, regardless of whether it is saved or not. No further tax is due. Whether this necessarily results in an undistorted level of savings depends, as with other ideal types of savings taxation, on factors not simply to do with savings taxation.

The second major difference between the ET and the tax-free savings accounts is that there is potentially a difficult area where it is not possible to easily say whether income should be taxed as labour or capital income. Under a tax-free savings account treatment, the more income which somebody can claim to be a return on capital, the less is the income tax left to be paid on the remainder which are earnings. Inevitably, unincorporated enterprises are an area where difficulties may arise.

A Flat Rate Tax on Investment Income

A flat rate tax on investment income (FRT) has been striven for in some countries and advocated by influential figures in others. Under an FRT system, all capital income is taxed at the same rate. In other words, savings are out of taxed income, but the return on the savings is taxed, although not at the same marginal personal tax rate as on labour income.

To some extent, tax-free savings accounts may therefore be seen as a special case of the FRT, where the tax rate is zero. Hence the effects on the level and timing of savings under an FRT are as they were under the tax-exempt option.

The effects on the allocation of savings of an FRT should, in the absence of inflation, be neutral. All that is required is that all capital income be taxed by means of a withholding tax at the rate of the flat-rate tax. This becomes much more difficult under inflationary conditions. Problems relating to capital gains etc. are the same as those encountered under the CIT. Hence there is the difficulty about how to tax unrealised capital gains, and how to adjust for inflation. Similarly, a problem exists at the dividing line between capital and labour, much as for under the tax-free accounts. However, the extent of this distortion depends on the difference in tax rates on capital and labour, which is less under the FRT than under tax-free accounts.

As regards the equity effects of an FRT, they lie between the CIT and the tax-free accounts. The closer that the flat rate of tax on capital income is to the tax rates on labour, the closer the tax will approximate a CIT — with the obvious large difference that under a CIT there can be a progressive rate schedule leading to those with large amounts of capital income paying proportionally more tax than those with less.

Practical Concerns

None of the four "ideal" types of taxation is without its problems. Given the possibility of creating a tax system from new, the likelihood is that governments would be tempted by the equity properties of a CIT, but the difficulties of indexation might lead them to prefer an ET on the grounds of practical simplicity. Unfortunately, moving towards one or the other of these two schemes is extremely difficult given that a range of savings treatments already exist.

The existence of "mixed systems" in savings taxation creates problems on several levels. First, if a particular savings instrument is taxed at a lower rate than other forms of saving, it may be chosen as a preferred form of saving by many savers. Any increase in the tax rate on that savings instrument will therefore affect many voters.

Second, the tax advantage may be capitalised in asset prices. This is perhaps most clearly the case with equities and government bonds, where the price of the asset is clearly related to the future stream of income attached to owning the asset, but it may well also be true for housing as well. At the limit, this can make special savings incentives nothing of the sort, any advantage being immediately capitalised so that the overall rate of return stays constant. Nevertheless, this does not make it any easier to remove the tax benefit; on the contrary, the fact that those who have bought the asset have done so at higher prices is a formidable barrier to changing the tax treatment with its attendant drop in asset values. The argument works equally in reverse: any more lenient tax treatment of an asset which is not phased in would give a one-off capital gain to those who already own the assets concerned.

Third, there are the revenue consequences of any change. A move to an expenditure tax would mean that the stock of new household savings (which, as was noted above, generally account for at least ten per cent of GDP) would be exempted from tax, but the return from this saving would not be taxed until the gains were consumed — potentially many years in the future. However appealing the principle of an expenditure tax, the consequences for public budgets in the short run may be unacceptable. It is for this reason that governments have often found the creation of tax-free savings account a more amenable route to tax reform — the immediate revenue consequences are limited.

Fourth (and closely related to the revenue consequences), there are problems of fairness. In the tax-free savings account, it is clearly important that the money which is going into the account has been taxed already, as otherwise the risk is that the income from the capital will not be taxed at any point. Yet this is in fact not simple to ensure. Much wealth is inherited, and exemption from tax of the returns to investing that inherited wealth is unlikely to be appealing politically. This is one reason why some governments have been attracted by the Flat Rate Tax, or why other governments have introduced tax-free savings accounts but have limited the amount which individuals can invest through them. Indeed, desire to ensure that there is no tax-exempt rentier class and efforts to limit revenue costs has led to widespread use of limits and thresholds throughout tax systems as they pertain to savings.

These are not the only problems which can arise in hybrid systems: in general there are always likely to be difficulties when marginal tax rates differ, both between different types of income and between income and deductions (typically, "round tripping" or borrowing with interest deductions to finance purchase of tax exempt assets). The general problem has been discussed by Stiglitz (1987) and many particular examples can be found in Steuerle (1985) and Aaron et al. (1988).

Evidence for the Effects of Taxation on the Allocation of Savings

The tax system may affect the level of private saving by reducing the taxation of income from capital and by providing tax benefits for current savers. Both of these measures work by increasing the after-tax rate of return on saving and therefore their effectiveness depends in part on the responsiveness of saving to the rate of return. Moreover, if the aim is to increase not just household saving but national saving, a tax incentive must increase private saving by more than it reduces government tax revenues.

However, before looking in particular at the effects of the tax treatment of household savings, it is important to note that other taxes not normally considered "savings taxes" will have an impact on saving. Under the life cycle approach to saving, tax variables in general, and not simply those specifically related to saving, appear in the household's budget constraint as drains on lifetime resources. The effect of a proportional tax on wages and salaries and that of a proportional consumption tax are equivalent from the household's point of view: they both effectively reduce the real purchasing power of lifetime resources, and thereby the level of the real consumption and saving streams. While this is true for the aggregate household sector, the substitution of a consumption tax for a progressive income tax may have an effect on after-tax income distribution across households. If the marginal propensity to save rises with income, such a tax change might tend to increase aggregate saving.

In addition, a tax on wages and salaries affects household saving through its impact on the work-leisure choice. An increase in the marginal tax rate on earned income will reduce work effort and income if the negative substitution effect from a lower after-tax marginal income is greater than the positive income effect. In this case, the level of saving will fall if there is no offsetting rise in the saving ratio. The direction of the change in the saving ratio cannot be determined *a priori* because a reduction in work effort could imply both fewer working hours before retirement and/or earlier retirement. The latter increases the need to save, while the effect of the former depends on whether leisure and consumption are substitutes or complements.

Capital taxes affect the trade-off between present and future consumption by altering the net rate of return on saving. This applies to corporate profit taxes and income taxes on dividends and interest and capital taxes. Corporate profits taxes, insofar as they are not shifted into higher prices or compensated by lower wages, will ultimately reduce the rate of return to holders of financial assets. After-tax rates of return will be lower than before-tax rates under an income tax. Saving may be discouraged by discriminating against future relative to current consumption. Whether such a distortion is, in fact, important depends on the size of the tax wedge (the difference between before and after-tax rates of return) and the elasticity of saving with respect to the after-tax rate of return. Because for a net saver the income and substitution effects are of opposing signs, the net effect of income taxation on saving is ambiguous. As noted earlier, empirical studies suggest that the responsiveness of saving to after-tax rate of return is still subject to debate.

A change in the tax on business profits may affect total private saving by changing the payout ratio of the firm. A tax system favouring retention leads to increasing business saving. The effect on total private saving depends on the household's reaction to this change. If, as seems likely, the household's marginal propensity to save out of capital gains is higher than that out of dividend income, the increase in business saving will be only partially offset by a reduction in household saving, leading to a rise in total private saving.

Deductibility of interest for tax purposes, when coupled with relatively high marginal tax rates, substantially reduces the cost of borrowing for consumption. In times of inflation, the deductibility of nominal interest can easily lead to negative real rates of interest, actually providing incentives to consume rather than to save. Deductibility of interest on housing and consumer loans varies widely among countries, and theory does not allow a clear cut conclusion on the likely effect of such deductibility on the level of private saving. If consumption is made cheaper through deductibility, a given level of current consumption can be achieved with more left to save, just as a higher rate of return may mean that a given level of future consumption can be achieved with less saving. The question is again an empirical one: is there evidence that countries that treat interest deductions liberally have low private saving rates relative to those that strictly limit interest deductions? Table 2 suggested that this was indeed so.

Finally, net wealth taxes have a series of effects on the incentive to save and on the allocation of saving. As described in a previous OECD publication (1988), one effect of such taxes is to encourage individuals to shift funds out of non-productive (or non-financially productive) forms and into those which have a yield out of which the tax could be paid. For example, paintings yield a return in the form of satisfaction, not money. A net wealth tax which included the value of such items might lead the owners to realise the value and invest the funds in shares. On the other hand, a net wealth tax reduces the return to saving and hence the rate of accumulation of wealth. The tax therefore gives rise to a substitution effect (immediate consumption seems more attractive than deferring that consumption and paying an extra tax). This substitution effect may potentially lead to dissaving — the owners of wealth may liquidate their holdings in order to consume it rather than pay the tax. In countries where there is a net wealth tax, some types of savings may be excluded from the net wealth tax base (e.g. savings in pension funds). Such exemptions may give rise to substitution towards the exempted types of savings.

Looking more particularly at household savings, the major difficulty encountered in assessing the effects of their tax treatment is that of distinguishing between effects on the composition of savings and the level of savings. There is no doubting the "success" of many special savings schemes with beneficial tax provisions in attracting funds. Whether these funds are new savings or simply represent a reallocation of household wealth to benefit from a new tax break is less easy to adjudicate. There is therefore general agreement that saving incentives alter the composition of saving, but no consensus on the effect of saving incentives on the total level of saving. This should not be surprising since the effectiveness of saving incentives will be determined in large part by the interest elasticity of saving, and as noted earlier, evidence on this subject is mixed.

There is broad agreement that taxation influences the composition of saving by changing the after-tax return on different types of assets. Tax provisions can influence the composition of household saving in a variety of ways. First, income invested in certain assets may be deductible (e.g., contributions to pension plans). Secondly, the

209

yield for an asset may be subject to a favourable tax treatment. Thirdly, the financial intermediary holding the funds may be tax exempt. The net tax incentive for any asset requires looking at each of these stages: the treatment at the time of purchase, during the holding period, at the time of disposal.

Saving incentives can seriously distort the allocation of funds in national capital markets and these distortions may be much more significant than any tax-induced increase of the activity as a whole. They have also been criticised as eroding the tax base and altering arbitrarily the distribution of the tax burden. A further criticism is that many of these incentives encourage taxpayers to place their funds with institutional investments (pension funds, insurance companies, etc.). It is argued that this may discourage risk-taking, because such institutions are generally reluctant to provide venture capital to newly established small companies which have been considered as being in the forefront of technological developments and providing large employment opportunities. But it is questionable that the removal of these incentives will necessarily lead to a change in investment behaviour of small savers, who may well be more concerned with the security of their investment than making a big gain.

The most important areas where tax incentives are given are:

i) *Home ownership* generally receives favourable tax treatment (at least for principal residences). Interest on loans incurred in respect of house purchase for principal residences is partially or fully deductible in all countries except Australia, Canada, New Zealand and Turkey. There are also other tax advantages provided to the housing sector under net wealth and capital gains taxation, as well as the absence of any tax on imputed income associated with home ownership in around half the OECD countries which allow a home ownership interest deduction. In those countries where imputed income is taxed, the imputed income is usually well below the market value and/or taxed at very low rates.

Such favourable tax treatment is likely to make the after-tax return on housing attractive relative to other non-residential investments. This favourable treatment, especially when extended to more than one residence, may have a crowding-out effect on the availability of capital for other investment and may distort consumption patterns. Consequently, a number of countries (Denmark, Ireland, Japan, New Zealand, the United Kingdom and the United States) now provide less favourable treatment for home ownership than previously.

ii) *Contributions to private pensions* are deductible from income subject to tax in most countries. A few governments have announced that they intend to shift the balance of pension provisions from the public to the private sector (e.g., Australia and the United Kingdom). In some cases, this policy has been implemented by providing a favourable tax treatment to the pension sector, either in the form of deductibility for contributions or a favourable treatment of the funds or the pension.

iii) *Contributions to life insurance* are generally deductible up to a ceiling. However, a number of countries have recently abolished reliefs for insurance premiums (Ireland, New Zealand, Norway, and the United Kingdom).

iv) *Banks, national savings schemes, etc.* Governments have also provided tax incentives for taxpayers saving through various savings vehicles and interest from such deposits is exempt from tax, subject to limits in Finland, Greece, New Zealand and the United Kingdom. Many incentives have, however, been recently tightened. In Japan, for example, the tax exemption for small savings was abolished (except for the aged and handicapped) from April 1988. The New Zealand exemption was abolished from 1991 and the Finnish interest tax relief has been made conditional on the rate of interest.

v) *Equity holdings.* For equity holdings, several countries have tried to use the tax system to encourage households to invest in equities. Also, almost all countries provide a favourable tax treatment of income from capital gains and share participation schemes provided by employers to their employees.

Work undertaken by the Institute for Fiscal Studies in London attempted to measure the importance of these tax differences in the United Kingdom (see Hills, 1984). The study estimates for a range of financial and non-financial assets the "degree of fiscal privilege", defined as the percentage difference between the saver's marginal income tax rate and the real effective tax rate on each asset. The effective tax rate is in turn defined as the percentage difference between the pre-tax and post-tax real rate of return. There was great variation across assets in the degree of fiscal privilege, even for individuals facing the same marginal income tax rate. The effective tax rate for savers is much more dependent on the asset chosen than the marginal income tax rate faced, and in some cases the degree of fiscal privilege exceeds that implicit in exempting the asset's return from tax completely.

The results are particularly sensitive to the rate of inflation, an increase in which further widens the dispersion of fiscal privilege and also changes the relative position of different assets. The study concluded that the vast majority of savings vehicles are sold primarily on the relative merits of their treatment by the tax system. The profitability of the underlying investment is often of secondary importance, to the obvious detriment of the ability of capital markets to channel savings into the most efficient investments. The share of personal saving being channelled into tax-privileged assets grew from 45 per cent in 1957 to 75 per cent in 1987.

A similar study in Ireland (Thom, 1988) found a similar pattern of divergent marginal effective tax rates, with a lower tax rate the more that the return takes the form of a capital gain.

A later United Kingdom study (Saunders and Webb, 1988) matched marginal effective tax rates to the incomes of households which saved with each particular instrument. They found that "the relatively rich and wealthy...are the main beneficiaries of the present pattern of fiscal privilege among financial assets". The Institute for Fiscal Studies study noted a correlation between the degree of fiscal privilege and movements in the composition of savings in the United Kingdom. There were, however, some notable exceptions to this, possibly reflecting the influence of other factors on savings behaviour and the fact that the estimated tax advantages may not fully accrue to savers but may be partly captured by the favoured institutions themselves.

211

There are two well known ways in which taxes may affect portfolio composition. First, differences in effective tax rates should lead to some portfolio specialisation or "clientele" effect. Households facing lower marginal tax rates should hold a greater proportion of more heavily taxed assets and those facing higher tax rates, a greater proportion of tax-exempt or tax-privileged assets. Secondly, taxes affect the trade-off between risk and return, although their impact on demand for risky assets is theoretically ambiguous (as discussed in Feldstein, 1976).

Certainly, the heterogeneity of household portfolio savings behaviour, particularly with respect to wealth, has been noted in several studies [for the United States, see Diamond and Hausman (1984) and King and Leape (1984)] and as discussed below, tax effects are significant. The earliest influential econometric study was that by Feldstein (1976), using 1962 Federal Reserve Board data for the United States. Estimating models of portfolio composition, he concluded that "the personal income tax has a very powerful effect on individuals' demands for portfolio assets, after adjusting for the effects of net worth, age, sex, and the ratio of human to non-human capital." However the major technical defect of the study was that in considering the decision to hold observed amounts of particular assets, all households not holding those assets at all were excluded, inducing sample selection bias and ignoring the "spillover" effect, that the proportion of an individual's wealth invested in a particular asset depends on the combination of assets in the portfolio. To overcome this problem it is necessary to adopt a two stage estimation procedure developed by Heckman (1979).

The early 1980s saw a series of studies based on large micro-data sets, which used the Heckman procedure to overcome the limitations of Feldstein's study. The most important are Dicks-Mireaux and King (1983) using 1977 data for Canada, King and Leape (1984) using 1978 data for the United States, Hubbard (1985) using 1979 data from a different source for the United States, and Agell and Edin (1990) using 1979 data for Sweden. Each study used a wide variety of explanatory variables but all found qualitatively similar and significant effects of the tax rate.

It is evident from the data used by these studies that in all countries most households choose to hold only a small number of the available savings assets. The first stage in the model used for each of these four studies is therefore for each household to decide whether to hold a particular asset at all — a discrete choice which will depend on information and transaction costs, and constraints on negative holdings of many assets, as discussed in detail in Auerbach and King (1983). The second stage is the continuous choice of how much of an asset to hold, conditional on the decision to hold it at all.

Each of the studies cited finds strong effects of taxes on the decision whether to hold a particular asset (i.e. the first stage); the influence of taxation on the decision as to how much to invest in a particular asset (the second stage) is less clear-cut.

As further explained in OECD (1994) the main difference between the studies is in the authors' preliminary decision as to how to group different assets and liabilities so as to make estimation manageable. A few categories are obvious (bonds, corporate equity, housing) but otherwise the choice of what to aggregate is less obvious and often depends on the data set. All the studies include liabilities, King and Leape and Agell and Edin separating out mortgages from other debt.

Considering first the effect of taxes on the stage 1 decision, all the significant coefficients for all countries have positive sign, suggesting that the higher the tax rate the more likely it is that all classes of asset and liability will be held. Generally, the effect is greater the higher the degree of privileged tax treatment. So for Canada, the highest coefficients are for registered retirement savings plans, stocks and shares and real estate equity, reflecting tax deductions and lower taxation of capital gains, although as the authors point out, because it is not possible to tell from the data whether individuals have exhausted their tax deductions or exemptions associated with particular assets, the exact interpretation is not clear cut.

This may explain the insignificant coefficient for registered home ownership savings plans, which are also tax privileged but only relevant for households saving for a first or larger house. For the United States, the King and Leape study surprisingly has the highest coefficients for liquid and contractual savings and other liabilities, although Hubbard's results (with much higher values, in part because of the smaller number of asset groups used) more predictably have the highest effects for bonds, savings bonds (many of which will be tax exempt but not distinguished in these data) and equities (capital gains being lightly taxed, with a maximum rate of 28 per cent on long-term gains following the Revenue Act of 1978). For Sweden, the highest coefficients are on "tax saving schemes", (deductible) mortgage debt and "other assets".

The figures for the stage 2 conditional asset demands are less easy to interpret. One would expect some of these coefficients to be positive and some negative, since they represent changes in shares of total net assets. It may seem surprising that so few are significant. The strongest effects were found by Dicks-Mireaux and King, with predicted decreases in the shares of home equity (lack of interest deductibility) and business equity (increasingly likely to incorporate) as the tax rate increases, and increases in stocks and shares, cash and deposits, and bonds. King and Leape also found a surprising predicted increase in checking accounts with higher taxes, as well as contractual savings and mortgage debt. Increased balances in checking accounts not paying interest may be due to the fact that transferring balances to interest paying deposit accounts is less attractive the higher the tax rate. Hubbard has positive effects for housing, equities and debt, and Agell and Edin find very strong effects on tax savings schemes and mortgage debt.

Not all the results in these studies are easy to explain in terms of a simple theory of household behaviour, and since each data set is very heterogeneous, analysis of sub-groups might give a richer picture. It is also clear that each country's tax system (for example interest deductibility and other means of sheltering taxable income) and other institutional features are important. However, given this heterogeneity the fact that tax rate effects are so significant is impressive.

To summarise, econometric studies using large micro-data sets on individual households find strong evidence that marginal tax rates affect the decision to hold certain assets and liabilities, and some evidence that the subsequent decision on how much of those assets and liabilities to hold is also affected. Governments *are* therefore likely to be able to influence the composition of household savings by choice of tax policy, even if there is no clear evidence (which there is not from these studies) that the overall level of saving will be affected. However since many other factors apart from taxation are also influential, the extent to which tax policy will be effective is likely to vary across countries.

Bibliography

AARON, H.J., H. GALPER and J.A. PECHMAN, eds. (1988), *Uneasy Compromise: Problems of a Hybrid Income/Consumption Tax*, The Brookings Institution, Washington, D.C.

AGELL, J. and P.-A. EDIN (1990), "Marginal Taxes and the Asset Portfolios of Swedish Households", *Scandinavian Journal of Economics*, Vol. 92.

AUERBACH, A.J. and M.A. KING (1983), "Taxation, Portfolio Choice and Debt-Equity Ratios: A General Equilibrium Model", *Quarterly Journal of Economics*, 98.

BAUM, D.N. (1988), "Consumption, Wealth and the Real Rate of Interest: A Re-examination", *Journal of Macroeconomics*, Vol. 10.

BEACH, C.M., R.W. BOADWAY and N. BRUCE (1988), *Taxation and Savings in Canada*, Economic Council of Canada, Ottawa.

BOSKIN, M.J. (1978), "Taxation, Saving and the Rate of Interest", *Journal of Political Economy*, Vol. 86.

BOSWORTH, B.P. (1984), *Tax Incentives and Economic Growth*, The Brookings Institution, Washington, D.C.

BOVENBERG, A.L. and O. EVANS, (1990), "National and Personal Saving in the United States: Measurement and Analysis of Recent Trends", *IMF Staff Papers*, Vol. 37, International Monetary Fund, Washington, D.C.

BURMAN, L., J. CORDES, and L. OZANNE (1990), "IRAs and National Savings", *National Tax Journal*, Vol. 43.

CARROLL, C. and L.H. SUMMERS (1987), "Why Have Private Saving Rates in the United States and Canada Diverged?", *Journal of Monetary Economics*, Vol. 20.

CULLISON, W.E. (1990), "Is Saving too Low in the United States", *Federal Reserve Bank of Richmond Economic Review*.

DIAMOND, P.A. and J.A. HAUSMAN (1984), "Individual Retirement and Savings Behaviour", Journal of Public Economics, Vol. 23.

DICKS-MIREAUX, L.-D.L. and M.A. KING (1983), "Portfolio Composition and Pension Wealth: An Econometric Study", in Z. BODIE and J.B. SHOVEN (eds.), *Financial Aspects of the United States Pension System*, University of Chicago Press, Chicago.

ELMESKOV, J., J.J. SHAFER and W. TEASE (1991) "Savings Trends and Measurement Issues", Economics Working Paper No. 105, OECD, Paris.

EVANS, O. (1983), "Tax Policy, the Interest Elasticity of Saving, and Capital Accumulation", *American Economic Review*, Vol. 73.

FEENBERG, D. and J. SKINNER, (1989), "Sources of IRA Saving", in *Tax Policy and the Economy 3*, ed. by L.H. SUMMERS, MIT Press, Cambridge, MA.

FELDSTEIN, M.S. (1976), "Social Security and Private Saving: International Evidence in an Extended Life-Cycle Model", in *The Economics of Public Services*, ed. by M.S. FELDSTEIN and R.P. INMAN, Macmillan, London.

FRIEND, I. and J. HASBROUCK (1983), "Saving and After-tax Rates of Return", *Review of Economics and Statistics*, Vol. 65.

GRAVELLE, J.G. (1989), "Capital Gains Taxes, IRAs and Savings", CRS Report for Congress, The Library of Congress, Congressional Research Service, Washington, D.C.

GYLFASON, T. (1981), "Interest Rates, Inflation, and the Aggregate Consumption Function", *Review of Economics and Statistics*, Vol. 63.

GYLFASON, T. (1993), "Optimal Saving, Interest Rates and Endogenous Growth", *Scandinavian Journal of Economics*, 95:4.

HALL, R.E. (1988), "Intertemporal Substitution in Consumption", *Journal of Political Economy*, Vol. 96 No. 2.

HAYASHI, F. (1986), "Why is Japan's Saving Rate So Apparently High?", in *NEBR Macroeconomics Annual 1986*, ed. by S. FISCHER, MIT Press, Cambridge, MA.

HECKMAN, J.J. (1979), "Sample Selection Bias as a Specification Error", *Econometrica, 47*.

HENDERSHOTT, P.H. and J. PEEK (1985), "Household Saving: An Econometric Investigation", in *The Level and Composition of Household Saving*, ed. by P.H. HENDERSHOTT, Ballinger, Cambridge, MA.

HILLS, J. (1984), *Savings and Fiscal Privilege*, Report Series No. 9, Institute for Fiscal Studies, London.

HORIOKA, C.Y. (1984), "The Applicability of the Life-Cycle Hypothesis of Saving to Japan", The *Kyoto University Economic Review*, Vol. 54.

HORIOKA, C.Y. (1990), "Why is Japan's Household Saving Rate So High? A Literature Survey", *Journal of Japanese and International Economies*, Vol. 1.

HOWREY, E.P. and S.H. HYMANS, (1978), "The Measurement and Determination of Loanable Funds", *Brookings Papers on Economic Activity: 3*, The Brookings Institution, Washington, D.C.

HUBBARD, R.G. (1984), "Do IRAs and Keoghs Increase Saving?", *National Tax Journal*, Vol. 37.

HUBBARD, R.G. (1985), "Personal Taxation, Pension Wealth and Portfolio Composition", *Review of Economics and Statistics,* Vol.67, No. 1, February.

Jump, G.V. (1982), "Tax Incentives to Promote Personal Saving: Recent Canadian Experience", in Saving and Goverment Policy, *Conference Series No. 25*, Federal Reserve Bank of Boston.

King, M.A. and J.L. Leape (1984), "Wealth and Portfolio Composition: Theory and Evidence", NBER Working Paper No. 1468, National Bureau of Economic Research, Cambridge, MA.

Kotlikoff, L.J. (1983), "National Savings and Economic Policy: The Efficacy of Investment and Savings Incentives", *American Economic Review*, Vol. 73.

Leape, J.I. (1987), "Taxes and Transaction Costs in Asset Market Equilibrium", *Journal of Public Economics,* Vol. 33

Leape, J.I. (1990), "The Impossibility of Perfect Neutrality: Fundamental Issues in Tax Reform", *Fiscal Studies*, Vol. 11 No. 2.

Makin, J.H. (1986), "Savings Rates in Japan and the United States: The Roles of Tax Policy and Other Factors", in *Savings and Capital Formation*, ed. by F.G. Adams, S.M. Wachter and D.C. Heath, Lexington, MA.

Makin, J.H. (1987), "Saving, Pension Contributions, and the Real Interest Rate", Working Paper No. 11, American Enterprise Institute, Washington D.C.

Meade, J.E. (1978), *The Structure and Reform of Direct Taxation*, The Institute for Fiscal Studies, Allen and Unwin, London.

Montgomery, E. (1986), "Where Did All the Saving Go?", *Economic Enquiry*, Vol. 24.

Oecd, *National Accounts of Oecd Countries* (various years), Paris.

Oecd (1988), *Taxation of Net Wealth, Capital Transfers and Capital Gains of Individuals*, Paris.

Oecd (1992), *Taxing Profits in a Global Economy: Domestic and International Issues*, Paris.

Oecd (1994), *Taxation and Household Saving*, Paris.

Poterba, J.M. (1987), "Tax Policy and Corporate Saving", *Brookings Papers on Economic Activity*: 2, The Brookings Institution, Washington, D.C.

Saunders, M. and S. Webb, (1988), "Fiscal Privilege and Financial Assets: Some Distributional Effects", *Fiscal Studies*, Vol. 9, No. 4.

Shibuya, H. (1987), "Japan's Household Savings Rate: An Application of the Life-Cycle Hypothesis", IMF Working Paper WP/87/15, International Monetary Fund, Washington, D.C.

Shibuya, H. (1988), "Japan's Household Savings: A Life-Cycle with Implicit Annuity Contract and Rational Expectations", unpublished, International Monetary Fund, Washington, D.C.

Skinner, J. and D. Feenberg, (1989), "The Impact of the 1986 Tax Reform on Personal Saving", Working Paper No. 90-3, The Office of Tax Policy Research, School of Business Administration, University of Michigan.

STEUERLE, E. (1985), *Taxes, Loans and Inflation,* The Brookings Institution, Washington, D.C.

STEWART, D.A. (1988), "Effects of Taxation on Saving", in Uneasy Compromise: Problems of a Hybrid Income-Consumption Tax, ed. by H.J. AARON, H. GALPER and J.A. PECHMAN, The Brookings Institution, Washington, D.C.

STIGLITZ, J. (1985), "The General Theory of Tax Avoidance", *National Tax Journal,* Vol. 38, No. 3, September.

SUMMERS, L.H. (1981), "Capital Taxation and Accumulation in a Life Cycle Growth Model", *American Economic Review*, Vol. 71.

TANZI, V. (1992), "The Need for Tax Coordination in an Economically Integrated World", mimeo, International Monetary Fund, Washington D.C.

THOM, R. (1988), *The Taxation of Savings*, Research report No. 2, Foundation for Fiscal Studies, Dublin.

VENTI, S.F. and D.A. WISE, (1987), "IRAs and Saving", in *The Effects of Taxation on Capital Accumulation*, ed. by M.S. FELDSTEIN, University of Chicago Press, Chicago.

WEBER, W.E. (1970), "The Effect of Interest Rates on Aggregate Consumption", *American Economic Review*, Vol. 60.

WEBER, W.E. (1975), "Interest Rates, Inflation, and Consumer Expenditures", *American Economic Review*, Vol. 65.

A Comment by Richard Disney

Normann and Owens have produced a useful survey of the literature on the effects of taxation on savings, and of alternative approaches to the taxation of savings. More briefly, they also provide a summary of recent trends in savings in OECD countries, discuss difficulties in measuring savings, and examine the major motives for saving by households. Since these last two points are uncontentious, these comments focus on the issues of the trend in saving by OECD consumers, on the evidence concerning the impact of the rate of return (gross and net of tax) on saving, and on the appropriate structure of taxation of savings.

Trends in Savings in OECD Countries

As the authors point out, there is considerable heterogeneity in savings behaviour across OECD countries in recent times. There are a number of underlying structural trends affecting savings behaviour in OECD countries. One is the demographic transition. As the OECD has frequently noted (e.g. OECD, 1990), there is a strong cross-section relationship between national old age dependency ratios, on the one hand, and domestic and national savings rates among OECD countries, on the other: greater old age dependency ratios will in due course reduce savings rates, although in the interim the transition may imply rising savings rates. These relationships *inter alia* are robustly confirmed by Weil (1994), Disney (1996) and Miles and Patel (1996) in models with country fixed effects and time controls. Of course, residual country heterogeneity ("fixed effects") in household savings rates may stem from differences in tax policy, which is our primary interest here, or from other institutional factors, especially the existence of large scale funded pension assets (Davis, 1995). Even if this relationship between old age dependency and savings is broadly consistent with the stylised life cycle hypothesis (LCH) of saving, there is the puzzle of why microeconometric evidence concerning the behaviour of consumers appears to exhibit less conformity to the LCH (see Deaton, 1992; Weil, 1994; and Disney, 1996).

A second important structural question concerns the fiscal (macroeconomic) stance of OECD countries, and its interaction with household saving. One key facet of this issue among EU members is the Maastricht convergence criteria and the fiscal contraction which may be required in order to achieve the target debt-GDP ratio and ceilings on inflation and budget deficits. There are at least three ways in which this might affect domestic saving: 1) transitory shocks to household income, 2) positive shocks to public saving and 3) any impact on private expectations about future tax rates consequent to monetary union or other harmonization of economic policies. A second, longer-run, structural issue which may impinge on the third of these effects is again the demographic transition, particularly given the existence of large, unfunded, social security liabilities in a number of OECD countries. The latter may cause household saving to increase not just because of Ricardian equivalence (about which Seater, 1993, contains some empirical evidence) but also because greater uncertainty about future social security pensions may induce an upsurge of precautionary saving. This latter point may be tested in a country such as Italy whose pension reforms from 1992 provide a "natural experiment".

The Interest Elasticity of Saving, and Tax Policies as "Natural Experiments"

Normann and Owens consider the issue of the interest elasticity of saving at some length. Given both income and substitution effects to changes in the interest rate in the standard n period model of the life-cycle utility maximising consumer, the authors confirm that empirical studies obtain no clear sign for the relationship, as should be confirmed *a priori*. However, it should be noted that under certain conditions the standard Euler equation, other things being equal, broadly predicts that the rate of consumption growth will be higher, the higher the expected real rate of return on savings, although the sign of the effect of changes in the rate of return on the level of consumption at any point in time cannot be determined. Moreover, positive *innovations* to the income process, which may include shocks to real returns, may raise both present and future consumption and the net impact on saving is again unclear (Deaton, 1992). In general, it is important to separate anticipated and unanticipated changes in variables, and know whether such changes are expected to be permanent (e.g. supply-side related) or transitory (e.g. cyclical). It is not clear that all the studies cited are testing the same propositions concerning consumption (savings) growth and level, and the impact of innovations.

This general debate has two implications for the issue of tax policy and macroeconomic performance. First, tax policies towards savings change real rates of return and the debate concerning the interest-elasticity of savings is directly pertinent here. In the "standard" capital accumulation model in which substitution effects dominate, taxing savings should in theory reduce the saving rate, at equilibrium lowering real capital per capita and thus steady state consumption per capita (consumption will, of course, initially jump). However, the equivalent indeterminate result in the presence of income effects is present also in this framework (Diamond, 1965). Again, to identify the impact on the savings rate, such policies as raising or reducing taxes must be unanticipated, and the form and levels of savings may well depend on whether the policies are perceived as, and treated as, permanent or transitory.

Secondly, subject to modelling these expectations, tax changes actually form a "natural experiment" from which the relevant elasticities could in principle be identified. Such legislation as the Tax Reform Act of 1986 in the United States, which limited the tax deductibility of Individual Retirement Accounts for middle- and high-income families, or the introduction of Personal Equity Plans (PEPs) and Tax Exempt Special Savings Accounts (TESSAs) in the UK in 1987 and 1991 respectively, are illustrations of such potential experiments. In the first case, the experiment is particularly interesting because the reform affected different income classes unevenly so standard theory would predict that the behaviour of those affected by the reform would change whereas those unaffected would remain the same. Likewise, permitting individuals to hold their PEPs wholly in the form of unit trusts (mutual funds) in 1992 changed the nature of the risks attached to PEPs and, presumably, their relative attractiveness to investors with differing degrees of risk aversion. As a final example, changes to limits (for example, ceilings on tax relief) should offer the potential for further experiments of this kind.

Unfortunately, the evidence from these "natural experiments" is far from clear and has resulted in a prolonged but largely inconclusive debate, particularly concerning the impact of IRAs on total saving (the most recent contributions are Gale and Scholz, 1994; Engen, Gale and Scholz, 1994, 1996; Poterba, 1994; Poterba, Venti and Wise, 1996).It is also clear from the empirical evidence that individual heterogeneity in savings behaviour is a key issue in analysing the responsiveness of savings rates to changes in after-tax real rates of return. This has led to the popularity of a "differences of differences" methodology in which individual panel data are used, ideally separating the sample by characteristics which affect savings preferences, and by looking at the responsiveness of sub-groups to changes in programmes (for an exposition, see in particular Poterba et al., 1996, Section 2). Again studies differ in their priorities concerning the appropriate groupings in the data and the issue has not yet been resolved to the satisfaction of all the participants.

Reshuffling of Asset Portfolios in Response to Differential Tax Treatment

The previous discussion has implicitly concerned the overall level of household saving. The debate appears to be on much firmer ground when the allocation of saving to different assets is considered. As Normann and Owens point out, the evidence that tax treatment affects household portfolio composition seems much more unequivocal than whether it affects the overall level of saving. As they also point out, the degree of substitutability of assets with differential tax treatment is a key consideration, as is the institutional structure governing savings decisions, a point recently emphasized by Bernheim (1996). Thus there would be greater reallocative effects if certain assets receive more favourable tax treatment, to the extent that those assets are substitutes for other assets. Conversely, when new assets with specialised characteristics are developed as a result of tax changes, there may be a potential for "ripple" effects across the household portfolio, and the reshuffling may involve changes in expenditure (for example, on consumer durables) as well as a reallocation of financial assets. Of course, this closely follows Friedman's (1957) analysis of consumption behaviour.

These points can be illustrated by evidence from the UK concerning the impact of TESSAs and PEPs on household saving. TESSAs are tax-free interest accounts held at UK banks and building societies for a minimum of five years subject to a ceiling on the total value of savings in this form. Given the finite horizon, they are not long-run saving for retirement, for example, nor are they "instant access" accounts like current accounts at banks (although withdrawals can be made at a penalty). So they should be close substitutes for other interest-bearing accounts (IBAs). Banks, Blundell and Dilnot (1994) estimate a pooled cross section regression of household holdings of IBAs on holdings of TESSAs, other wealth and household characteristics. The implied elasticity of IBA holdings on TESSAs is -0.95 (t ratio -20.7), indicating almost complete reshuffling of holdings into the new, tax-privileged TESSAs. A similar exercise for holdings of equities with respect to PEPs, and a similar set of controls, gives a coefficient of -0.07 (t ratio -3.23), indicating that the inability of investors in PEPs to hold a fully-diversified portfolio prior to 1992 limited the substitutability of PEPs for other forms of equity holding (usually in the form of diversified portfolios such as unit trusts, or holdings of equity in newly privatised utilities). Interestingly, the use of a dummy variable for whether an individual holds a PEP increases the substitution elasticity considerably, which might imply that saver heterogeneity is a key issue in the holding of somewhat riskier assets such as equity. These examples are entirely in accord with the general tenor of the discussion by Normann and Owen.

The Taxation of Savings: What Regime, How Much Neutrality?

In their discussion of the appropriate taxation of savings, Normann and Owen follow the approach of Leape (1990) fairly closely. In line with both papers, the conclusion seems correct that a comprehensive income tax or expenditure tax is probably impossible in terms of administrative convenience and equity considerations. Flat rate taxes on investment income, and tax-free savings accounts, which are closer in spirit to an expenditure tax but are generally only applied to certain classes of assets, may be pragmatic middle ways.

An important issue is the extent of welfare losses attributable to non-neutral tax treatment of savings. As Leape, and Normann and Owen point out, in the presence of other distortionary taxes (such as taxes on labour income), a second best solution may involve the taxation of saving. In addition, where certain kinds of saving are intermediated, or where investors differ in their financial sophistication and ability to arbitrage differences in tax treatment, non-neutrality across assets may also incur low deadweight losses. These are both, of course, illustrations of market segmentation.

Secondly, where investors differ in their attitudes to risk and where assets differ in their portfolio risk, non-neutrality may be used to widen coverage by certain assets. For example, the development of the market for Personal Pensions in the UK after 1987 (which are a tax-privileged form of individual retirement savings account) may have required significant tax incentives because defined-contribution pension schemes of this kind expose investors explicitly to market risk, and because the bulk of higher-income, asset-rich investors were already covered by company-provided defined-benefit pension plans. Broadening and deepening the market requires "excessively" favourable tax treatment at the start even though the windfalls were probably too generous and lasted too long (Disney and Whitehouse, 1992). Many assets fulfil both a saving and an insurance function, and the optimal tax treatment of assets from the two points of view need not be identical.

Finally, the importance of capitalisation of tax treatment should be emphasized. The distributional impact on the housing market of the tax relief provided to owner occupation in the UK is well known, but a decrease in such tax relief to restore a level playing field should be implemented during a cyclical upturn in house prices, which dampens the speculative component of such periods. The point also applies to equity markets, where the values are undoubtedly in part underpinned by the tax privileges of pension funds in order to provide defined-benefit and, increasingly, defined-contribution pensions in the future. Changes in corporate tax treatment, by affecting the magnitude of recovered tax relief obtained by untaxed institutions such as pension funds, can also affect fund values and thus the contribution rates needed to provide actuarial balance in such schemes. These points imply that the achievement of neutrality in the taxation of savings may not be the primary goal of tax policy, although straightforward and well-perceived opportunities for arbitrage ought to be minimised.

Bibliography

BANKS, J., BLUNDELL, R. and DILNOT, A. (1994), "Tax-Based Saving Initiatives in the UK", mimeo, paper for NBER/OECD Conference on International Comparisons of Household Saving, Paris, May.

BERNHEIM, B.D. (1996), "Rethinking Saving Incentives", mimeo, Stanford,March.

DAVIS, E.P. (1995), *Pension Funds: Retirement-Income Security and Capital Markets: An International Perspective*, Oxford University Press, Oxford.

DEATON, A. (1992), *Understanding Consumption*, Clarendon Press, Oxford.

DIAMOND, P.A. (1965), "National Debt in a Neo-Classical Growth Model", *American Economic Review*, 55, December.

DISNEY, R. (1996), *Can We Afford to Grow Older: A Perspective on the Economics of Aging*, MIT Press, Cambridge, MA.

DISNEY, R. and E. WHITEHOUSE (1992), "The Personal Pension Stampede", Report Series, Institute for Fiscal Studies, London.

ENGEN, E.M., W.G. GALE and J.K. SCHOLZ (1994), "Do Saving Incentives Work?" *Brookings Papers on Economic Activity*, Washington, D.C., No. 1.

ENGEN, E.M., W.G. GALE and J.K. SCHOLZ, (1996), "Effects of Tax-Based Saving Incentives on Saving and Wealth: A Critical View of the Literature", mimeo, The Brookings Institution, Washington, D.C., May.

FRIEDMAN, M. (1957), *A Theory of the Consumption Function*, Princeton University Press, Princeton.

GALE, W.G. and J.K. SCHOLZ, (1994), "IRAs and Household Saving", *American Economic Review*, 84, December.

LEAPE, J. (1990), "The Impossibility of Perfect Neutrality: Fundamental Issues In Tax Reform", *Fiscal Studies*, 11, May.

MILES, D. and N. PATEL (1996), "Savings and Wealth Accumulation in Europe", Merrill Lynch Financial Research, June.

OECD (1990) OECD *Economic Surveys: Japan 1989/90*, Paris.

POTERBA, J.M. (1994), "Personal Saving Behavior and Retirement Income Modelling: A Research Assessment", mimeo, MIT, June.

POTERBA, J.M., S.M. VENTI and D.A. WISE (1996), "Personal Retirement Saving Programs and Asset Accumulation: Reconciling the Evidence, National Bureau of Economic Research". Working Paper No. 5599, May.

SEATER, J.J. (1993), "Ricardian Equivalence", *Journal of Economic Literature*, XXXI, March.

WEIL, D.N. (1994), "The Saving of the Elderly in Micro and Macro Data", *Quarterly Journal of Economics*, 109, February.

A Comment by A. Lans Bovenberg

Normann and Owens provide an excellent overview of several issues involving saving in OECD countries. They make a number of important points, for example, that labour and capital income are not easily separated. Some of the issues raised here go beyond the scope of their paper but deserve some attention during a conference on Latin America.

Corporate Saving

The authors focus on household rather than corporate saving on the grounds that the links between taxation and corporate saving are obscure. At the same time, however, they acknowledge that the impact of taxes on household saving is not simple either. Clearly, household and corporate saving should be analysed together because the two types of saving are close substitutes for one other.

This can be illustrated with cross-country comparisons of household saving. In some countries, small businesses are mainly in the household sector. In other countries, in contrast, they tend to be in the corporate sector. In fact, tax considerations play a major role in determining the dividing line between the household and corporate sectors. In particular, in countries with low corporate but high personal tax rates, entrepreneurs face incentives to incorporate and thus save through their businesses. Hence, in these countries, most saving occurs through the business rather than the household sector. Actually, this follows from one of the authors' main messages, namely that the composition of saving is rather sensitive to tax considerations. Indeed, high tax countries with relatively low corporate rates, such as the Netherlands, Denmark, and Norway, feature relatively high corporate saving. This may explain their finding that in many OECD countries corporations tend to be a more important source of saving than households. Of course, the sheer size of corporate saving is another reason to devote attention to this type of saving.

One should be aware that the dividing line between household and corporate saving is not fixed, not only in cross-country comparisons but also when analysing time series. This was shown by the US Tax Reform Act of 1986 which reduced the

227

statutory corporate rate compared to the average statutory personal rate. This encouraged agents to shift their income away from the household into the corporate sector, thereby boosting corporate returns and corporate saving.

Intangible Assets

The authors acknowledge that the national accounts measure saving rather imprecisely by ignoring spending on education, R&D, and other intangibles. Nonetheless, they argue that the saving trends over time would not be affected much by accounting for various kinds of intangible investments. This is doubtful because investments in knowledge and human-capital accumulation appear to have become more important in recent years. For example, firms spend more and more resources on training their work force as learning becomes a lifelong process. Moreover, human capital is becoming an increasingly important asset. Also here, the authors should have heeded their main message that the composition of saving is sensitive to the tax treatment of different assets. This finding is likely to apply also to the allocation of the portfolio over tangible assets, human capital and other intangible assets. Hence, an analysis of the impact of taxation on human capital and other intangible assets would be welcome.

The Level of Saving

The authors provide an excellent survey of recent research on the link between the after-tax return and the level of saving. Thus their conclusion is rather disappointing since the evidence is not clear cut. Some researchers find large effects, others small and insignificant impacts. Nevertheless, the authors seem a bit sceptical of the claims of some academics that lower taxes on saving could significantly raise the overall level of national saving by raising the after-tax rate of return. The authors suggest that some of the significant effects of taxes on private saving that have been found are due mainly to non-tax factors, such as advertising and increased public awareness about the merits of saving.

This seems a sensible conclusion. Indeed, one could argue that the government should employ more direct instruments for raising national saving rather than trying to affect private saving through tax policy. For example, the government could reduce the budget deficit. Alternatively, it could require people to save part of their income for their retirement, as Chile has done.

In this connection, there should have been a little more attention given to transmission channels other than the rate of return by which taxes can affect private saving. For example, the tax system may affect private saving through the timing of the tax collections. This can be seen by comparing taxes on labour and expenditure.

Compared to labour taxes, expenditure taxes tend to fall more at the end than at the beginning of the life cycle. This encourages people to save more in order to maintain their consumption levels during the latter part of the life cycle.

Further analysis of the reasons why different studies arrive at such different conclusions would also be welcome. Is it because these studies employ different estimation techniques and procedures? Indeed, time-series seem to yield lower estimates than do microeconometric techniques using variations in person-specific tax rates. The low time-series estimates may reflect the temporary nature of fluctuations in the rate of return.

Composition of Saving

Turning to the allocation of saving, as already mentioned, the authors' message is clear: taxes play an important role in affecting the allocation of saving to different assets. This is an important point, and as also mentioned, it should have been taken a bit further by exploring the allocation of saving between the business and the household sectors as well as between tangible and intangible assets.

There is in fact another reason why the allocation of saving is important. This relates to our theme, namely the perspectives for Latin America. International capital markets can channel high levels of OECD saving to Latin America. Indeed, there seems ample scope for mutually advantageous intertemporal trade between the OECD and Latin America. In particular, if OECD countries whose population is ageing invest their pension savings in Latin America, both parties may well gain; the OECD countries would reap high returns on their saving while Latin America would benefit from higher investment and growth. The authors largely ignore the international aspects of taxation. This is a pity because tax policy in the OECD countries can affect net capital flows towards the non-OECD countries by affecting the allocation of saving within the OECD countries. For example, if the tax policy encourages OECD residents to invest in domestic rather than foreign assets by favouring owner-occupied housing, education, and consumer durables, this discourages capital outflows. Another example is provided by German tax law, which encourages firms to keep their pension reserves in their own firm in the form of book reserves. This reduces capital flows to young German firms and also to other countries. This shows how domestic tax policy may distort the international capital market. Indeed, tax policy favouring domestic investment may be one of the explanations for the finding by Feldstein and Horioka that saving and investment are rather closely correlated across countries.

Imperfections in Capital Markets

Another reason for this finding involves imperfections in capital markets, such as asymmetric information giving rise to credit rationing and agency problems. These capital market imperfections tend to be particularly relevant for small firms and poor households, especially in Latin America but also in the OECD countries. With imperfect capital markets, average, rather than marginal tax rates become more important. High average tax rates hinder investment by reducing cash flow. The authors do not pay much attention to capital market imperfections, although these imperfections are very important determinants of the welfare effects of capital income taxation. For that reason, neutrality may no longer be desirable in the presence of market imperfections, as second-best considerations call for particular policy interventions. At the same time, some non-neutral policies may exacerbate non-tax distortions. Indeed, capital market imperfections can be viewed as implicit taxes.

Capital market imperfections are relevant also because they do not conform to the textbook equivalence between taxation on expenditure and labour taxation. Moreover, they allow for an explicit role for tax policy in helping small firms and entrepreneurs with liquidity constraints.

Tax Design: The Case of Latin America

The paper contains a good discussion of the advantages and disadvantages of various tax systems. Unfortunately, the discussion remains a bit abstract. The authors should do two things to make their analysis more practical and timely. First, they should explore how the strengths and weaknesses of the various tax systems are affected by major developments like the globalisation of international capital markets and the deregulation of domestic financial markets. These developments are likely to put pressure on residence-based, comprehensive income taxes. In this connection, the choice between source- and origin-based taxes on the one hand, and destination- and residence-based taxes on the other hand, is likely to become increasingly important. Under source-based taxes, income (or cash-flow) that is earned within a country's jurisdiction is taxed. Under destination-based taxes, in contrast, consumption that occurs within a jurisdiction is taxed.

Finally, the authors should apply their analysis to Latin America. These countries would be well-advised to adopt a mixture of destination-based consumption taxes and source-based income taxes. An important argument in favour of a mix of both principles is that tax distortions would probably be smoothed out over various margins. Getting the revenue eggs from several baskets makes the overall tax system less vulnerable to efficiency losses and administrative problems.

Indeed, international differences in both types of taxes distort economic activity, but dissimilarly. In particular, international differences in destination-based taxes encourage cross-border shopping. Differences in origin-based tax rates, in contrast, provide multinationals with incentives to employ transfer prices and other financial constructions to shift their taxable profits to countries having low statutory tax rates. Moreover, these corporations are induced to move rents that are non-location specific to low-tax countries. Countries should balance the distortions induced by destination-based and origin-based taxes in such a way that the marginal costs of the two taxes are equalised.

As labour mobility increases, some coordination between Latin American countries is needed in selecting the best mix between destination-based and origin-based taxes. This is necessary in order to avoid arbitrage across different tax mixes. For example, if Brazil relies mainly on origin-based taxes, while Chile collects primarily destination-based taxes, individuals are encouraged to work in Chile, which levies low origin-based taxes, and spend their income in Brazil, which has low destination-based taxes. They can spend the money in Brazil during retirement or by sending their earnings to their families living in Brazil.

As far as the source-based income tax is concerned, it would be preferable to have a flat rate on investment income. This would allow capital taxes to be levied at the source through withholding. This counters tax evasion that is increasingly facilitated by the liberalisation and globalisation of international capital flows. The authors contend that a comprehensive income tax which, in principle, taxes both capital and labour income at a progressive rate, would be less regressive. In practice, however, many income taxes fail to tax high-income earners effectively because high incomes can exploit various tax-arbitrage opportunities. This erodes the revenue base and distorts the allocation of risk, property rights and corporate governance. Indeed, the most important advantage of a flat tax on capital income is that it would reduce tax arbitrage, something that becomes increasingly important as capital markets are liberalised. Indeed, while countries should adopt a mix between destination- and origin-based taxes, they should adopt consistent principles with respect to origin-based capital taxation. Indeed, several OECD countries have moved in this direction in recent years.

To protect their tax base, Latin American countries may have to agree on minimum source-based taxes on capital income. The centrally imposed floor on capital taxation must be rather low in order to prevent a substantial increase in the cost of capital in Latin America. If co-ordination with the rest of the world is possible, a somewhat higher rate may be feasible. In fact, the OECD may be able to play an important role in facilitating international co-operation in this area.

The Limits of Foreign Savings

Helmut Reisen

The current account deficits that this paper will address share three important common features. First, they are 'private-sector driven' in the (non-Ricardian) sense that they do not reflect government budget deficits. We look into four Asian and four Latin American countries that do not have public-sector deficits and that have received heavy capital imports over the 1990s. We thus ignore the public budget and assume full private capital mobility as given. We are thus obliged to view the current account not as a net export balance, as in the old elasticities approach, but as a private-sector savings-investment balance. Second, (apart from shortly ahead of currency crisis) the current account deficits are 'overfinanced', implying a positive overall balance of payments and rising levels of foreign exchange reserves. Third, a part of the deficit is financed by capital flows that are largely determined by cyclical factors, as has been generally the case for an important share of the emerging-market flows of the 1990s (see, e.g., Calvo, Leiderman and Reinhart, 1996). Their cyclical determination makes these flows akin to reversal.

The abundance of private capital flows confronts many Asian and Latin American authorities with a specific transfer problem. They have to make the basic decision of whether to accept or resist the capital inflow, or how much to accept or how much to resist. We aim to inform that decision, from the perspective of long-term development. Advice on *how* (if any) foreign savings should be resisted (macroeconomic restraint, sterilised intervention, capital controls, *et al.*) will not be given here. Likewise, it is not intended to advise authorities on financial crisis prevention (excellent surveys now abound; see Goldstein, 1996, for example).

The chapter is structured as follows. First, the benefits of foreign savings (rather than of gross capital mobility *per se*) are reviewed along different theoretical strands in the literature. The potential benefits of foreign savings are growth enhancement through higher investment and consumption-smoothing through risk sharing. We thus provide capsule summaries of neo-classical and new growth models as well as of the intertemporal approach to the current account. Second, we present and calibrate various notions of long-term sustainability of debt-augmenting capital flows, in view of a country's intertemporal solvency. Since large current account deficits will not be financed by foreigners forever, authorities need to know the required size and time profile of the subsequent adjustment back to payments balance. Third, since an unsustainable deficit is not necessarily an "excessive" deficit, the size of the current account deficit does not give rise to normative judgements; what matters, by contrast, is the *source* of the deficit. We make a case for resisting part of foreign savings when unsustainable currency appreciation, excessive risk-taking in the banking system and a sharp drop in private savings coincide. The policy response has then to strike a balance between the benefits of consumption-smoothing and of financing viable investment versus the economic costs of excessive private borrowing. A case can be made that foreign direct investment is less likely than other capital flows to stimulate excessive private consumption and to cause a real appreciation problem.

The Benefits of (Net) Capital Inflows

It will perhaps be surprising that the role for development that the economic literature assigns to foreign savings, rather than to capital mobility (and gross flows) *per se*, is fairly modest. This in stark contrast to the earlier "two-gap" literature (Chenery and Bruno, 1962; McKinnon, 1964), according to which growth was not only limited by a country's ability to save, but also by foreign savings to buy necessary imported inputs. Since the abundance of foreign exchange (rather than the scarcity) motivates this paper, we omit discussion of the two-gap literature. We can immediately move from structuralist to mainstream economic thinking.

Neo-classical Considerations

In the neo-classical general equilibrium framework, the benefits of capital inflows into (capital-) poor countries are essentially derived from divergences in the marginal productivity of capital. Labour in advanced countries is equipped with better and more capital than the workers in developing countries, and capital can be used more productively by being sent south.

The simplest of the neo-classical models, the two-country Kemp-MacDougall model (see, e.g., Lal, 1990) can provide some basic insights about the benefit of capital inflows as well as the optimal size of these inflows. Savings rates are constant and a fixed proportion of per capita income in both countries. The marginal product of capital is higher in the poor country than in the rich country in autarchy, and diminishing in both countries with rising capital/labour ratios. With perfect capital mobility, the poor country will benefit from capital inflows, until its marginal product of capital is equal to that of the rich country; both in turn determine (and are equal to) the world interest rate.

The size of the optimal net capital inflow rises with the difference between the autarchic marginal product of capital and the world interest rate, and falls the faster marginal capital productivity declines with a higher capital labour ratio. The poor country gains per capita income — the marginal output of capital times the capital inflow minus the income payments on the capital stock located at home. (The rich country, of course, gains as well from the capital export: the output loss due to capital relocation is more than compensated by interest and dividend payments). In the new, long-run equilibrium, output will grow at the same rate as in the closed economy.

The Kemp-MacDougall theory crucially assumes that the capital inflow is invested, not consumed, and that the capital ratio is raised by the inflow, until the steady-state capital ratio is reached. The inflow is not consumed, because the world interest rate exceeds the country's rate of time preference. This fulfils an important requirement of the full debt cycle, so that the deficits first incurred on trade and current accounts will give way to a trade surplus and later a surplus on current account. Concerns about debt stocks and the size of the financial and real transfer are unwarranted because they will adjust in a sort of automatic way. Foreign investors are assumed to bring in capital goods and take away part of the additional production, thereby resolving the transfer problem. The traditional neo-classical model thus seems more appropriate to describe FDI inflows than other capital flows.

Mere capital accumulation does not guarantee that a country will benefit from capital inflows; first, in the presence of sufficiently misguided policies, inflows can "immiserize"; and, second, an upward-sloping supply of capital will mean that the cost of capital inflows rises at the margin. Even on standard neo-classical grounds, governments can be justified to resist part of the capital inflows.

Models of "immiserizing" inflows have been developed by Bhagwati (1973), Johnson (1967), and Brecher-Diaz Alejandro (1977). Tariff-induced inflows of capital magnify the welfare losses due to distorted consumption and production patterns by stimulating capital accumulation in protected sectors and by attracting foreign capital into these sectors, if foreign capital receives the full (untaxed) value of its marginal product. As Calvo (1996) suggests, drastic structural reform in most capital importing countries has made the "immiserizing inflow" argument less relevant today in its original presentation. These reforms do not guarantee that countries have moved to Pareto optimum. Distortions persist that may stimulate private credit booms, for example, by maintaining high marginal tax rates with full deductability of interest payments. Moreover, distortions may be reintroduced in the case of a capital-outflow crisis.

There is also an 'optimum tariff'-type case for taxing capital inflows. Harberger (1985) suggests levying an optimal tax on foreign borrowing, if the recipient country faces an upward-sloping supply of credit, to equate its tax-inclusive average cost to the higher marginal cost. A related argument can be built for the group of capital-importing net debtor countries, if such a tax succeeds in improving their joint capital terms of trade by dampening interest rates.

Further evidence that capital inflows will not play a crucial role in the standard neo-classical framework comes from growth accounting (Krugman, 1993). Adding human capital accumulation to the standard Solow growth model, output growth can be written as

$$\dot{Y} = \alpha\dot{K} + \beta\dot{H} + (1 - \alpha - \beta)\dot{L} + \dot{\theta} \qquad (1)$$

where dots represent growth rates of output Y, physical capital K, human capital H and labour L, α and β are the physical and human capital shares in national income and θ is the growth rate of Solow residual. Mankiw, Romer and Weil (1992) have found that the three variables K, H and L of their augmented Solow model explain almost 80 per cent of the cross-country variation in income per capita of the full Summers/Heston country sample of 98 non-oil countries. Their estimates imply a physical capital share α of 0.31 and a human capital share β of 0.28. Taking an average capital/output ratio of 2.5 and an average current account deficit of 4 per cent of GDP (a stylised description of major capital importers), the Solow model would predict an increase in the growth rate of capital of 1.6 per cent; and the resulting increase in short-run growth of output would merely reach 0.50 per cent.

Implications of the Endogenous Growth Literature

Endogenous •-growth models, unlike neo-classical models which imply decreasing returns to capital, are characterised by the assumption of non-decreasing returns to the set of reproducible factors of production. Equation (1) becomes an endogenous growth model if $\alpha + \beta = 1$, so that

$$\dot{Y} = \alpha\dot{K} + \beta\dot{H} \qquad (2)$$

Equation (2) says that long-term growth can be explained entirely by growth in capital, without any appeal to a Solow residual. This implies external economies to capital accumulation: the elasticity of output with respect to capital greatly exceeds its share of GNP at market prices. Such externalities create a presumption that the benefits of capital inflows must be much higher than those stipulated by the standard neo-classical approach[1]. In the neo-classical growth model, countries benefiting from large inflows could see large increases in capital accumulation; their growth rates should peak on impact, to gradually reach the steady state. To change the growth rate of the capital recipient permanently, though, the inflow must not only lift the economy to a higher capital equipment (and income level), but it also has to change the economy's production function. In contrast with the Solow growth framework (where technological change is exogenously given), the new growth literature highlights the dependence of growth rates on the state of technology relative to the rest of the world. Despite the optimistic predictions of the endogenous growth model for the benefits of inflows, Cohen (1993) finds for a sample of 34 developing debtor countries that benefited from renewed access to the world financial markets in the seventies, capital accumulation was actually less than for other developing countries, an observation which is not explained by endogenous factors — the initial output per capita and the initial stock of capital. Rather, capital accumulation failed to increase because much of the capital inflow leaked into consumption.

For foreign direct investment flows, in contrast to debt-creating flows, the optimistic assessment of endogenous growth has been validated recently by Borensztein, De Gregorio and Lee (1995). They find in a cross-country regression framework for 69 developing countries over the period 1970-89 that for each percentage point of increase in the FDI-to-GDP ratio, the rate of growth to the host economy increases by 0.8 percentage points. The contribution of FDI to long-term growth results from two effects. FDI adds to capital accumulation, because it stimulates domestic investment, rather than crowding out domestic investment by competing in domestic product markets or financial markets. The complementarity of FDI and domestic investment is explained by their complementarity in production and by positive technology spillovers. The second growth effect of FDI stems from the embodied transfer of technology and efficiency, provided the host country has a minimum threshold stock of human capital; FDI can increase the growth rate of the host economy only by interacting with that country's absorptive capacity.

FDI flows, then, have the potential to speed up convergence through two channels. First, by stimulating capital accumulation (rather than consumption), FDI raises the initial starting ratio of poor country to rich country GNP, R. Second, by helping change a country's production function through introducing higher efficiency, FDI flows raise a country's growth rate and the differential between the poor country and rich country growth rate, D. The time to convergence (of per capita income between rich and poor countries), t, can be written as a function of R and D:

$$t = - (\ln R) / D \qquad\qquad (3)$$

What difference for the time to convergence does a rise in the FDI-to-GDP ratio make? Assuming R to be a fourth, and taking the above results by Borensztein and co-authors to mean that a rise in the FDI ratio will increase the growth differential by 0.8 percentage points from 2 per cent to 2.8 per cent, the time needed for convergence declines from 69 years to 50 years, a decline of 27 per cent.

It is also interesting to compare what difference a FDI flow makes in the neo-classical compared to the endogenous growth model. In the neo-classical model, only the level of GNP is affected, not its growth rate. Assuming capital's share in income α to be 0.31 (Mankiw, *et al.*, 1992) and a capital-output ratio of 2.5, the marginal product of capital is 12.4 per cent $(\alpha/K/Y)$. An inflow worth 4 per cent of GNP that only raises the initial starting ratio of poor country to rich county GNP will raise R from 0.25 to 0.26, producing little reduction in the time to convergence (from 69 to 67 years).

The Intertemporal Approach to the Current Account

In the models considered so far, the benefits of capital inflows are derived from net capital inflows that are fully invested and raise the level or the growth rate of GDP. However, the benefits of capital flows are not only derived from directing world savings to the most productive investment opportunities, but also from allowing individuals to smooth consumption over different states of nature by borrowing or diversifying portfolios abroad. Developing countries are likely to benefit greatly from the international pooling of country-specific risks that would result in intertemporal smoothing of consumption levels[2]. First, poor countries tend to be more shock-prone than richer ones; second, since per capita income is low, any downside adjustment will hurt more than in countries with higher consumption levels. Table 1 illustrates the point for five Latin American countries (for which data were easily available).

Table 1. **Gains from the Elimination of Consumption Variability**

Country	Annual per cent consumption gain[a]	Real GDP per capita, 1990[b] (US= 100)	Std. Dev. of GDP growth[c]
Argentina	1.94	19	4.83
Brazil	1.80	14	5.43
Chile	2.75	22	6.34
Mexico	0.54	29	3.77
Venezuela	2.22	30	4.65

a. Obstfeld (1993): The calculations assume that the logarithm of per capita consumption follows a random walk with trend and that individuals have generalized isoelastic utility functions with annual time discount factor 0.95, relative risk aversion parameter 1, and intertemporal substitution elasticity 0.25.
b. Heston and Summers (1993) ; GDP is PPP adjusted.
c. IADB, *Annual Report 1995*; the observation period is 1970-92 for annual real GDP.

In principle, the intertemporal approach to the current account can be helpful in answering the question of how much to accept (in terms of the size of the current account deficit) of capital flows offered by foreign investors. International capital mobility opens the opportunity to trade off present levels of absorption against future absorption; if saving falls short of desired investment, foreigners have to finance the resulting current account deficit, leading to a rise in the country's net foreign liabilities. The intertemporal approach views the current account as the outcome of forward-looking dynamic saving and investment decisions (Obstfeld and Rogoff, 1994), which are driven by expectations of future productivity growth, interest rates and other factors. Finally, the approach is able, in principle, to provide a benchmark for defining "excessive" current account deficits in the context of models that yield predictions about the equilibrium path of external imbalances (Milesi-Ferretti and Razin, 1996).

Without writing down the whole maximisation problem for the representative consumer (among the many assumptions necessary to produce behavioural predictions are intertemporal separability of preferences and perfect foresight; see Obstfeld and Rogoff, 1994), Table 2 collects some important predictions of the intertemporal approach to the (first-period) current account from the two impulses that have figured prominently in the discussion on the determinants of recent capital flows to emerging markets.

Table 2 yields some important insights about how the 'equilibrium' current account of the developing-country recipients should have responded to the drop in world interest rates, or, alternatively, to the reform-induced rise of productivity:

Table 2. **Current Account Effects Predicted by the Consumption-Smoothing Approach**

Shock	Temporary			Persistent		
	Saving	Investment	Current account	Saving	Investment	Current account
1. Drop in world interest rates below permanent average rate						
- Net debtor countries	+	0	+	not applicable		
- Net creditor countries	-	0	-			
2. Rise in productivity						
- Country-specific	+	0	+	-	+	-
- Global	+	0	+	+	+	0

Source: Discussions in Glick and Rogoff (1992), Obstfeld and Rogoff (1994) and Razin (1995).

— The capital-importing countries, being net foreign debtors, should have raised the saving rate in response to cyclical portfolio flows, which are interest-driven. The current accounts should have moved towards lower deficits (or into surplus) as people smooth consumption in the face of temporarily low interest payments. For net creditor countries, temporarily low interest rates would have resulted in opposite current account effects. If a net debtor country widens current account deficits in response to temporary interest rate reductions, the response may well destabilise rather than smooth the intertemporal consumption path.

— Likewise, the intertemporal approach does not necessarily predict widening current account deficits when capital flows are attracted by country-specific productivity surges. The "equilibrium" response of the current account depends crucially on the expectation of whether the productivity surge is temporary or permanent. In both cases, the productivity surge will raise output immediately, but only a persistent rise in productivity will cause permanent income to rise. The reason is that only a permanent productivity surge will induce investment and a higher future capital stock. The rise in permanent income will also cause consumption to rise more than output, resulting in a strong current account deficit as a result of lower saving and higher investment. A transitory increase in productivity, by contrast, should result in an opposite current account effect (a lower deficit), since there is no effect on investment and agents save part of any transitory increase of income (in the permanent income model of consumption).

239

— Productivity surges must not necessarily be interpreted as country-specific, but can be part of a broader global shock. A persistent productivity-enhancing shock common to all countries will raise the world rate of interest. This should dampen consumption in net debtor countries sufficiently to compensate for the consumption effects arising from higher permanent income brought about by higher investment. Since all countries cannot improve their current accounts, world interest rates rise until global savings and investment are balanced. A global transitory productivity shock will produce excess world saving and thereby exert downward pressure on interest rates. A temporary drop in world interest rates should result in lower current-account deficits for net debtor countries, as analysed above.

It is noteworthy that — among the capital-flow determinants discussed here — the intertemporal approach predicts a widening of current account deficits (for net debtor countries) only if the country enjoys a permanent idiosyncratic productivity boom. However, the predictive power of the intertemporal approach to the current account may remain very limited for developing countries, in spite of their higher financial openness. Heymann (1994) raises some important questions, notably in the context of recurrent episodes of private-sector overindebtedness: How plausible is the assumption of rational expectations during a period when there is a "regime change" in the economy? How correct can forecasts be about the expected value of future prices and quantities, and how realistic and binding is the intertemporal budget constraint to induce agents to plan according to these forecasts? Such questions raise deep doubts about the claim that "The intertemporal approach to the current account offers a viable framework for assessing macroeconomic policy" (Obstfeld and Rogoff, 1994).

The Evidence on Benefits

How much economic benefit have our sample countries derived from foreign savings? Have current account deficits been excessive in view of the benefits (on costs, see below)? Let us consult some data to confront the theories surveyed so far with them. Note that the standard neo-classical approach assumes that foreign savings are invested and that the investment will raise the country's capital ratio (with respect to labour). The country will import foreign savings as a function of the difference between the efficiency and the borrowing cost of investment. Table 3 shows that all sample countries should have benefited from foreign savings in principle, given the strong difference between efficiency and cost measures. That difference is particularly strong for Thailand, Malaysia and Chile; it is weaker for Mexico, Peru and the Philippines, with Argentina and Indonesia in between. Strikingly, labour was only equipped with more capital where capital was most efficient (Argentina, Chile, Indonesia, Malaysia and Thailand). By contrast, the capital-labour ratio fell strongly in Mexico during the inflow period, excluding any benefits there on standard neo-classical grounds.

Table 3. **Efficiency, Average Borrowing Cost and Capital-Output Rations**
(in per cent)

Country	Efficiency[a] avg. 1987-94	Real interest cost[b] avg. 1988-94	First year of inflow	Capital-labour ratio[c] % change up to 1993
Argentina	18.9	3.5	1991	+8.0
Chile	24.4	3.8	1990	+21.2
Mexico	13.2	4.3	1989	-23.1
Peru	n.d.	3.2	1992	-1.0
Indonesia	20.4	3.0	1990	+18.1
Malaysia	22.7	2.9	1989	+24.0
Philippines	13.5	3.0	1992	+1.2
Thailand	27.8	3.3	1988	+40.6

Sources: a. J.P. Morgan, *Emerging Markets Economic Outlook*, September 1995. Efficiency is defined here as the inverse of the investment rate to the real GDP growth rate.
b. World Bank, *World Debt Tables 1996*, Vol. 2. Defined as average terms of new commitments in US dollar terms minus US CPI inflation rate.
c. World Bank data files.

Figure 1 displays the Solow residual derived from estimating equation (1). We see marginal productivity rise during the inflow period, except in Peru, Indonesia and the Philippines (and in the G7 countries). The evidence gives some support for the presumption on standard neo-classical grounds, that foreign savings were highly beneficial if they were invested, above all in Thailand, Malaysia and Chile.

Figure 1. **Solow Residuals**

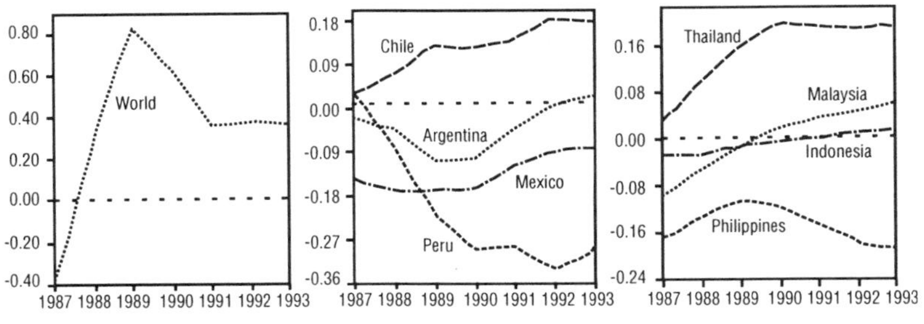

Sources: Author's calculations; IMF, National Accounts.

What happened to growth and convergence since the inflows started? Table 4 reports actually some decline for Mexico's and the Philippines' PPP adjusted per capita income, while the other recipient countries catch up strongly. We also observe, with the noticeable exception of Mexico and Peru, that the inflow period coincides with *actual* GDP growth rates that exceed our estimates of *potential* growth rates, which

241

refer to the period since the sample countries have "opened up" according to Sachs and Warner (1995). (The potential growth rates have been obtained by the simple peak-to-peak method, as will be explained below.) However, it is still too early to arrive at any solid judgement on whether the recent capital inflows have raised efficiency and the growth rate permanently.

Table 4. Income Growth and Convergence

Country	PPP estimates[a] of GNP per capita (US = 100)		Potential GDP growth rate since classified as "open" by Sachs/Warner[b]		Actual GDP growth rate since first year of inflow until 1995[c]
	1990	1994	Year	Growth potential	
Argentina	21.9	33.7	1991	4.3	5.4
Chile	29.0	34.4	1976	4.2	6.4
Mexico	28.0	27.2	1986	1.8	1.7
Peru	12.7	13.9	1991	7.8	5.9
Indonesia	11.0	13.9	1970	6.1	7.1
Malaysia	27.6	32.6	1970	6.5	8.9
Philippines	10.9	10.6	1988	2.6	3.8
Thailand	21.6	26.9	1960	7.2	9.7

Sources: a. World Bank, *World Development Report*, 1992 and 1996.
   b. Peak-to-Peak method; see text.
   c. JP Morgan, *World Financial Markets*, various issues.

How well then does the intertemporal approach explain actual current account balances in our eight sample countries? It is still too early, in view of the limited number of reliable observations of productivity developments in the sample countries for the recent capital-inflow period, to estimate investment and current-account equations for the individual sample countries[3]. We therefore present for the period 1988-93 panel estimates for the current-account equation

$$CA_t = b_0 + b_1 I_{t-1} + b_2 \Delta \theta^c_t + b_3 \theta^w_t + b_4 CA_{t-1} + b_5 TOT_t + b_6 r^w_t \qquad (4)$$

where CA is the current account deficit as a fraction of GDP, I is gross domestic investment as a fraction of GDP, θ^c and θ^w are domestic and global productivity (the Solow residual derived from Cobb-Douglas production functions), TOT is the terms of trade index, and r^w is the real US treasury bill interest rate (see Table 5, first panel).

The second panel estimate in Table 5 introduces a government budget reaction function similar to Summers (1988), where

$$BD_t = b_0 + b_1 (S^{pr} - I)_t \qquad (5)$$

the government budget deficit BD_t responds to changes in the balance between private savings S^{pr} and investment (all variables as a fraction of GDP). Equation (5) can be taken as evidence of current-account targeting, so that equation (4) has to be estimated in a simultaneous equation system.

As seen in Table 5, there is a strong negative correlation between the size of the private current account and the size of the budget deficit. The results for the current-account equation are largely the same, however, in the direct and the simultaneous panel estimate. All parameters show the expected sign as predicted in Table 2, but only global productivity enters significantly among the determinants stressed by the intertemporal approach.

Table 5. **Panel Estimates on Current-Account Equations, 1988-93**

(t = values in brackets)

1. $$CA_t = b_1 I_{t-1} + b_2 \Delta\theta^c_t + b_3\theta^w_t + b_4 CA_{t-1} + b_5 TOT_t + b_6 r^w_t$$

	-0.2	-0.02	-0.06	+0.6	-0.001	+0.01
	(-0.87)	(-0.14)	(-1.7)	(2.52)	(-1.02)	(0.31)

Estimation: Fixed effect model using OLS framework;

number of observations: 48 ; $R^2 = 0.59$; DW = 2.53

---

2. $$BD_t = b_1 (S^{pr} - I)_t$$

-0.4 $R^2 = 0.84$; DW = 1.48 ; number of obs. = 48
(-10.2)

$$CA_t = b_1 I_{t-1} + b_2 \Delta\theta^c_t + b_3\theta^w_t + b_4 CA_{t-1} + b_5 TOT_t + b_6 r^w_t$$

-0.1	+0.1	-0.1	+ 0.5	-0.001	+0.003
(-0.45)	(1.16)	(-2.54)	(3.42)	(-0.48)	(0.89)

$R^2 = 0.58$; DW = 2.62; number of obs. = 48

Estimation: Simultaneous equation system with GMM estimation (= 3 SLS).

Sources: Instrumental variable method was used; residuals were heteroskedastic-consistent.
Current account, gross domestic investment, terms of trade index: all World Bank data base.
US treasury bill interest rate minus change in CPI index/private savings: all IMF.
Domestic productivity, world productivity (GDP-weighted average for G7 countries) are Solow residuals from Cobb-Douglas production functions: all Wold Bank data base; national accounts.

The results in Table 5 lead to the tentative conclusion that econometric tests derived from the intertemporal approach to the current account cannot explain actual current account deficits in major capital-flow recipient countries. This means that either the observed current account deficits have been excessive, or that the benchmark (derived from the intertemporal approach) is ill-defined or insufficiently represented in our estimates. While global productivity (as defined in Table 5) has stagnated during the observation period 1988-93, country-specific productivity surges were observed in Argentina, Chile, Malaysia, Mexico and Thailand. These countries could be predicted by the intertemporal approach to run current account deficits, due to transitorily higher investment levels (and possibly lower saving rates), assuming that the productivity surges were permanent.

243

Table 6. **Saving-Investment Balances in Selected Countries**

Country	Change in annual averages as % of GDP from first year of inflow to 1994 against 1986 to first year of inflow[b]				Memo:		
	Current account	Investment	Saving	Private consumption	First year of inflow	Year when CA deficit peaked	Peak CA deficit[a], % of GDP
Argentina	-2.1	+0.4	-1.7	+4.2	1991	1994	3.5
Chile	+1.3	+4.3	+5.6	-0.2	1990	1993	2.1
Mexico[c]	-5.3	+1.8	-3.5	+5.8	1989	1994	7.8
Peru	-2.5	-0.8	-3.4	+3.9	1992	1995	6.4
Indonesia	+1.1	+4.6	+5.7	-4.3	1990	1996	4.0
Malaysia	-8.2	+8.8	+0.6	+2.4	1989	1995	8.5
Philippines	-2.4	+3.5	+1.1	+3.6	1992	1994	4.5
Thailand	-5.4	+11.8	+6.4	-5.6	1988	1995	8.3

Sources:
a. J.P. Morgan, *World Financial Markets*, Second Quarter 1996; data for 1995 are estimates and for 1996 forecasts.
b. Based on national account data; saving rates were derived as residual; IMF, *International Financial Statistics*.
c. IMF, *World Economic Outlook*, May 1995.

Table 6 explores the issue in more country detail by means of a simple shift analysis. The table (apart from the memo columns) is structured as Table 2 which summarised the main predictions of the intertemporal model. As Table 6 shows, the observed shift in savings-investment balances often does not suit the theoretical predictions:

— Argentina and Peru engage in excessive private consumption. Only a permanent rise in productivity, which should give rise to higher investment rates, or a temporary drop of actual output below potential could have justified the observed rise in private consumption rates. There is, however, no rise in observed investment rates, while actual output has been rising strongly.

— The Mexican story is slightly different, because output growth remained extremely low during the inflow period. There was some moderate rise in investment rates, but most of the switch in the current account balance was due to a private consumption boom. That boom could partly be justified by higher public savings, current income levels below potential, and expectations of higher permanent income (as indicated by higher investment); but the size of the switch in private consumption is clearly excessive.

— There is also a rise in private consumption, as a fraction of GDP, in Malaysia and the Philippines. The rise is compensated by a sufficient rise in public savings and validated by higher investment rates (indicating expectations of higher permanent income levels). It should be noted, however, that the rise in the Philippine investment rate goes along with a fall in the Solow residual (Figure 1) during the inflow period.

— Chile, Indonesia and Thailand respond to capital inflows with a drop in private consumption rates, although their output growth rises on impact above potential, although public savings rise (implying no Ricardian offset), and although a strong rise in investment rates and rising productivity would quite solidly warrant expectations of a higher permanent income. Note finally that Indonesia and Chile reduce their external deficit as a result of strong increases in savings. Indonesia is different from Chile and Thailand, however, in one respect: productivity (Figure 1) declines during the inflow period, suggesting a future drop in the country's investment rate and current account deficit.

The evidence suggests two lessons, one for theorists and one for practitioners. The insight for theory is that the intertemporal approach fails to predict the macroeconomic responses of most capital-flow recipient countries. In the case of Chile, the existence of effective capital controls may provide a part of the explanation for the failure of the intertemporal approach (which assumes full capital mobility). In the case of the other sample countries (for which full openness can be assumed), "excessive" private consumption (Argentina, Mexico, Peru) and "excessive" savings responses (Thailand) must be explained by the determinants not captured by the consumption-smoothing approach.

The insight for the practitioners is that current account deficits were excessive in Mexico and are probably more in Peru by 1996. Malaysia's and Thailand's deficits, although high, cannot be labelled as "excessive", however. They are used for investment which exploits high efficiency and rising total factor productivity; moreover, foreign savings are so far supported by rising national savings in these countries.

Long-term Sustainability

Debt Dynamics

It is a common fallacy to confuse unsustainability with undesirability. Foreign savings must not necessarily be resisted because they finance a current account deficit that is unsustainably large. In particular during reform episodes, a deficit may represent a sound stock adjustment from financial assets into real assets in the case of an investment boom, because the expected profitability of real assets has improved. The corresponding deficit in the current account will inevitably be temporary, yet desirable. This is a valuable lesson from the intertemporal approach.

Nonetheless, a large deficit will not be financed by foreigners forever; there will at one point inevitably have to be adjustment back to payments balance. It is thus not only important to know the *sources* of the current account deficit (see below), but also the *size* and the *time profile* of the balancing adjustment. And that makes long-term sustainability of the current account deficit a benchmark of which authorities should be aware.

Building on work by Milesi-Ferretti and Razin (1996) and Edwards, Steiner and Losada (1995)[4], let us first consider an economy in steady state, with liabilities as a fraction of the country's GDP that foreigners are willing to hold in equilibrium, denoted by d. d can be seen as an 'equilibrium portfolio share'. Note that foreign direct investment is *not* governed by portfolio considerations; multinational companies seek to internalise agglomeration benefits by concentrating (rather than diversifying) their FDI flows. Consequently, FDI flows will not be covered by the subsequent discussion on long-term sustainability. In equilibrium, i.e. with d to be held constant, the country can accumulate net liabilities, equal to both the current account deficit plus net accumulation of international reserves, as a fraction of GDP, CA and FX, in proportion to its long-run GDP growth, γ.

$$CA + \Delta FX = \gamma d \qquad (6).$$

Long-run GDP growth also exerts two indirect effects on the steady state current account that is consistent with a stable debt-to-GDP ratio. First, as the economy expands, the desired level of international reserves will also grow. The literature on the demand for international reserves has empirically identified two different determinants (Heller and Khan, 1978). The first is the level of imports (not the import ratio, which is ambiguous), with an elasticity of demand for reserves close to unity. The second is the variability in the balance of payments which, by creating uncertainty, increases the demand for reserves. We ignore the uncertainty in the balance of payments, which is difficult to forecast; yet, it can in principle be incorporated into the analysis, by making predictions about the coefficient of variation from the time trend in the foreign reserve ratio. Denoting real annual import growth by η, the change in the desired reserve ratio can be written as

$$\Delta FX = [(1 + \eta)/(1 + \gamma)]FX - FX \qquad (7).$$

Incorporating (7) into (6) yields

$$\gamma d = CA + [(\eta - \gamma)/(1 + \gamma)]FX \qquad (8).$$

A second channel through which GDP growth indirectly impacts on debt dynamics is the Balassa-Samuelson effect. In the long run, *relative* growth will lead to real exchange rate appreciation, largely driven by the evolution of productivity differentials between the traded and non-traded goods in the domestic economy and in the rest of the world. Real exchange rate appreciation per unit of GDP growth, denoted by ε, reduces both debt and foreign exchange reserves as a fraction of GDP, so that equation (8) is enlarged to

$$(\gamma + \varepsilon)d = CA + [(\eta + \varepsilon - \gamma)/(1 + \gamma)]FX \qquad (9).$$

Equation (9) describes the steady-state current account deficit that can be sustained over the long run if the debt ratio remains constant and desired reserves are raised in proportion to import growth:

$$CA = (\gamma + \varepsilon)d - [(\eta + \varepsilon - \gamma)/(1 + \gamma)]FX \qquad (9').$$

Table 7 provides numerical examples of equation (9') for four Latin American and four Asian countries. The variables d (total external debt/GDP) and FX (international reserves/GDP) refer to 1995 estimates as given in JP Morgan, *World Financial Markets* (March 29, 1996). The variables γ, ε, and η, ideally, should be estimated on the basis of best guesses about *future* trends.

Table 7. **Debt-Related Current Account Deficits in Steady State**

Country	CA	$= (\gamma+\varepsilon)d^*$	-	$[(\eta+\varepsilon-\gamma)/(1+\gamma)]FX^*$	Memo: d	FX
Argentina	0.016	(0.043+0.007)0.5	-	[(0.318+0.007-0.043)/1.043]0.035	0.33	0.050
Chile	0.020	(0.042+0.006)0.5	-	[(0.069+0.006-0.042)/1.042]0.114	0.34	0.220
Mexico	-0.006	(0.018+0.000)0.5	-	[(0.126+0.000-0.018)/1.018]0.140	0.68	0.058
Peru	0.038	(0.078+0.009)0.5	-	[(0.152+0.009-0.078)/1.078]0.065	0.51	0.127
Indonesia	0.030	(0.061+0.004)0.5	-	[(0.073+0.004-0.061)/1.061]0.099	0.54	0.088
Malaysia	0.017	(0.065+0.014)0.5	-	[(0.111+0.014-0.065)/1.065]0.396	0.42	0.291
Philippines	-0.006	(0.026+0.001)0.5	-	[(0.112+0.001-0.026)/1.026]0.166	0.59	0.087
Thailand	0.028	(0.072+0.010)0.5	-	[(0.133+0.010-0.072)/1.072]0.197	0.48	0.192

* See text for explanation.

247

For γ, we estimate the potential real GDP growth rate for two periods, for 1960-95 and for the countries' respective period of "openness" as classified by Sachs and Warner (1995). Since GDP can be seen as the result of a transformation of key factors of production, a theoretically appropriate way to estimate potential GDP is to feed the available volume of factor inputs in the business sector into a numerically specified production function. However, even small estimation errors for the individual parameters of the production function (output elasticities; rate of technical progress; degree of slack) can add up quickly to produce rather implausible estimates for potential output. We thus opt for a very simple approach, which only uses actual GDP data as input for the derivation of potential GDP estimates, the so-called *peak-to-peak method*.

In a first step, we identified the peak of actual GDP in each cycle and connected these data points by interpolation. The procedure is applied for two different observation periods, for 1960-95 (for Malaysia 1970-95) and since the countries' opening until 1995. For Argentina and Peru, Sachs and Warner (1995) classify the year of opening as 1991, for the Philippines 1988, for Mexico 1986 and for Chile 1976; in the other cases the observation periods coincide. We use annual GDP data, except for Peru and the Philippines where good quarterly data are available and where the reform period is relatively short. The resulting GDP series can be seen as an approximation of the highest attainable level of output at any given point in time.

In a second step, we calculated the average ratio of actual GDP to the highest attainable GDP for each cycle — a measure for the 'normal' degree of slack in the eight economies — and applied this ratio to the series of highest attainable GDP to derive estimates for potential GDP. The *annual growth rate* of potential GDP is then obtained by regressing the series of potential GDP on a time trend. The results show largely plausible parameter values, except possibly for Mexico and the Philippines where the opening of the economy actually seems to have reduced the growth rate of potential GDP relative to the total observation period. For want of any better estimates, the growth rates of potential GDP obtained for the period since reform are used in Table 7.

For ε, we rely on Larraín (1996) who has estimated with the Instrumental Variables Method the determinants of real exchange rates (viz. the dollar) for a sample of 28 Asian and Latin American countries through the period 1960-90. The impact of GDP relative to the US level on real exchange rates is corrected for other determinants, namely government spending, degree of openness and terms of trade. The calculation of ε, the annual 'equilibrium' real exchange rate appreciation is not only driven by the annual growth rate of potential GDP, but also by the country's relative income level. Since the relationship between real exchange rates and relative GDP levels is non-linear, a given estimate for the growth rate of potential GDP will lead to more real equilibrium exchange rate appreciation at higher relative income levels; witness the difference, for example, between Malaysia and Indonesia.

248

Finally, estimates about the future annual real import growth rate, η, are simply extrapolated out of the reform-period sample for each country. Argentina's annual import growth may seem implausibly high, but it has to be recognised that Argentina is still a very closed economy in terms of the import ratio m and that the potential for natural trade (Mercosur) is far from exhausted.

Table 7 displays the calibration of equation (9') for the long-run equilibrium current account ratio which holds debt and reserve levels steady in terms of GDP. Since a high debt ratio can be sustained by a larger deficit in the current account than a smaller debt ratio, we assume for all sample countries that foreign investors are comfortable with tolerating a debt ratio of 50 per cent. This is at about the level in Peru or Thailand, countries about which the financial press has started to worry recently. Likewise, for the foreign exchange reserves we assume a target level of half the import ratio (six months of imports) for all countries. Note that because of low estimates of potential growth rates, neither Mexico nor the Philippines can afford a steady-state deficit in the debt-related current account.

Table 8 considers a hypothetical adjustment of the current debt-GDP ratio to 0.5 and of foreign exchange reserves to a target level of half the import-GDP ratio. The resulting 'transitional' current account deficits vary largely across countries. To reach the targeted debt-GDP and reserve levels within five years, Mexico would have to run a current-account *surplus* worth more than five per cent of GDP (excluding the part financed by FDI). Chile, by contrast, could enjoy a five-year period of current-account *deficits* (plus FDI) of five per cent of GDP to find herself at the imposed levels of debt stocks and foreign exchange levels.

Table 8. **Transitional Current Account Deficits**
(five-year adjustment to d*= 0.5 and FX*= 0.5m)

Country	1/5CA	=	d*-(1-γ-ε)d	-	|FX*-((1-η-ε)/1+γ)FX|
Argentina	0.0367	=	0.1865	-	0.0027
Chile	0.0515	=	-0.1763	+	0.0813
Mexico	-0.0516	=	-0.1678	-	0.0902
Peru	0.0136	=	0.0344	+	0.0338
Indonesia	-0.0045	=	-0.0049	-	0.0173
Malaysia	-0.0087	=	0.1132	-	0.1569
Philippines	-0.0330	=	-0.0741	-	0.0908
Thailand	0.0032	=	0.0594	-	0.0435

*   See text for explanation.

Table 9 displays the various concepts for actual, cyclically corrected, FDI-corrected, steady-state and transitional current deficits for the year 1994 (the last year for which FDI data were available). Then, taking account of FDI and cyclical correction (the residual), current account deficits were higher than steady-state deficits in Argentina, Mexico and the Philippines. By contrast, high-deficit countries such as Malaysia and Thailand were clearly within long-term sustainable ranges.

Table 9. **Various Concepts of Current Account Balances**
(in per cent of GDP)

	Memo: Actual 1994	Cyclical correction	-	FDI	=	Residual	Memo: Steady-state	Memo: Transitional
Arg	-3.5	-3.0	-	0.4	=	-2.6	-1.6	-3.7
Chi	-1.5	-1.5	-	3.6	=	+2.1	-2.0	-5.2
Mex	-7.8	-7.1	-	2.2	=	-4.9	+0.1	+5.2
Per	-4.5	-3.5	-	4.7	=	+1.2	-3.8	-1.4
Ind	-1.6	-0.4	-	1.3	=	+0.9	-3.0	+0.5
Mal	-5.9	±0.0	-	6.5	=	+6.5	-1.7	+0.9
Phi	-4.4	-4.3	-	1.5	=	-2.8	+0.6	+3.3
Tha	-5.9	-1.1	-	3.1	=	+2.0	-2.8	-0.3

Note: The cyclically corrected deficit corrects imports for the difference in actual and potential GDP.

Problems with Excessive Current Account Deficits

The benefits of foreign savings — consumption-smoothing and growth of income — will not materialise when current account deficits represent excessive current consumption or when foreign funds are misallocated. A hard landing to payments balance will thus be unavoidable. We have first to recall, however, some arguments of those who think that excessive consumption and unsound investment surges are unlikely to happen in the absence of public-sector deficits and distortions.

The Lawson Doctrine

Commenting on concerns over the UK balance of payments in a speech to the IMF, the UK Chancellor Nigel Lawson concluded in September 1988 (a year before a deep crisis with falling output and surging unemployment set in): "we are prisoners of the past, when UK current account deficits were almost invariably associated with large budget deficits, poor economic performance, low reserves and exiguous net overseas assets. The present position could not be more different". What came to be internationally known as the Lawson doctrine, is a proposition that has been most eloquently expressed by Max Corden (1977; and, with some qualifications, 1994):

"The current account is the net result of savings and investment, private and public. Decentralised optimal decisions on private saving and investment will lead to a net balance — the current account — which will also be optimal. There is no reason to presume that governments or outside observers know better how much private agents should invest and save than these agents themselves, unless there are government-imposed distortions. It follows that an increase in a current account deficit that results from a shift in private sector behaviour should not be a matter of concern at all. On the other hand, the public budget balance is a matter of public policy concern and the focus should be on this." (Corden, 1994).

The fact, however, that large current account deficits reflected primarily a private-sector saving-investment imbalance did not prevent private capital markets from attacking currencies in Chile (early 1980s), in the UK and the Nordic countries (late 1980s) and in Mexico and Argentina (mid 1990s). So what was wrong with the Lawson doctrine?

— *First*, in a forward-looking rational-expectations framework, current account balances are always the result of private-sector decisions, with or without public-sector deficits. With Ricardian equivalence, a public budget deficit will immediately stimulate private savings to pay for future taxes. People who subscribe to the Lawson doctrine are thus saying that they do not believe in Ricardian equivalence (they believe in optimal private-sector decisions, but not in rational expectations). In fact, the Ricardian offset coefficient has been estimated to average 0.5 for developing countries (Edwards, 1995); other things being equal, a deterioration in the current account worth 5 per cent of GDP thus would require the public-sector deficit to worsen by 10 per cent of GDP.

— *Second,* current private-sector liabilities are often contingent public-sector liabilities. Foreign creditors may force governments, as happened in Chile after 1982, to turn private-sector debt into public-sector obligations. Furthermore, private-sector losses tend to be absorbed eventually by the public sector, either in terms of tax revenue foregone or through costly resolutions of banking crises, in particular when financial institutions are deemed 'too large to fail'. Balance-of-payments and financial crises are often caused by common factors, such as domestic financial liberalisation, implicit deposit insurance or exchange rate-based stabilisation plans (Kaminsky and Reinhart, 1996).

— *Third,* observed and expected returns to saving and investment are distorted by various market failures: *a)* Private borrowers do not internalise the rising marginal social cost of their private borrowing that arise from the upward-sloping supply of foreign capital (Harberger, 1985). *b)* Excessively optimistic expectations about permanent income levels after major changes in the policy regime lead to over-borrowing, because financial market institutions fail as efficient information conduits between depositors and borrowers (McKinnon and Pill, 1995). Financial market bubbles add to such boom mentality by discouraging private savings through the wealth effect.

— *Fourth,* a movement into current account deficit may lead to an unsustainable appreciation in the real exchange rate. The appreciation is in conflict with development strategies based on the expansion of exports and efficient import substitution, which centrally relies on a reliable and competitive exchange rate. Overvalued exchange rates cause sub-optimal investments which are costly to reverse, undermine active trade promotion, export diversification and productivity growth and breed capital flight. Large swings in real exchange rates, often a result of temporary capital flows, have been found to significantly depress machinery and equipment investment and thus long-run growth performance (Agosin, 1994).

— *Fifth* (as now also stressed by Corden, 1994), markets are concerned with country risk and do look at a country's total debt ratio. Therefore, the current account as a whole, and not just the sources of its changes, become relevant. Once debt ratios and current account deficits exceed certain levels (see above), decentralised decision making can lead to excessive borrowing from a national point of view (again, due to the Harberger externality), particularly when increased borrowing is for consumption rather than for investment.

Table 10 displays three hard-landing episodes in Latin America where the required switch in the current account went along with sharp drops in real GDP, even sharper cuts in private per capita consumption, and often strong depreciation in real exchange rates. During the bust, the benefits of consumption-smoothing and growth enhancement through foreign savings do indeed ring hollow.

Table 10. **Corrections of Private-Sector Driven Current Account Deficits**

Country	Year (period ag.)	Current account % of GDP	Real GDP Growth % p.a.	Real priv. cons. % p.a. per cap.	RER appreciation % p.a.
Chile	1980	-7.1	7.8	1.5	22.0
	1981	-14.5	5.6	2.4	8.4
	1982	-9.5	-14.1	-12.4	-20.6
	1983	-5.6	-0.7	-5.1	-20.4
Mexico	1993	-6.5	0.6	-2.1	5.8
	1994	-7.8	3.5	3.7	-3.7
	1995	-0.3	-6.9	-9.2	-28.1
Argentina	1993	-2.9	6.0	1.2	7.4
	1994	-3.5	7.4	3.7	1.7
	1995	-0.8	-4.4	-9.2	0.4

Sources: IMF, *International Financial Statistics*; J.P. Morgan, *World Financial Markets*; own calculations.

Private Spending Booms

As defined above, large current account deficits may represent "excessive" private consumption, as was suggested above for Argentina, Mexico and Peru. The empirical link between consumption booms, surges in bank lending and subsequent banking crises is well documented (Gavin and Hausmann, 1996). Therefore, payments deficits owing to private spending booms suggest great risks to the public sector — risks of tax revenue losses and costly bank crisis resolutions, as documented by Table 11.

Table 11. **Episodes of Systemic Banking Crises with Heavy Capital Inflows**

Country	Scope of crisis	Cost of rescuing banks, % of GDP
Argentina 1980-82	16% of assets of commercial banks; 35% of total assets of finance companies	55.3
Chile 1981-83	45% of total assets	41.2
Israel 1977-83	Entire banking sector	30.0
Finland 1991-93	Savings banks affected	8.2
Mexico 1995-?	Commercial banks past due to gross loan ratio reaches 9.3% in February 1995	12-15

Sources: Bank for International Settlements, *63rd Annual Report*, 1993; G. Caprio and D. Klingebiel (1996).

While it seems obvious that such costs imposed on the public sector suggest that governments engage in some stabilising measures to moderate private spending booms (restrictive fiscal policies or credit restrictions for private borrowers), it is less straightforward that the resistance to large current account deficits is part of such measures. Distortions should be corrected at the source; the twin payment and banking crises seem to originate in either domestic financial deregulation, implicit deposit insurance, or protracted exchange rate-based stabilisation plans:

— Since the 1980s, the link between banking crises and balance-of-payments crises has strengthened. Kaminsky and Reinhart (1996) trace 71 balance-of-payments crises and 25 banking crises during the period 1970-95; while they report only 3 banking crises vs. 25 balance-of-payments crises during 1970-79, they find 22 banking crises vs. 46 payments crises over 1980-95. They find that financial liberalisation (which occurred mostly since the 1980s) plays a significant role in explaining the probability of a banking crisis preceded by a private lending boom. A banking crisis, in turn, helps to predict a currency crisis. There is also clear evidence for the OECD countries that quick and extensive financial deregulation has tended to lower household savings by lessening liquidity constraints (Blundell-Wignall and Browne, 1991). While most of that drop in private savings could be interpreted as a temporary stock adjustment to a higher consumption path, there is evidence that household saving rates have remained low, unless financial deregulation occurred gradually or already in the 1950s and 1960s (Andersen and White, 1996).

— Information asymmetries, reinforced by the lack of institutions that monitor and supervise credit risk, produce moral hazard and adverse selection. Firms with a high risk-return profile have an incentive to borrow heavily, as their exposure is limited by bankruptcy laws. Consumers incur excessive debt when they feel that their debt is not comprehensively monitored. In principle, banks and other intermediaries may attempt to reduce credit risk through credit rationing. This would set a limit to the extent to which liberalisation can ease liquidity constraints. But when the government insures deposits against adverse outcomes, it alters how the banking system views the risks associated with making loans — it introduces moral hazard. This results in higher bank lending, which in turn can underpin excessively optimistic expectations about the success of reform (McKinnon and Pill, 1995)[5].

— Exchange rate-based stabilisation plans have often been accompanied by a boom in bank lending, which in turn has fuelled a boom in consumption spending. Unlike under money-based stabilisation, disinflation produces a rise in real-money balances, as a result of central bank intervention to peg the currency and of higher money demand as domestic wealth holders convert their assets back into domestic currency. The unsterilised intervention on the foreign exchange market is fully intermediated into the banking system. This allows a boom in credit to agents who have been rationed previously as a result of inflation and financial repression (Sachs, 1996; Reisen, 1993). Subsequently, overvaluation due to inflation inertia will cause recession and a deterioration of bank assets as a result of non-performing loans and lower asset prices.

While the source of these private spending booms is domestic and not the fact that they are financed by foreign savings, we have to ask whether foreign savings do worsen the boom (Corden, 1994). In the absence of foreign capital inflows, the spending boom would manifest itself not in a current account deficit, but in higher interest rates. The critical question, then, is what kind of investment would be crowded out by the rise in domestic interest rates. With ineffective bank supervision (as a result of too rapid financial deregulation, for example), the average productivity of borrowing may decline as risk-averse investors withdraw from the pool of potential borrowers. The failure to finance productive investment would be the cost of the decision not to accept capital inflows; the excess of the risk-adjusted domestic interest rate over the world interest rate would be a measure of the distortion created by that decision. The result on the decision whether to accept or resist inflows would be ambiguous.

In the McKinnon-Pill model the closed-economy financial market failure is reflected in higher financial yields, but its effect on quantities — borrowing and consumption — is ambiguous, depending on offsetting income and substitution effects. Excessively optimistic expectations about future permanent income levels, resulting in both over-consumption and over-investment, are financed by excessive borrowing from the rest of the world. The distortion (crazy expectations; boom mentality) is reinforced by foreign savings. The McKinnon-Pill solution to the distortion is similar to a Pigou-Harberger tax (nominally, a reserve requirement on foreign deposits) so as to incite the optimal choice between consumption-smoothing and excessive borrowing.

The first-best solution to the boom distortion triggered by exchange rate-based stabilisation is to announce, at the start of the stabilisation plan, that a peg will be temporary, to be followed by more nominal exchange rate flexibility. While this is easier said than done, it will not do away with the immediate remonetisation and real exchange rate appreciation that characterise the first phase of disinflation. Temporary support from selective controls on short-term capital controls may well be needed (Hausmann and Reisen, 1996).

The Real Appreciation Problem

If the scope for sterilised intervention is limited or exhausted[6] and if foreign savings are partly spent on nontradables, a protracted current account deficit will be associated with real appreciation of the exchange rate. But there is no mechanical link between the size of the deficit and the size of appreciation. To the extent that the shift in the current account balance represents higher investment, the increased resource transfer is likely to be spent on additional imports of capital goods and intermediate goods. In such a case, the real transfer will be 'effected' largely through the transfer of purchasing power, with little effect on relative prices. But when the current account deficit largely represents a consumption boom, the transfer of purchasing power will not solve the real transfer problem by itself, since a large part of the additional purchasing power is likely to fall on nontradables. In such cases, a shift in relative prices — a real appreciation of the exchange rate in the recipient country — will be necessary. This lesson from the inter-war transfer debate is fully supported by Table 12.

The table suggests that the real appreciation problem only appeared when capital inflows were mostly consumed rather than invested, as was noted for Argentina, Mexico and Peru. The degree of 'unwarranted' appreciation (the residual) is derived from data in the UN Income Comparison Project, as reported in the World Bank's *World Development Reports*. What is known as the Balassa-Samuelson effect, is that poor countries tend to be 'cheap' in PPP terms, since services tend to be cheaper in poor countries. In fact, there is a strong non-linear correlation between the PPP-adjusted per capita income of a country relative to the US and the deviation of the currency below PPP (Reisen, 1993). Already in 1990, neither Argentina nor Peru had been 'cheap' countries in PPP terms as determined by their comparative per capita income. Since then, however, their currencies have strongly appreciated, as did the Mexican peso until 1994. Only a small part of that appreciation (in Mexico's case, none) is due to the "catch-up" effect: the fact that relative growth (compared to US levels) will lead to trend appreciation of the real exchange rate. The table again employs the results obtained by Larraín (1996). The 'residual' appreciation is likely to be in conflict with development strategies based on the expansion of exports and efficient import substitution, which centrally relies on a reliable and competitive exchange rate, similar to the "Dutch disease" effects of a major discovery of natural resources (Edwards and van Wijnbergen, 1989).

Table 12. **Consumption, Import Structure and Real Exchange Rate Appreciation**

Country	Change in domestic saving rate since inflows started (from Table 6)	Degree of undervaluation (US = 100) Current vs. PPP-adj. income per cap.			Catch-up effect	Residual (Change minus catch-up effect)
		1990	1994	Change		
Argentina	-1.7	50	93	+43	8	35
Chile	+5.6	31	40	+9	3	6
Mexico	-3.5	32	60	+28	0	28
Peru	-3.4	42	59	+17	1	16
Indonesia	+5.7	24	24	±0	1	-1
Malaysia	+0.6	38	41	+3	7	-4
Philippines	+1.1	31	35	+4	0	4
Thailand	+6.4	30	35	+5	5	0

Sources: World Bank, *World Development Report*, 1992 and 1996 ; Larraín (1996).

Is Foreign Direct Investment Special?

From 1970 to 1982, Singapore ran a current account deficit worth 12.1 per cent of GDP on average; in the early 1970s, the deficit peaked at around 20 per cent of GDP several times. Almost half of the corresponding net capital inflows consisted of foreign direct investment (FDI). Real GDP growth averaged more than 8.6 per cent per year over the period; the domestic saving rate doubled from 21 per cent in 1970 to more than 40 per cent in 1982; a balance-of-payments crisis never developed. Such anecdotal evidence is supported by Frankel and Rose (1996), who find in a panel of annual data for over 100 developing countries from 1971 through 1991 that a high ratio of FDI to debt is associated with a low likelihood of a currency crash. This raises the question whether FDI is special with respect to its macroeconomic implications. There is a strong presumption that indeed it is:

— First, foreign direct investment is largely determined by non-cyclical considerations. Being rather governed by long-term profitability expectations, it is less subject to sudden shifts in investor sentiment. While on an annual basis, large fluctuations of foreign-direct-investment *flows* are regularly observed, foreign-direct-investment *stocks* are largely illiquid and irreversible[7]. Foreign direct investment, which is little dependent on financial market sentiment, has bad-weather qualities. This observation is reinforced by Mexico's capital account in 1995, which showed only a slightly reduced net inflow of foreign direct investment.

— Second, the Harberger externality does not apply to foreign direct investment. Even if the supply schedule of FDI was upward-sloping, FDI is likely to produce positive external spillovers, comparable to agglomeration benefits. This conjecture implies that higher inflows of FDI will carry positive externalities, by improving the host country's production function (Borensztein *et al.*, 1995). Moreover, returns on FDI are state-contingent and sovereign risk seems to apply less than to other forms of foreign capital inflows. As a result, foreign investors do not observe an upper limit of engagement, in contrast to debt ratios and the like.

— Third, to the extent that FDI is not induced by privatisation (which represents, other things being equal, just a change in ownership), FDI inflows will exert less upward pressure on the real exchange rate, minimising the risk of 'Dutch disease' (see Table 13). Since FDI is likely to crowd in domestic investment and to the extent that it is 'green plant' investment, it will stimulate a corresponding movement in the demand for foreign exchange by stimulating imports. Moreover, by stimulating investment rather than consumption, FDI creates an *ex ante* home goods excess supply in the recipient country; equilibrium in the home goods market requires a depreciation of the real exchange rate to stimulate the demand for home goods (Artus, 1996).

Table 13. **Foreign Direct Investment and Privatisation, 1990-94**

	Latin America	East Asia (excl. China)
Net Private Capital Inflows, $ billion	173.8	110.0
- of which: raised through privatisation	22.2	3.8
Net Foreign Direct Investment Inflows, $ billion	71.3	47.2
- of which: raised through privatisation	13.0	2.0
"Traditional" Foreign Direct Investment, $ billion	58.3	45.2
% of "Traditional" FDI in Net Inflows	33.5	1.1

Sources: World Bank, *World Debt Tables 1996;* own calculations.

Conclusions

This chapter has first surveyed several theoretical strands in the economic literature for their hypotheses regarding the benefits of *net* capital inflows (as opposed to capital mobility and gross capital flows). Perhaps surprisingly, in the current context of heavy portfolio flows and non-binding foreign exchange constraints (which were emphasised earlier on by the two-gap literature), the benefits of large net inflows are mostly found to be small.

Even if net capital inflows were fully invested rather than consumed, neo-classical growth models do not promise grandiose benefits. The resulting rise in the capital ratio will only affect short-term growth, not a country's long-term growth rate, as long as capital flows do not affect the production function. But even such modest benefit may not be realised, when capital flows are immiserising due to distortions, or when the rising marginal costs of foreign borrowing are not appropriately factored in by the economic agents. Endogenous growth models promise more (but they do not promise large capital flows to capital-poor countries when marginal capital returns are non-decreasing). The requirement for high benefits is, however, that capital flows carry externalities that improve a country's efficiency, externalities which can only be exploited when a certain level of human capital is already present in the country.

The intertemporal approach to the current account identifies circumstances that justify welfare-enhancing current account deficits. Among the determinants for recent capital flows to emerging markets, however, the approach predicts a large current account deficit only when a country-specific productivity surge will raise permanent income. Permanent productivity increases and technological spillovers emphasised by the new growth literature are most likely embodied in foreign direct investment inflows to a largely undistorted economy.

We here provide illustrations of references against which to judge the size of actual current account deficits to determine their long-term sustainability. It was found that actual deficit numbers alone cannot provide information about long-term sustainability. Any judgement would need to consider debt-GDP ratios (current versus tolerated by investors), official foreign exchange reserves (current versus targeted), the potential GDP growth rate, import growth, the Balassa-Samuelson effect, and the structure of capital inflows. Sustainability considerations do not make sense for FDI flows, as long as there is no widely held notion about the sustainability of net foreign liabilities for the stock of FDI invested in a country.

The size of the current account deficit does not give rise to normative judgements; a deficit worth 3 per cent of GDP may be 'excessive' in one country, while a deficit worth 12 per cent of GDP may be justified for another country. What distinguishes such deficits is not so much whether they are driven by public-sector or private-sector decisions, since there is some evidence for a Ricardian offset and since private debt is a contingent public-sector liability. What matters for governments is, by contrast, the source of the current account deficit. Some foreign savings should be resisted when they are seen to finance excessive consumption or unproductive investment.

How much foreign savings should be resisted in such a case? The answer depends primarily on the nature of the source that ultimately gives rise to a spending boom and on the structure of the capital inflow. Private spending booms mostly originate in prior domestic deregulation, in the interaction of implicit or explicit deposit insurance with an existing boom mentality, and in disinflation brought about by exchange rate-based stabilisation. Resisting foreign savings is thus not necessarily a first-best policy response. If more nominal exchange rate flexibility, effective prudential regulation and bank supervision and gradual domestic financial reform succeed in keeping private savings rates stable and productive investment financed, all the better. If, by contrast, unsustainable currency appreciation, excessive risk-taking in the banking system and a sharp drop in private savings coincide, there is a case for resisting foreign capital inflows. The policy response has then to strike a balance between the benefits of consumption-smoothing and financing viable investment and the risks of excessive borrowing.

A case can be made for the open economy to accept all foreign direct investment, unless it creates new distortions as a result of new trade restrictions and as long as it can be absorbed by the existing stock of human capital. Foreign direct investment has staying power; it is little constrained by considerations of sovereign risk and portfolio limits from the perspective of the investor; and by crowding in domestic investment and having a minor initial effect on consumption (possibly unless privatisation-induced), foreign direct investment is unlikely to generate a real appreciation problem.

Notes

1. However, if returns to capital are constant, then the rate of return on capital will not be decreasing in the capital-labour ratio. There is thus no incentive in the endogenous-growth model for capital to flow from rich to poor countries, because returns on capital need not be larger in poor countries (Krugman, 1993).

2. The benefits of portfolio diversification are particularly present in the case of fully-funded pensions. Ageing industrial countries can escape part of the demographic problems by investing in emerging markets, while poor countries can diversify away some of their idiosyncratic risks stemming from higher exposure to country-specific shocks by investing some of their pension assets in industrial countries (Reisen, 1994a; Reisen, 1996a).

3. Individual country estimates for the period 1970-90, following the reduced-form regression in Glick and Rogoff (1992), do not find a significant impact of domestic productivity on changes in the current account. It should be noted, however, that Glick and Rogoff are only able to obtain a low level of explanatory power in their estimates on current-account determinants for even the industrial countries. The R^2 in their individual country time-series regressions range between 3 and 49 per cent, indicating an incomplete model.

4. We ignore interest payments on outstanding debt and the resource transfer (the non-interest current account) here to keep the focus on the sustainable current account deficit. The loss of information is minor to the extent that average interest costs do not vary largely across the sample countries.

5. In other words, bank lending supports excess credibility of liberalisation and stabilisation programmes. Earlier, when liberalisation was seen as temporary (a hypothesis which does not seem apt to describe existing policy regimes in the capital-importing countries), it was *lack* of credibility which could explain temporary spending booms as residents exploited a 'window of opportunity' (Calvo, 1987).

6. On sterilised intervention in Asia and Latin America, see Reisen (1994b).

7. Using quarterly balance-of-payments flow data for changes in *net* claims of FDI, portfolio equity, "long-term" and "short-term" flows, Claessens *et al.* (1995) find that capital-account labels do not provide any information about the volatility of the flow. In particular, they argue that FDI and long-term flows are not more persistent than others. However, the primary policy concern here is with *reversals* of foreign investment of large magnitude, a concern not addressed by Claessens and co-authors who base their analysis on quarterly time-series properties of net, rather than gross, inflows.

Bibliography

AGOSIN, M.R. (1994), "Saving and Investment in Latin America", *UNCTAD Discussion Papers*, No. 90.

ANDERSEN, P.S. and R.W. WHITE (1996), "The Macroeconomic Effects of Financial Sector Reforms: An Overview of Industrial Countries", mimeo, Bank for International Settlements, Basle.

ARTUS, P. (1996), "Le financement de la croissance par endettement extérieur", *Document de travail No. 1996-05/T*, Caisse des dépôts et consignations, Paris.

BANK FOR INTERNATIONAL SETTLEMENTS (1993), *63rd Annual Report*, Washington, D.C.

BHAGWATI, J.N. (1973), "The Theory of Immiserizing Growth: Further Applications", in M.B. CONNOLLY and A.K. SWOBODA (eds.), *International Trade and Money*, Toronto University Press, Toronto.

BLUNDELL-WIGNALL, A. and F. BROWNE (1991), "Macroeconomic Consequences of Financial Liberalisation: A Summary Report", *ESD Working Paper No. 98*, Organisation for Economic Co-operation and Development, Paris.

BORENSZTEIN, E., J. DE GREGORIO and J-W. LEE (1995), "How Does Foreign Direct Investment Affect Economic Growth?", *NBER Working Paper No. 5057*, National Bureau of Economic Research, Cambridge, MA.

BRECHER, R.A. and C.F. DIAZ ALEJANDRO (1977), "Tariffs, Foreign Capital, and Immiserizing Growth", *Journal of International Economics*, 7.4.

CALVO, G. (1987), "On the Costs of Temporary Policy", *Journal of Development Economics*, 27.

CALVO, G. (1996), "Varieties of Capital-Market Crises", *Working Paper No. 15*, Center for International Economics, University of Maryland at College Park.

CALVO, G., L. LEIDERMAN and C. REINHART (1996), "Inflows of Capital to Developing Countries in the 1990s", *Journal of Economic Perspectives*, 10.2.

CAPRIO, Jr., G. and D. KLINGEBEIL (1996), "Bank Insolvency: Bad Luck, Bad Policy, or Bad Banking?", The World Bank, Washington, D.C.

CHENERY, H.B. and M. BRUNO (1962), "Development Alternatives in an Open Economy: the Case of Israel", *Economic Journal*, 57.

CLAESSENS, S., M.P. DOOLEY and A. WARNER (1995), "Portfolio Capital Flows: Hot or Cold?", *The World Bank Economic Review*, 9.1.

COHEN, D. (1993), "Convergence in the Closed and in the Open Economy", in A. GIOVANNINI (ed.), *Finance and Development: Issues and Experience*, Cambridge University Press, Cambridge.

CORDEN, W.M. (1977), *Inflation, Exchange Rates and the International System*, Oxford University Press, Oxford.

CORDEN, W.M. (1994), *Economic Policy, Exchange Rates and the International System*, Clarendon Press, Oxford.

EDWARDS, S. (1995), "Why are Saving Rates So Different Across Countries?: An International Comparative Analysis", *NBER Working Paper No. 5097*, National Bureau of Economic Research, Cambridge, MA.

EDWARDS, S., R. STEINER and F. LOSADA (1995), "Capital Inflows, the Real Exchange Rate and the Mexican Crisis of 1994", mimeo, The World Bank, Washington, D.C.

EDWARDS, S. and S. VAN WIJNBERGEN (1989), "Disequilibrium and Structural Adjustment", in H. CHENERY AND T.N. SRINIVASAN (eds.), *Handbook of Development Economics*, Vol. 2, Elsevier, Amsterdam.

FRANKEL, J. and A.K. ROSE (1996), "Currency Crashes in Emerging Markets: Empirical Indicators", *NBER Working Paper No. 5437*, National Bureau of Economic Research, Cambridge, MA.

GAVIN, M. and R. HAUSMANN (1996), "The Roots of Banking Crises: The Macroeconomic Context", *Working Paper Series 318*, Inter-American Development Bank, Washington, D.C.

GLICK, R. and K. ROGOFF (1992), "Global versus Country-Specific Productivity Shocks and the Current Account", *NBER Working Paper No. 4140*, National Bureau of Economic Research, Cambridge, MA.

GOLDSTEIN, M. (1996), "Presumptive Indicators/Early Warning Signals of Vulnerability to Financial Crises in Emerging-Market Economies", mimeo, Institute for International Economics, Washington, D.C.

HARBERGER, A. (1985), "Lessons for Debtor-Country Managers and Policymakers", in G.W. SMITH and J.T. CUDDINGTON (eds.), *International Debt and the Developing Countries*, The World Bank, Washington, D.C.

HAUSMANN, R. and H. REISEN (eds.) (1996), *Securing Stability and Growth in Latin America: Policy Issues and Prospects for Shock-Prone Economies*, Organisation for Economic Co-operation and Development, Paris.

HELLER, H.R. and M.S. KHAN (1978), "The Demand for International Reserves Under Fixed and Floating Exchange Rates", *IMF Staff Papers* 25.4, Washington, D.C.

HESTON, A. and R. SUMMERS (1993), *The Penn World Table: An Extended Set of International Comparisons, 1950-1988*, Cambridge, MA.

HEYMANN, D. (1994), "En la interpretacion de la cuenta corriente", *Economia Mexicana*, 3.1.

JOHNSON, H. (1967), "The Possibility of Income Losses from Increased Efficiency or Factor Accumulation in the Presence of Tariffs", *Economic Journal, 77.*

KAMINSKY, G. and C.M. REINHART (1996), "The Twin Crises: The Causes of Banking and Balance-of-Payments Problems", *Working Paper No. 17,* Center for International Economics, University of Maryland at College Park.

KRUGMAN, P. (1993), "International Finance and Economic Development", in A. GIOVANNINI (ed.), *Finance and Development: Issues and Experiences,* Cambridge University Press, Cambridge.

LAL, D. (1990), "International Capital Flows and Economic Development", in M. SCOTT and D. LAL (eds.), *Public Policy and Economic Development: Essays in Honour of Ian Little,* Clarendon Press, Oxford.

LARRAÍN, G. (1996), "Productividad del gasto publico y tipo de cambio real", in F. MORANDE (ed.), *Estudios empiricos de tipo de cambio real in Chile,* CEP/ILADES Georgetown University, Santiago de Chile.

MACDOUGALL, G.D.A. (1960), "The Benefits and Costs of Private Investment from Abroad: A Theoretical Approach", *Economic Record, 36.*

McKINNON, R. (1964), "Foreign Exchange Constraints in Economic Development and Efficient Aid Allocation", *Economic Journal, 74.*

McKINNON, R. and H. PILL (1995), "Credible Liberalizations and International Capital Flows", mimeo, Stanford University.

MANKIW, N.G., D. ROMER and D.N. WEIL (1992), "A Contribution to the Empirics of Economic Growth", *Quarterly Journal of Economics,* 107.2.

MILESI-FERRETTI, G.M. and A. RAZIN (1996), "Sustainability of Persistent Current Account Deficits", *NBER Working Paper No. 5467,* National Bureau of Economic Research, Cambridge, MA.

OBSTFELD, M. (1993), "International Capital Mobility in the 1990s", *NBER Working Paper No. 4534,* National Bureau of Economic Research, Cambridge, MA.

OBSTFELD, M. and K. ROGOFF (1994), "The Intertemporal Approach to the Current Account", *NBER Working Paper No. 4893,* National Bureau of Economic Research, Cambridge, MA.

RAZIN, A. (1995), "The Dynamic-Optimizing Approach to the Current Account: Theory and Evidence", in P. KENEN (ed.), *Understanding Interdependence: The Macroeconomics of the Open Economy,* Princeton University Press, Princeton, NJ.

REISEN, H. (1993), "Integation with Disinflation: Which Way?", in R. O'BRIEN (ed.), *Finance and the International Economy, 7,* The Amex Bank Review Prize Essays, Oxford University Press, Oxford.

REISEN, H. (1994a), "On the Wealth of Nations and Retirees", in R. O'BRIEN (ed.), *Finance and the International Economy, 8,* The Amex Bank Review Prize Essays, Oxford University Press, Oxford.

REISEN, H. (1994b), *Debt, Deficits and Exchange Rates*, Edward Elgar Publishing Limited, Aldershot.

REISEN, H. (1996a), "Liberalizing Foreign Pension Fund Investment: Positive and Normative Aspects", forthcoming, *World Development*.

REISEN, H. (1996b), "Managing Volatile Capital Inflows: The Experience of the 1990s", *Asian Development Review*, 14.1.

SACHS, J. and A. WARNER (1995), "Economic Reform and the Process of Global Integration", *Brookings Papers on Economic Activity*, 1.

SACHS, J., A. TORNELL and A. VELASCO (1996), "Financial Crises in Emerging Markets: The Lessons from 1995", *NBER Working Paper No. 5576*, National Bureau of Economic Research, Cambridge, MA.

SUMMERS, L. (1988), "Tax Policy and International Competitiveness", in J.A. FRENKEL (ed.), *International Aspects of Fiscal Policies*, University of Chicago Press, Chicago.

WORLD BANK (1992, 1996), *World Development Report*, Washington, D.C.

A Comment by Assaf Razin

Reisen's paper adds to the growing literature which seeks an answer to the question: Are persistent current account deficits sustainable? The paper follows the right track. It argues: *1)* a distinction should be made between external deficits which reflect high consumption spending and high investment spending; *2)* if greater rate exchange rate flexibility, prudential regulation and bank supervision succeed in keeping the saving rate from falling, and ensure that social returns to low-risk investments are high, then deficits can be sustained for long periods; *3)* and with FDI flows domestic investment could be crowded in with small adverse effects on domestic savings.

The paper consists of three parts associated with those issues. It blends theory and illustrative evidence but overlooks a number of issues. In a recent paper (Milesi-Ferreti and Razin, 1996; see also Frenkel, Razin, and Chi-Wa Yuen, 1996, Chapters 7 and 17), we distinguished between cases in which *i)* protracted current account deficits are associated with severe domestic macroeconomic problems, and *ii)* when they are not, but may still reflect an external problem.

In cases of the first type, the macroeconomic imbalances *per se* would be an indicator of the "unsustainability" of current policy, and therefore of an impending domestic crisis, such as runaway inflation or public sector insolvency. The crisis may also have an adverse external dimension, with (partial) default on external obligations. A policy reversal designed to address these domestic imbalances would in all likelihood reduce external problems as well. Public sector imbalances, for example, may be the driving force of a high inflation process, as well as creating fiscal solvency problems. In the presence of imperfect substitution between private and public savings, they could also be associated with large external imbalances. However, with a high degree of substitution between private and public savings, fiscal imbalances would be an indicator of domestic problems, rather than impinging on current account sustainability.

In cases of the second type, the evaluation of current account sustainability is more complex, because there is no clear "policy reversal" needed to address some domestic macroeconomic problem (for example, the fiscal balance may be in surplus and inflation under control).

Structural Indicators

Investment/savings. The current account balance is determined by the difference between national savings and domestic investment. For a given current account balance, the *levels* of savings and investment can have implications for the sustainability of the external position, for a given current account imbalance. High levels of investment, *ceteris paribus*, imply higher future growth through the build-up of a larger productive capacity, and therefore enhance intertemporal solvency. High savings and investment ratios can also act as a signal of creditworthiness to international investors, because they act as a form of commitment to higher future output and thus raise the perceived ability to service and reduce external debt. Higher investment would be reflected in a higher present value of output (a higher Y), reducing default risk.

The discussion above assumes that investment is necessarily growth-enhancing and that it increases the ability to repay external debt. Investment projects, however, may be chosen inefficiently, because of financial market distortions or because they are driven by political priorities. For example, relative price distortions may skew investment towards the nontraded goods sector, therefore failing to enhance a country's ability to generate future trade surpluses. Therefore, one should look not only at "excessive consumption" but also at "excessively risky investment" in gauging external weaknesses.

Economic growth. Countries with a high growth rate can sustain persistent current account deficits without increasing their external indebtedness relative to GDP. Thus far we have emphasised how the accumulation of physical capital through investment enhances a country's ability to service its external obligations; the same role is played by other engines of economic growth, such as the accumulation of human capital and increases in total factor productivity.

The sectoral composition of growth may be an additional indicator of potential external difficulties. In particular, low export growth could reflect an exchange rate misalignment, which may point to the need for a policy reversal. A related argument is that a high level of foreign trade can imply a more diversified input base for production in a small open economy, and hence higher productivity growth. A positive impact on productivity can also come from access to technology embodied in internationally traded goods.

Openness and trade. The degree of openness can be defined as the ratio of exports to GDP. A country must produce traded goods to obtain foreign exchange for servicing and reducing its external indebtedness. Clearly, countries with a large export sector can service external debts more easily, because debt service will absorb a smaller fraction of their total export earnings. A country must shift resources towards the export sector to generate foreign exchange for servicing external debt in case of an interruption in capital flows. Since this shift cannot occur instantaneously a sharp reduction in imports may become necessary, which will have adverse consequences on the domestic industries relying on imported inputs (Sachs, 1985 and Sachs and

MODERN HOTELS

Level "A"

Scott

Avda. Rius i Taulet, 1-3 08004 BARCELONA
Telf. (93) 426 22 23 Fax (93) 425 50 47

I have your
Suitcase up in
the Graciela Room

Warner, 1995). This reduction in imports may be more costly in a relatively closed economy because it is more likely to entail cuts of "essential" imported inputs (Williamson, 1985).

Insofar as debt default is associated with trade disruptions (such as difficulties in obtaining export credits) it may be more costly for an open economy. The constituency opposing actions that would entail trade disruptions is also likely to be stronger, the larger the size of the export sector. Higher costs of default would reduce the likelihood of sudden reversals of capital inflows, because foreign investors will perceive the country, *ceteris paribus*, as less risky.

How is the vulnerability to external shocks related to the degree of openness and the composition of trade? Obviously a more open economy is more vulnerable to external shocks such as fluctuations in the terms of trade or foreign demand shocks, *ceteris paribus*. In this regard, vulnerability is reduced by a well diversified commodity composition of trade. Fluctuations in commodity prices have a larger impact on the terms of trade of countries with a narrow export base, especially when they are highly dependent on raw material imports, thus weakening their ability to sustain current account deficits. Ghosh and Ostry (1995) found support for the view that large current account deficits are more likely to be unsustainable in countries with a less diversified export base in the context of a model based on precautionary savings. Mendoza (forthcoming) presents evidence that the *volatility* of terms of trade is associated with lower economic growth in a wide sample of countries.

Composition of external liabilities. The composition of external liabilities may have an impact on a country's ability to absorb a shock smoothly. In general terms, we can distinguish between "debt" and "equity" instruments. In principle, equity financing allows asset price adjustments to absorb at least part of negative shocks, so that part of the burden is borne by foreign equity investors. In contrast, a country with foreign currency debt bears most of the burden, provided it does not default. The structure of equity and debt liabilities is also important in order to evaluate a country's vulnerability to shocks. With regard to equity, it is often argued that portfolio investment is potentially more volatile than foreign direct investment. The vulnerability of debt to shocks is affected by its maturity structure, currency denomination and whether it carries fixed or floating interest rates. The risk of external shocks is increased by short-term maturities, foreign currency denomination and variable interest rates because they magnify the impact on the debt burden.

Financial structure. The links between the structure of the financial sector, macroeconomic policy and the likelihood of financial crises have been extensively researched recently, following the resumption of large capital flows to developing countries in the early 1990s and the Mexican crisis of 1994-95 (see, for example, Rojas-Suárez and Weisbrod, 1995; and Goldstein, 1996). In developing countries, financial intermediation is typically dominated by banks: bank deposits are the most important form of private savings and bank loans the main source of finance for firms. The disciplinary effect of competition with alternative forms of financial intermediation is limited, and therefore the role of bank supervision is critical. The fact that it is more likely that banks will be bailed out by the central bank (government), relative to other financial institutions, can also imply more risk-taking behaviour in a bank-dominated financial system. Problems are likely to occur when the central bank itself is involved in direct lending, financed through high reserve requirements, because of the conflict this implies with an arm's length supervision role. The quality of bank portfolios can also be affected by political influence on lending decisions, for example, to state-owned enterprises.

As underscored by Goldstein (1996), the central bank's ability to exercise its role as a lender of last resort is limited when the exchange rate regime is not flexible. Under these circumstances, monetary policy is "tied to the mast" because of the need to defend the exchange rate peg, making the banking system more vulnerable to sudden reversals in capital flows.

Capital account regime. When the capital account is very open, *de jure* or *de facto*, a country is more vulnerable to sudden reversals in the direction of capital flows. Such reversals can involve domestic as well as foreign capital. Clearly, the degree of *de facto* opening of the capital account is endogenous, and depends in particular on the strength of the incentives to export capital (risk-adjusted rate of return differentials due to domestic policy misalignments, political instability etc.). Capital controls are a distortion that puts a wedge between rates of return on capital in the domestic economy and abroad. They can also affect the consistency of the macroeconomic policy stance: for example, capital controls can allow a government to pursue temporarily an expansionary monetary policy with a fixed exchange rate, thereby weakening the current account. An open capital account can provide a disciplining device, since this policy inconsistency would result in the collapse of the peg. A related argument is that an open capital account could serve as a signal of a country's commitment to the pursuit of "sustainable" policies, and thereby raise foreign investors' perception of the country's creditworthiness. This would contribute to reducing the cost of capital for the country and/or to increasing the supply of foreign funds. On the other hand, economic research and practical experience have also highlighted the potential dangers associated with poor financial supervision and a weak banking system when the capital account is open (see, for example, Diaz-Alejandro, 1985).

In sum, capital account openness *per se* is an ambiguous indicator of current account sustainability. While greater openness increases the exposure to adverse external shocks, it also offers a disciplining role for domestic policies.

Macroeconomic Policy Stance

Degree of exchange rate flexibility and exchange rate policy. Reisen emphasises that the degree of exchange rate flexibility in response to external shocks can contribute to explaining the ability of an economy to sustain current account deficits. A rigid exchange rate regime buffeted by external shocks may be the target of speculative attacks that precipitate an external crisis (see Krugman, 1979; and Flood and Garber, 1984). In this context, the level of the real exchange rate is an important indicator of sustainability. A persistent real exchange rate appreciation can be driven by "fundamental" factors such as high productivity growth in the traded goods sector, or favourable terms-of-trade shocks. However, in the context of a fixed or managed exchange rate system, it could reflect a fundamental inconsistency between the monetary policy stance and exchange rate policy, giving rise to "overvaluation".

In this case, the overvaluation would typically be maintained by high domestic interest rates and/or by the presence of capital controls. An overvalued exchange rate would encourage a decline in savings as domestic residents substitute present for future consumption. It can also cause a decline in economic activity, both because of the high interest rates needed to maintain the exchange rate peg and because the traded goods sector is "priced out" of world markets. These effects would contribute to a widening of current account imbalances and loss of foreign exchange reserves. The drain of foreign reserves can be reinforced by expectations of a future devaluation that encourage capital outflows. Finally, the weakening of the export sector hinders the ability of the country to sustain external imbalances.

There is also the possibility, however, that a real exchange rate appreciation would result from large capital inflows; to the extent that these are not driven by long-term fundamentals, they can result in an overvaluation. Weaknesses in domestic financial intermediation and supervision can hinder the efficient allocation of capital inflows between consumption and investment, and contribute to the overvaluation.

In practice, however, it is difficult to make an operational definition of real exchange rate overvaluation in the absence of a well-established framework of real exchange rate behaviour. In developing countries that have undertaken structural reforms, a real exchange rate appreciation may reflect increases in productivity and in the return to capital. If current account deficits also emerge because of the underlying increase in permanent income, this would not be an indicator of unsustainability.

Fiscal balance. In order to examine the relation between fiscal and external imbalances, Reisen begins with a benchmark "debt neutrality" case (Barro, 1974), where there is no correlation between the public sector deficit and current account imbalances: the current account is independent of the time profile of taxation, and therefore of the budget deficit. Among other things, the debt neutrality result relies on the fact that consumption depends only on lifetime income and that taxes are not distortionary. Distortionary taxes would have an effect on the level of output and investment, and would therefore affect the current account. Furthermore, if consumption depends also on disposable income, for example, because some consumers are unable to borrow on the same terms as the government, lower current taxes would induce higher consumption (see Jappelli and Pagano, 1994). Similarly for the firms, an effective easing of borrowing constraints associated with lower current taxes could induce an increase in investment. Analogous effects would obtain if future tax obligations are not expected to fall entirely on current period taxpayers.

269

All the effects discussed so far imply, among other things, imperfect substitutability between private and public savings and a positive correlation between budget deficits and current account deficits. The discussion also suggests that the strength of this correlation may depend on the degree of development of domestic financial markets. In countries with underdeveloped or highly regulated financial markets we would expect to find stronger links between the fiscal stance and the current account balance, and therefore between government solvency and current account sustainability.

The degree of private sector saving offset by a given increase in public sector saving may also depend on the level of public debt (Sutherland, 1995). With low public debt the current generation could view a future debt stabilisation policy (via fiscal surpluses) as remote, thus the future tax liabilities are perceived to be small and fiscal adjustments affect aggregate demand and savings. In contrast, with high public debt the future debt stabilisation looks imminent and debt neutrality is at full force. The link between the twin deficits may therefore be stronger the lower is the level of public debt. Another implication of this line of reasoning is that the effects of fiscal stabilisation on aggregate demand are weaker the greater is the public debt burden.

To sum up, in the presence of high substitutability between private and public savings, large budget deficits may signal fiscal sustainability problems, but would be only weakly related to current account developments. With low substitutability between private and public savings, there would instead be a correlation between fiscal and external sustainability.

Current account deficits are not sustainable if a continuation of the current policy stance and the current private sector behaviour is going to entail the need for a drastic policy shift (such as a sudden policy tightening causing a major recession), or an external financial crisis (such as an exchange rate collapse leading to inability to service the debt). It will be necessary to build on the work of Reisen and other authors to untangle the complex economic fundamentals that could provide an "early warning signal" of the need for shifting policy.

Bibliography

BARRO, R.J. (1974), "Are Government Bonds Net Wealth?", *Journal of Political Economy*, 82, November.

DIAZ-ALEJANDRO, C.F. (1985), "Good bye Financial Repression, Hello Financial Crash", *Journal of Development Economics*, 19, September-October.

FRENKEL, J., A. RAZIN with C.-W. YUEN (1996), *Fiscal Policy in the World Economy*, 3rd Edition, MIT Press, Cambridge, Mass.

FLOOD, R. and P. GARBER (1984), "Collapsing Exchange Rate Regimes: Some Linear Examples", *Journal of International Economics*, 17.

GHOSH, A.R. and J.D. OSTRY (1995), "The Current Account in Developing Countries: A Perspective from the Consumption Smoothing Approach", *World Bank Economic Review*, 9, May.

GOLDSTEIN, M. (1996), "Presumptive Indicators/Early Warning Signals of Vulnerability to Financial Crises, in Emerging Market Economies", mimeo, Institute for International Economics, January.

JAPPELLI, T. and M. PAGANO (1994), "Saving, Growth and Liquidity Constraints", *Quarterly Journal of Economics*, 109, February.

KRUGMAN, P. (1979), "A Model of Balance-of-Payments Crises", *Journal of Money Credit and Banking*, 11.

MENDOZA, E.G. (forthcoming), "Terms of Trade Uncertainty and Economic Growth: Are Risk Indicators Significant in Growth Regressions?", *Journal of Development Economics*.

MILESI-FERRETI, G.M. and A. RAZIN (1996), *Current Account Sustainability*, Princeton Studies in International Finance, University Press, Princeton, NJ.

ROJAS-SUÁREZ, L. and S. WEISBROD (1995), "Financial Fragilities in Latin America: the 1980s and the 1990s", IMF Occasional Paper No. 132, Washington, D.C., October.

SACHS, J. (1985), "External Debt and Macroeconomic Performance in Latin America and East Asia", *Brookings Papers on Economic Activity*, 1, Washington, D.C.

SACHS, J. and A. WARNER (1995), "Economic Reform and the Process of Global Integration", *Brookings Papers on Economic Activity*, 1, Washington, D.C.

SUTHERLAND, A. (1995), "Fiscal Crises and Demand: Can High Public Debt Reverse the Effects of Fiscal Policies?", CEPR Discussion Papers, No. 1246, September.

WILLIAMSON, J. (1985), "Comments on Sachs", *Brookings papers on Economic Activity*, 1, Washington, D.C.

Promoting Savings in Latin America: Some Insights

Helmut Reisen

The Seventh International Forum on Latin American Perspectives not only debated whether to promote savings in Latin America, it also succeeded in designing savings-enhancing policies. Very much as an investor — who cannot predict the rate of return on a specific asset — diversifies his investments, the policy maker who observes the lack of consensus among economists about the growth-savings nexus, who knows that eastern Asia did not wait for growth to stimulate savings but that it actively promoted them, or who simply wants to sustain high growth through high investment rates but shies away from the risks implied by foreign savings to finance investment, will want to diversify his policy instruments by targeting higher growth and higher savings simultaneously. East Asia did not experience a temporary drop in savings as a result of structural reform: consequently, a trade-off between targeting savings and targeting growth did not materialise there.

Price Stabilisation

It is often held that Latin America's record of high inflation explains the region's low level of savings (and investment), because wealth risks being confiscated in a bout of unexpectedly high inflation. However, while substantial progress has been made in Latin America in bringing inflation down, the process of price stabilisation has depressed savings even further unless stabilisation was money-based. Exchange rate-based stabilisation plans have often been accompanied by a boom in bank lending, which in turn has fuelled a boom in consumption spending. Unlike under money-based stabilisation, disinflation produces a rise in real-money balances, as a result of central bank intervention to peg the currency and of higher money demand after disinflation sets in. The unsterilised intervention on the foreign exchange market is fully intermediated into the banking system. This allows a boom in credit to agents who have been rationed previously as a result of inflation and financial regression. Inflation inertia leads to an overvalued exchange rate which further depresses savings as residents intertemporally substitute present for future consumption.

Monetary policy in Latin America can thus promote savings by opting for money-based rather than exchange rate-based stabilisation, which implies a higher degree of nominal exchange rate flexibility than has been observed in many countries of the region. However, a restrictive monetary policy under floating exchange rates does not only imply the control of domestic monetary aggregates, but it also operates through an exchange rate appreciation. The problem of monetary policy in Latin America is thus the optimal rate of inflation and the optimal speed of disinflation towards such rate. Under almost unrestricted capital mobility, a savings-enhancing policy is wise not to be overambitious and single-minded with inflation targets in the low-level single-digit rate.

Financial-Sector Reform

In the past, Latin American financial systems could be characterised as bank-dominated, low-confidence systems with high corporate-to-household liquidity ratios and low savings rates. Recent reform, however, has increased confidence in the domestic financial system which has been reflected in a large rise of financial savings placed in Latin America. Notwithstanding earlier theories that predicted a positive savings response to deregulated (typically higher) interest rates and financial deepening, financial reform in Latin America has, as in many OECD countries, resulted in a drop of private savings rates.

We have learned, meanwhile, that savings-enhancing financial reform has to avoid the rise of excessive risk taking in the banking system, to slow the removal of liquidity constraints and to reduce the transaction costs for low-income savers to access profitable savings instruments. The pace of financial reform should therefore not exceed a country's capacity to build appropriate institutions that monitor and supervise credit risk within a newly established framework of prudential regulation. Comprehensive monitoring of consumer lending, tight credit lines for mortgage lending, the credible removal of bank deposit insurance and the enforcement of bankruptcy claims against ailing debtors should help avoid any substantial expansion in consumption, mortgage and high-risk corporate lending. In order to tilt the balance of financial reform further towards raising the national savings rate, a dense network of accessible financial institutions, such as the postal savings banks common to many East Asian countries or public savings institutions as in continental Europe should be seriously considered. Such institutions will help to raise the confidence of low-income savers that they can expect reliable and decent returns for thrift.

While pension reform (from pay-as-you-go to fully-funded schemes) is justified on many grounds other than savings, some governments aim to raise their country's savings rate with such reform. However, the hope for pension reform to enhance savings is at times based on a misreading of Chile's experience where the reform *per se* did not contribute much to the impressive rise of the country's savings rate; the transition from an unfunded to a funded system of old-age security was more tax-financed than seems possible in the rest of Latin America, and it was the growth- and incentive-induced rise in corporate savings that explains most of Chile's higher savings. Moreover, cross-country evidence does suggest that the importance of funded pension assets (as a fraction of GDP) and a country's savings rate is not significantly different from zero. Several explanations can be advanced for the lack of pension reform to stimulate savings: high returns on pension assets require a lower rate of savings for achieving a targeted pension level (inducing early retirement); the rise of pension assets stimulates the supply of loanable funds, facilitating household access to consumer and mortgage lending credits; funded pensions, implying greater credibility of future pension benefits than in unfunded systems, reduce the need for precautionary savings. Consequently, for pension reform to result in high savings it must be heavily tax financed, mandatory with high contribution rates and be accompanied by liquidity constraints in the rest of the financial sector. Singapore and Switzerland, where these requirements have been met, have indeed combined a high importance of pension assets with a high national savings rate, in contrast to most Anglo-Saxon countries.

Public Savings

While public savings have increased significantly in most of Latin America, the corresponding decline in private savings has denied many countries in the region a rise in total domestic savings. Most estimates of the Ricardian offset coefficient put it at 50 per cent for Latin America, meaning that private savings tend to decline by 50 cents for every dollar by which public savings increase. An important finding, however, is that the average Ricardian offset coefficient conceals two very different saving responses to fiscal policy for normal times, and for crisis periods, respectively. Unlike in OECD countries, fiscal policy behaves very procyclically in Latin America, largely due to financial distress during crisis periods. This implies a Ricardian offset coefficient much higher than average during bad times, and much lower during good times.

In the absence of any crisis, raising national savings by one percentage point would require an increase in fiscal surplus of a full 5 percentage points. Raising tax rates further to achieve a national savings target would intensify economic distortions, possibly up to a point where it would be counterproductive even from the perspective of raising the domestic savings rate.

The appropriate way out is to strengthen budgetary institutions in order to increase the public sector's creditworthiness by making better use of surpluses in good times and reassuring investors in bad times. This must be complemented by effective bank regulation and supervision, for any major bank crisis will usually involve extremely high fiscal spending on bank crisis resolution. This strategy does not exclude the need to raise public savings in good times, if the destabilising mix of procyclical fiscal policies and low offset coefficients is to be avoided during recessions. The way to do it, more in Latin America than anywhere else, is not to raise taxes, but to combine lower taxes with a strict enforcement of tax base broadening. The removal of tax exemptions and tax holidays is certain to meet opposition from forceful interest groups, but the economic reward of ignoring such opposition will be very high.

Tax Incentives

A government seeking to encourage savings can in principle choose between global tax incentives and targeted incentives. In practice, a comprehensive income tax treatment or an expenditure tax treatment will be difficult to implement in Latin America because of shortcomings in income accounting and tax administration. Moreover, the comprehensive income tax — very much like flat rate taxes on investment income — raises the problem of taxing unrealised capital gains. The expenditure tax — like the tax-free savings account — is regressive. On the other hand, a flat rate tax on investment income allows capital taxes to be levied at source through withholding, which combats tax evasion — notorious in Latin America and increasingly facilitated by the globalisation of international capital flows. Source-based income taxation should be coupled with residence-based consumption taxes, in order to minimise overall tax distortions and to make the tax system less vulnerable to administrative problems. In order to avoid incentives to employ transfer prices and other financial constructions by multinational corporations, some co-ordination between Latin American countries is needed in selecting the best mix between source- and residence-based taxation. Likewise, co-ordination with the OECD countries in needed in this area.

Targeted incentives on specific savings instruments, such as for vehicles of retirement savings, will not have a great impact on Latin America's savings rates. Such incentives do have an important impact on household portfolio composition and they do change the real return on savings. However, the induced change in the asset mix does not raise the overall level of savings, nor will a rise in the real rate of return to savings achieve higher savings as negative income effects outweigh positive substitution effects. This at least is what OECD evidence suggests.

PROGRAMME

VIIth International Forum on Latin American Perspectives

Thursday, 7th November, 1996

Co-Presidents	Jean Bonvin, President, OECD Development Centre
	Ricardo Hausmann, Chief Economist, IDB
Preliminary Remarks	Jean Bonvin, President, OECD Development Centre
	Ricardo Hausmann, Chief Economist, IDB

Session 1

Saving Behaviour in Latin America: Overview and Policy Issues

Authors	Michael Gavin, IDB
	Ricardo Hausmann, IDB
	Ernesto Talvi, IDB
Discussants	Daniel Cohen, CEPREMAP, Paris
	Marco Pagano, Università degli Studi di Napoli

Session 2

Financial Development, Savings and Growth Convergence: A Panel Data Approach

Authors	Jean-Claude Berthélemy, OECD Development Centre
	Aristomène Varoudakis, OECD Development Centre
Discussants	Jorge Braga de Macedo, Universidade Nova de Lisboa
	José De Gregorio, Ministry of Finance, Chile

Session 3

Financial Markets and the Behaviour of Private Savings in Latin America

Authors	Liliana Rojas-Suárez, IDB
	Steven R. Weisbrod, IDB
Discussants	Bernhard Fischer, HWWA
	Stephany Griffith-Jones, Institute of Development Studies

Session 4

Why Low Inequality Spurs Growth: Savings and Investment by the Poor

Authors	Nancy Birdsall, IDB
	Thomas C. Pinckney, Williams College
	Richard H. Sabot, Williams College
Discussants	François Bourguignon, DELTA, Paris
	Eliana Cardoso, Ministry of Finance, Brazil

Friday, 8th November, 1996

Session 5

Fiscal Policy and Private Saving in Latin America in Good Times and Bad

Authors	Michael Gavin, IDB
	Roberto Perotti, IDB
Discussants	Guillermo Perry, World Bank
	Luigi Spaventa, Università degli Studi di Roma "La Sapienza"

Session 6

Tax Effects on Household Saving: Evidence from OECD Member Countries

Authors   Göran Normann, OECD

                         Jeffrey Owens, OECD

Discussants   Richard Disney, Institute of Fiscal Studies, London

                         A. Lans Bovenberg, Netherlands Bureau of Economic
                         Policy Analysis, The Hague

Session 7

The Limits of Foreign Savings

Author   Helmut Reisen, OECD Development Centre

Discussant   Assaf Razin, Tel-Aviv University

LIST OF AUTHORS AND PARTICIPANTS

Co-Chair

Jean Bonvin   President, OECD Development Centre

Ricardo Hausmann   Chief Economist, Inter-American
                             Development Bank

Authors

Jean-Claude Berthélemy   OECD Development Centre

Nancy Birdsall   Executive Vice President, Inter-American
                             Development Bank

Michael Gavin   Inter-American Development Bank

Ricardo Hausmann   Chief Economist, Inter-American Development
                             Bank

Göran Normann   OECD, Fiscal Affairs Division

Jeffrey Owens   OECD, Fiscal Affairs Division

Roberto Perotti   Columbia University, New York, United States

Thomas C. Pinckney   Williams College, MA., United States

Helmut Reisen   OECD Development Centre

Liliana Rojas-Suárez   Inter-American Development Bank

Richard H. Sabot   Williams College, MA., United States

Ernesto Talvi   Inter-American Development Bank

Aristomène Varoudakis   OECD Development Centre

Steven R. Weisbrod   Inter-American Development Bank

Discussants

François Bourguignon   DELTA, Paris, France

A. Lans Bovenberg   Netherlands Bureau of Economic Policy
                             Analysis, The Hague, Netherlands

Jorge Braga de Macedo   Universidade Nova de Lisboa
                             Lisbon, Portugal

Eliana Cardoso   Ministry of Finance, Brazil

Daniel Cohen   École Normale Supérieure, CEPREMAP,
                             Paris, France

285

José De Gregorio	Ministry of Finance, Chile
Richard Disney	Institute of Fiscal Studies, London, United Kingdom
Bernhard Fischer	HWWA Institute for Economic Research, Hamburg, Germany
Stephany Griffith-Jones	Institute of Development Studies, University of Sussex, United Kingdom
Marco Pagano	Università degli Studi di Napoli Federico II, Italy
Guillermo Perry Rubio	The World Bank, Washington, D.C., United States
Assaf Razin	Tel Aviv University, Israel
Luigi Spaventa	Università degli Studi "La Sapienza", Rome, Italy

Other participants

Alvaro Calderón	Instituto de Relaciones Europeo-Latinoamericanas, Madrid, Spain
Emil-Maria Claassen	Université Dauphine, Paris, France
Luiz de Mello	University of Kent, United Kingdom
Dan Dorrow	Merrill Lynch, New York, United States
Richard Erb	Erb International, Inc., Paris, France
Stephen Fidler	Financial Times, London, United Kingdom
Helan Jaworski	Istituto Italo-Latinoamericano, Rome, Italy
Steven Kamin	Bank for International Settlements, Basle, Switzerland
Françoise Lachaud	Banque de France, Paris, France
Alessandro Merli	Il Sole - 24 Ore, London, United Kingdom
Heinz Mewes	Deutsch-SüdamerikanischeBank, Hamburg, Germany
Françoise Nicolas	Institut français des relations internationales, Paris, France
John Praveen	Merrill Lynch, New York, United States

Carlos Quenan	Sistema Economico Latinamericano, Ivry-sur-Seine, France
Reiner Schaefer	Dresdner Bank AG, Frankfurt/Main, Germany
Eberhard Schulz	Deutsche Bank, Franfurt/Main, Germany
Carlos Seiglie	The State University of New Jersey, United States
Jérôme Sgard	Centre d'Études Prospectives et d'Informations Internationales, Paris, France
Frans van Loon	ING Bank International, Amsterdam, Netherlands
Antonio Vidal Balué	Groupement européen des caisses d'épargne, Bruxelles, Belgique
Leonardo Villar Gomez	Vice Minister of Finance, Colombia

Diplomatic Representatives

Argentina

Mario Bossi de Ezcurra	Minister, Argentine Embassy, Paris
Horacio Doval	Minister, Argentine Embassy, Paris
Felipe Gardella	Counsellor, Argentine Embassy, Paris

Austria

Peter Jankowitsch	Ambassador, Austrian Delegation to the OECD
Doris Bertrand	Minister Plenipotentiary, Delegation of Austria to the OECD

Belgium

Xavier Hawia	Financial Counsellor, Delegation of Belgium to the OECD
Adelin Hudsyn	Embassy Counsellor, Delegation of Belgium to the OECD

Brazil

Denis Fontes de Souza Pinto	Counsellor, Brazilian Embassy, Paris
S. Hazan Menasce	Brazilian Embassy, Paris

Canada

Kimon Valaskakis   Ambassador, Delegation of Canada to the OECD

Hunter McGill   Counsellor, Delegation of Canada to the OECD

Colombia

Nestor Humberto Martinez Neira   Ambassador, Colombian Embassy, Paris

Commission of European Communities

Inés Garcia Pintos Balbas   DG1 BB, European Commission, Brussels

Robert Dhonte   Consultant, European Commission, Brussels

Ecuador

Carlos Jatiza   Chargé d'Affaires, Embassy of Ecuador, Paris

Finland

Kirsti Aarnio   Counsellor, Delegation of Finland to the OECD

Germany

Gregor Haas   Attaché, Delegation of Germany to the OECD

Italy

Eugenio d'Auria   First Counsellor, Delegation of Italy to the OECD

Japan

Miho Kawahatsu   Attaché, Delegation of Japan to the OECD

Mexico

Carlos Hurtado   Ambassador, Delegation of Mexico to the OECD

Rogelio Arellano   Minister, Delegation of Mexico to the OECD

Alfredo Genel   Minister, Delegation of Mexico to the OECD

David Topete   Counsellor, Delegation of Mexico to the OECD

Netherlands

Rudolf S. Bekink   Counsellor, Deputy Permanent Representative, Delegation of the Netherlands to the OECD

Portugal

Jorges de Lemos Godinho   Ambassador, Delegation of Portugal to the OECD

Ana Maria Ribeiro da Silva   Embassy Secretary, Delegation of Portugal to the OECD

Spain

José Maria Ridao	Counsellor, Delegation of Spain to the OECD

Switzerland

Holger Tausch	Direction du développement et de la Coopération (DDC), Berne
Roger Pasquier	Embassy Counsellor, Delegation of Switzerland to the OECD

United Kingdom

Sarah Bernard	Overseas Development Administration, United Kingdom

United States

Daniel Dolan	Minister-counsellor, Delegation of the United States to the OECD
Lee Roussel	Minister-counsellor, Delegation of the United States to the OECD

International Monetary Fund

Christian Brachet	Director, Office in Europe, International Monetary Fund, Paris
Robert Hagemann	Senior Economist, Office in Europe, International Monetary Fund, Paris

OECD Secretariat*

Makoto Taniguchi	Deputy Secretary-General
Richard Carey	Directorate for Co-operation and Development
Satish Mishra	Centre for Co-operation with the Economies in Transition
Hans Blommestein	Directorate for Financial, Fiscal and Enterprise Affairs
Andrea Goldstein	Economics Directorate
Anne Vourc'h	Economics Directorate
Bruce McMullen	International Energy Agency

Inter-American Development Bank*

Andrés Bajuk	Special Representative in Europe, IDB European Office
Rod Chapman	Senior Press and Information Officer, IDB European Office
Ziga Vodusek	Senior Economist, IDB European Office

OECD Development Centre*

Ulrich Hiemenz	Director for Co-ordination
Giulio Fossi	Head, External Co-operation Programme
Catherine Duport	Principal Administrator
Kiichiro Fukasaku	Head of Division
Colm Foy	Head of Publications Unit
Henny Helmich	Administrator, External Co-operation Progamme
Guillermo Larraín	Consultant

*   Except those listed as authors or discussants

MAIN SALES OUTLETS OF OECD PUBLICATIONS
PRINCIPAUX POINTS DE VENTE DES PUBLICATIONS DE L'OCDE

AUSTRALIA – AUSTRALIE
D.A. Information Services
648 Whitehorse Road. P.O.B 163
Mitcham. Victoria 3132   Tel. (03) 9210.7777
Fax: (03) 9210.7788

AUSTRIA – AUTRICHE
Gerold & Co.
Graben 31
Wien 1   Tel. (0222) 533.50.14
Fax: (0222) 512.47.31.29

BELGIUM – BELGIQUE
Jean De Lannoy
Avenue du Roi, Koningslaan 202
B-1060 Bruxelles Tel. (02) 538.51.69/538.08.41
Fax: (02) 538.08.41

CANADA
Renouf Publishing Company Ltd.
5369 Canotek Road
Unit 1
Ottawa. Ont. K1J 9J3   Tel. (613) 745.2665
Fax: (613) 745.7660

Stores:
71 1/2 Sparks Street
Ottawa. Ont. K1P 5R1   Tel. (613) 238.8985
Fax: (613) 238.6041

12 Adelaide Street West
Toronto. QN M5H 1L6   Tel. (416) 363.3171
Fax: (416) 363.5963

Les Éditions La Liberté Inc.
3020 Chemin Sainte-Foy
Sainte-Foy. PQ G1X 3V6 Tel. (418) 658.3763
Fax: (418) 658.3763

Federal Publications Inc.
165 University Avenue. Suite 701
Toronto. ON M5H 3B8   Tel. (416) 860.1611
Fax: (416) 860.1608

Les Publications Fédérales
1185 Université
Montréal. QC H3B 3A7   Tel. (514) 954.1633
Fax: (514) 954.1635

CHINA – CHINE
Book Dept., China National Publiations
Import and Export Corporation (CNPIEC)
16 Gongti E. Road. Chaoyang District
Beijing 100020 Tel. (10) 6506-6688 Ext. 8402
(10) 6506-3101

CHINESE TAIPEI – TAIPEI CHINOIS
Good Faith Worldwide Int'l. Co. Ltd.
9th Floor. No. 118. Sec. 2
Chung Hsiao E. Road
Taipei   Tel. (02) 391.7396/391.7397
Fax: (02) 394.9176

**CZECH REPUBLIC –
RÉPUBLIQUE TCHÈQUE**
National Information Centre
NIS – prodejna
Konviktská 5
Praha 1 – 113 57   Tel. (02) 24.23.09.07
Fax: (02) 24.22.94.33
E-mail: nkposp@dec.niz.cz
Internet: http://www.nis.cz

DENMARK – DANEMARK
Munksgaard Book and Subscription Service
35. Nørre Søgade, P.O. Box 2148
DK-1016 København K   Tel. (33) 12.85.70
Fax: (33) 12.93.87

J. H. Schultz Information A/S.
Herstedvang 12.
DK – 2620 Albertslung   Tel. 43 63 23 00
Fax: 43 63 19 69
Internet: s-info@inet.uni-c.dk

EGYPT – ÉGYPTE
The Middle East Observer
41 Sherif Street
Cairo   Tel. (2) 392.6919
Fax: (2) 360.6804

FINLAND – FINLANDE
Akateeminen Kirjakauppa
Keskuskatu 1. P.O. Box 128
00100 Helsinki

Subscription Services/Agence d'abonnements :
P.O. Box 23
00100 Helsinki   Tel. (358) 9.121.4403
Fax: (358) 9.121.4450

*FRANCE
OECD/OCDE
Mail Orders/Commandes par correspondance :
2, rue André-Pascal
75775 Paris Cedex 16 Tel. 33 (0)1.45.24.82.00
Fax: 33 (0)1.49.10.42.76
Telex: 640048 OCDE
Internet: Compte.PUBSINQ@oecd.org

Orders via Minitel, France only/
Commandes par Minitel. France
exclusivement : 36 15 OCDE

OECD Bookshop/Librairie de l'OCDE :
33. rue Octave-Feuillet
75016 Paris   Tel. 33 (0)1.45.24.81.81
33 (0)1.45.24.81.67

Dawson
B.P. 40
91121 Palaiseau Cedex   Tel. 01.89.10.47.00
Fax: 01.64.54.83.26

Documentation Française
29, quai Voltaire
75007 Paris   Tel. 01.40.15.70.00

Economica
49, rue Héricart
75015 Paris   Tel. 01.45.78.12.92
Fax: 01.45.75.05.67

Gibert Jeune (Droit-Économie)
6, place Saint-Michel
75006 Paris   Tel. 01.43.25.91.19

Librairie du Commerce International
10. avenue d'Iéna
75016 Paris   Tel. 01.40.73.34.60

Librairie Dunod
Université Paris-Dauphine
Place du Maréchal-de-Lattre-de-Tassigny
75016 Paris   Tel. 01.44.05.40.13

Librairie Lavoisier
11. rue Lavoisier
75008 Paris   Tel. 01.42.65.39.95

Librairie des Sciences Politiques
30. rue Saint-Guillaume
75007 Paris   Tel. 01.45.48.36.02

P.U.F.
49. boulevard Saint-Michel
75005 Paris   Tel. 01.43.25.83.40

Librairie de l'Université
12a. rue Nazareth
13100 Aix-en-Provence   Tel. 04.42.26.18.08

Documentation Française
165, rue Garibaldi
69003 Lyon   Tel. 04.78.63.32.23

Librairie Decitre
29, place Bellecour
69002 Lyon   Tel. 04.72.40.54.54

Librairie Sauramps
Le Triangle
34967 Montpellier Cedex 2 Tel. 04.67.58.85.15
Fax: 04.67.58.27.36

A la Sorbonne Actual
23, rue de l'Hôtel-des-Postes
06000 Nice   Tel. 04.93.13.77.75
Fax: 04.93.80.75.69

GERMANY – ALLEMAGNE
OECD Bonn Centre
August-Bebel-Allee 6
D-53175 Bonn   Tel. (0228) 959.120
Fax: (0228) 959.12.17

GREECE – GRÈCE
Librairie Kauffmann
Stadiou 28
10564 Athens   Tel. (01) 32.55.321
Fax: (01) 32.30.320

HONG-KONG
Swindon Book Co. Ltd.
Astoria Bldg. 3F
34 Ashley Road. Tsimshatsui
Kowloon, Hong Kong   Tel. 2376.2062
Fax: 2376.0685

HUNGARY – HONGRIE
Euro Info Service
Margitsziget, Európa Ház
1138 Budapest   Tel. (1) 111.60.61
Fax: (1) 302.50.35
E-mail: euroinfo@mail.matav.hu
Internet: http://www.euroinfo.hu//index.html

ICELAND – ISLANDE
Mál og Menning
Laugavegi 18, Pósthólf 392
121 Reykjavik   Tel. (1) 552.4240
Fax: (1) 562.3523

INDIA – INDE
Oxford Book and Stationery Co.
Scindia House
New Delhi 110001   Tel. (11) 331.5896/5308
Fax: (11) 332.2639
E-mail: oxford.publ@axcess.net.in

17 Park Street
Calcutta 700016   Tel. 240832

INDONESIA – INDONÉSIE
Pdii-Lipi
P.O. Box 4298
Jakarta 12042   Tel. (21) 573.34.67
Fax: (21) 573.34.67

IRELAND – IRLANDE
Government Supplies Agency
Publications Section
4/5 Harcourt Road
Dublin 2   Tel. 661.31.11
Fax: 475.27.60

ISRAEL – ISRAËL
Praedicta
5 Shatner Street
P.O. Box 34030
Jerusalem 91430   Tel. (2) 652.84.90/1/2
Fax: (2) 652.84.93

R.O.Y. International
P.O. Box 13056
Tel Aviv 61130   Tel. (3) 546 1423
Fax: (3) 546 1442
E-mail: royil@netvision.net.il

Palestinian Authority/Middle East:
INDEX Information Services
P.O.B. 19502
Jerusalem   Tel. (2) 627.16.34
Fax: (2) 627.12.19

ITALY – ITALIE
Libreria Commissionaria Sansoni
Via Duca di Calabria. 1/1
50125 Firenze   Tel. (055) 64.54.15
Fax: (055) 64.12.57
E-mail: licosa@ftbcc.it

Via Bartolini 29
20155 Milano   Tel. (02) 36.50.83

Editrice e Libreria Herder
Piazza Montecitorio 120
00186 Roma   Tel. 679.46.28
Fax: 678.47.51

Libreria Hoepli
Via Hoepli 5
20121 Milano   Tel. (02) 86.54.46
                          Fax: (02) 805.28.86
Libreria Scientifica
Dott. Lucio de Biasio 'Aeiou'
Via Coronelli. 6
20146 Milano   Tel. (02) 48.95.45.52
                          Fax: (02) 48.95.45.48

JAPAN – JAPON
OECD Tokyo Centre
Landic Akasaka Building
2-3-4 Akasaka. Minato-ku
Tokyo 107   Tel. (81.3) 3586.2016
                          Fax: (81.3) 3584.7929

KOREA – CORÉE
Kyobo Book Centre Co. Ltd.
P.O. Box 1658. Kwang Hwa Moon
Seoul   Tel. 730.78.91
                          Fax: 735.00.30

MALAYSIA – MALAISIE
University of Malaya Bookshop
University of Malaya
P.O. Box 1127. Jalan Pantai Baru
59700 Kuala Lumpur
Malaysia   Tel. 756.5000/756.5425
                          Fax: 756.3246

MEXICO – MEXIQUE
OECD Mexico Centre
Edificio INFOTEC
Av. San Fernando no. 37
Col. Toriello Guerra
Tlalpan C.P. 14050
Mexico D.F.   Tel. (525) 528.10.38
                          Fax: (525) 606.13.07
E-mail: ocde@rtn.net.mx

NETHERLANDS – PAYS-BAS
SDU Uitgeverij Plantijnstraat
Externe Fondsen
Postbus 20014
2500 EA's-Gravenhage Tel. (070) 37.89.880
Voor bestellingen: Fax: (070) 34.75.778

Subscription Agency/Agence d'abonnements :
SWETS & ZEITLINGER BV
Heereweg 347B
P.O. Box 830
2160 SZ Lisse   Tel. 252.435.111
                          Fax: 252.415.888

**NEW ZEALAND –
NOUVELLE-ZÉLANDE**
GPLegislation Services
P.O. Box 12418
Thorndon. Wellington   Tel. (04) 496.5655
                          Fax: (04) 496.5698

NORWAY – NORVÈGE
NIC INFO A/S
Ostensjoveien 18
P.O. Box 6512 Etterstad
0606 Oslo   Tel. (22) 97.45.00
                          Fax: (22) 97.45.45

PAKISTAN
Mirza Book Agency
65 Shahrah Quaid-E-Azam
Lahore 54000   Tel. (42) 735.36.01
                          Fax: (42) 576.37.14

PHILIPPINE – PHILIPPINES
International Booksource Center Inc.
Rm 179/920 Cityland 10 Condo Tower 2
HV dela Costa Ext cor Valero St.
Makati Metro Manila   Tel. (632) 817 9676
                       Fax: (632) 817 1741

POLAND – POLOGNE
Ars Polona
00-950 Warszawa
Krakowskie Prezdmiescie 7 Tel. (22) 264760
                           Fax: (22) 265334

PORTUGAL
Livraria Portugal
Rua do Carmo 70-74
Apart. 2681
1200 Lisboa   Tel. (01) 347.49.82/5
                          Fax: (01) 347.02.64

SINGAPORE – SINGAPOUR
Ashgate Publishing
Asia Pacific Pte. Ltd
Golden Wheel Building. 04-03
41. Kallang Pudding Road
Singapore 349316   Tel. 741.5166
                          Fax: 742.9356

SPAIN – ESPAGNE
Mundi-Prensa Libros S.A.
Castelló 37. Apartado 1223
Madrid 28001   Tel. (91) 431.33.99
                          Fax: (91) 575.39.98
E-mail: mundiprensa@tsai.es
Internet: http://www.mundiprensa.es

Mundi-Prensa Barcelona
Consell de Cent No. 391
08009 – Barcelona   Tel. (93) 488.34.92
                          Fax: (93) 487.76.59

Libreria de la Generalitat
Palau Moja
Rambla dels Estudis. 118
08002 – Barcelona
           (Suscripciones) Tel. (93) 318.80.12
           (Publicaciones) Tel. (93) 302.67.23
                           Fax: (93) 412.18.54

SRI LANKA
Centre for Policy Research
c/o Colombo Agencies Ltd.
No. 300-304. Galle Road
Colombo 3   Tel. (1) 574240. 573551-2
                       Fax: (1) 575394. 510711

SWEDEN – SUÈDE
CE Fritzes AB
S–106 47 Stockholm   Tel. (08) 690.90.90
                          Fax: (08) 20.50.21

For electronic publications only/
Publications électroniques seulement
STATISTICS SWEDEN
Informationsservice
S-115 81 Stockholm   Tel. 8 783 5066
                          Fax: 8 783 4045

Subscription Agency/Agence d'abonnements :
Wennergren-Williams Info AB
P.O. Box 1305
171 25 Solna   Tel. (08) 705.97.50
                          Fax: (08) 27.00.71

Liber distribution
Internatinal organizations
Fagerstagatan 21
S-163 52 Spanga

SWITZERLAND – SUISSE
Maditec S.A. (Books and Periodicals/Livres
et périodiques)
Chemin des Palettes 4
Case postale 266
1020 Renens VD 1   Tel. (021) 635.08.65
                          Fax: (021) 635.07.80

Librairie Payot S.A.
4. place Pépinet
CP 3212
1002 Lausanne   Tel. (021) 320.25.11
                          Fax: (021) 320.25.14

Librairie Unilivres
6. rue de Candolle
1205 Genève   Tel. (022) 320.26.23
                          Fax: (022) 329.73.18

Subscription Agency/Agence d'abonnements :
Dynapresse Marketing S.A.
38. avenue Vibert
1227 Carouge   Tel. (022) 308.08.70
                          Fax: (022) 308.07.99

See also – Voir aussi :
OECD Bonn Centre
August-Bebel-Allee 6
D-53175 Bonn (Germany) Tel. (0228) 959.120
                        Fax: (0228) 959.12.17

THAILAND – THAÏLANDE
Suksit Siam Co. Ltd.
113. 115 Fuang Nakhon Rd.
Opp. Wat Rajbopith
Bangkok 10200   Tel. (662) 225.9531/2
                          Fax: (662) 222.5188

**TRINIDAD & TOBAGO, CARIBBEAN
TRINITÉ-ET-TOBAGO, CARAÏBES**
Systematics Studies Limited
9 Watts Street
Curepe
Trinidad & Tobago. W.I. Tel. (1809) 645.3475
                         Fax: (1809) 662.5654
E-mail: tobe@trinidad.net

TUNISIA – TUNISIE
Grande Librairie Spécialisée
Fendri Ali
Avenue Haffouz Imm El-Intilaka
Bloc B 1 Sfax 3000   Tel. (216-4) 296 855
                          Fax: (216-4) 298.270

TURKEY – TURQUIE
Kültür Yayinlari Is-Türk Ltd.
Atatürk Bulvari No. 191/Kat 13
06684 Kavaklidere/Ankara
                    Tel. (312) 428.11.40 Ext. 2458
                    Fax : (312) 417.24.90

Dolmabahce Cad. No. 29
Besiktas/Istanbul   Tel. (212) 260 7188

UNITED KINGDOM – ROYAUME-UNI
The Stationery Office Ltd.
Postal orders only:
P.O. Box 276. London SW8 5DT
Gen. enquiries   Tel. (171) 873 0011
                          Fax: (171) 873 8463

The Stationery Office Ltd.
Postal orders only:
49 High Holborn. London WC1V 6HB
Branches at: Belfast. Birmingham. Bristol.
Edinburgh. Manchester

UNITED STATES – ÉTATS-UNIS
OECD Washington Center
2001 L Street N.W.. Suite 650
Washington. D.C. 20036-4922
                          Tel. (202) 785.6323
                          Fax: (202) 785.0350
Internet: washcont@oecd.org

Subscriptions to OECD periodicals may also
be placed through main subscription agencies.

Les abonnements aux publications périodiques
de l'OCDE peuvent être souscrits auprès des
principales agences d'abonnement.

Orders and inquiries from countries where Dis-
tributors have not yet been appointed should be
sent to: OECD Publications. 2. rue André-Pascal. 75775 Paris Cedex 16. France.

Les commandes provenant de pays où l'OCDE
n'a pas encore désigné de distributeur peuvent
être adressées aux Éditions de l'OCDE. 2. rue
André-Pascal. 75775 Paris Cedex 16. France.

12-1996

OECD PUBLICATIONS, 2, rue André-Pascal, 75775 PARIS CEDEX 16
PRINTED IN FRANCE
(41 97 05 1) ISBN 92-64-15462-0 – No. 49357 1997